D0824473

JAPANESE NATIONAL RAILWAYS
ITS BREAK-UP AND PRIVATIZATION

Japanese National Railways

Its Break-up and Privatization

HOW JAPAN'S PASSENGER RAIL SERVICES
BECAME THE ENVY OF THE WORLD

by

Yoshiyuki Kasai

GLOBAL ORIENTAL

JAPANESE NATIONAL RAILWAYS
ITS BREAK-UP AND PRIVATIZATION

By Yoshiyuki Kasai

First published 2003 by
GLOBAL ORIENTAL
PO Box 219
Folkestone
Kent CT20 2WP

Global Oriental is an imprint of Global Books Ltd

English edition copyright © 2003 by Central Japan Railway Company

ISBN 1-901903-45-1

Originally published in Japanese
as *Mikan no 'kokutetsu kaikaku'*
by Toyo Keizai Inc., Tokyo 2001
Copyright © 2001 by Yoshiyuki Kasai

All rights reserved. No part of this publication
may be reproduced or transmitted in any form or by
any means without prior permission in writing
from the Publishers, except for the use of short extracts
in criticism.

British Library Cataloguing in Publication Data
A CIP catalogue entry for this book is available
from the British Library

Set in Garamond 11.5 on 12.5 by Mark Heslington, Scarborough, North Yorkshire
Printed and bound in England by The Cromwell Press Ltd, Trowbridge, Wilts.

To my wife Shoko
for her unstinting support

Contents

Contents

Foreword

It did not take many meetings with Yoshiyuki Kasai for me to recognize the pragmatic, yet distinctly visionary qualities of a man who spent many years with Japanese National Railways, helping to guide it through its many restructurings on the route to privatization. It took, however, the reading of this book for me to truly appreciate the long and full extent of his particular involvement in the privatization process of Japanese National Railways. Today, Mr Kasai is the CEO and President of JR Central and the fact that this company operates the most profitable and technologically advanced Shinkansen line affirms his extensive capabilities.

My own involvement in the British privatization process dates back to the early 1980s, a time when the British Government was a pioneer in the relatively young field of privatization. The privatization and liberalization of Britain's electricity, gas and telecoms industries are major developments of which the country can today remain justifiably proud. There were of course many detractors at the time when both Britain and Japan were advancing in this area, and Mr Kasai's experiences relating to the obstacles to change, in particular obstacles to privatization, both within and outside his organization, are all too familiar to me.

The difficulties in carrying the privatization process through the political process in the context of, at times, troubled industrial relations bear parallels to the United Kingdom's experience of privatization, and makes fascinating reading. The publication of Mr Kasai's book coincides with the rebirth of the troubled privatized UK railway network, and if Britain can boast of its pioneering record in privatization generally, railway privatization was, to put it mildly, a less unequivocal success. It remains only a distant dream to see our trains run uniformly across the network at the enviable 270 km (168 m) per hour now achieved by the Tokaido Shinkansen!

Mr Kasai's unique experience gained in senior management positions in various departments of Japanese National Railways and his direct involvement in the political aspects of JNR's privatization, allows him to comment with insight not only on the relationship with the political process but also on management's changing relationship with the labour work-force and unions, and key strategic and financial aspects of privatization, e.g., debt forgiveness and asset separation. The result is a very detailed and comprehensive account of the politico-economic process of one of the largest and complex Japanese privatizations to date, concluding with a panel discussion on railway privatization, where many of the key issues highlighted by Mr Kasai are discussed in the broader context of railway reforms in the UK, Germany and Japan.

Many privatization programmes, particularly of Western European and some Asian countries, are now at a relatively advanced stage and this naturally provides an opportunity to review and evaluate the results different privatization approaches have yielded. Such a review is of particular importance not only for future policy formation in countries which are in the process of contemplating privatization but also in industries where private ownership is not yet the norm. In this context, Mr Kasai's book makes a valuable contribution – in particular given the small number of precedents for railway reform and privatization and the special importance the railway sector has for any economy.

That is why Mr Kasai's book is particularly timely and interesting for a broad international audience and provides a unique insider's view of the privatization of the Japanese national railway system. But it also will be of the greatest interest to all readers who wish to be better informed regarding the political and industrial climate of Japan at this critical time in its development. Mr Kasai has demonstrated to us all in the course of his successful career and in the writing of this invaluable book the truth of the Chinese saying he quotes in his opening pages – '*Yu fa zi*' – There is a way.

Lord Brittan of Spennithorne

Acknowledgements

The publication of the English edition of my book on the break-up and privatization of Japanese National Railways would not have been successful without the support of many friends and helpers. In particular, I am deeply indebted to my esteemed friend George Olcott for his help in completing the present English edition. Mr Olcott, who, having been brought up in Japan, has an excellent command of both Japanese and English, was educated at Oxford University. Following a successful career in investment banking, he is currently participating in the doctoral programme at Cambridge University, where he is conducting research on the impact of foreign capital participation in Japanese corporations.

The rationale, character and process of JNR's break-up and privatization and the history of its implementation is a highly specialized subject even for most Japanese readers. Hence the conversion of the Japanese original edition into an English edition, which would be easily comprehensible for readers interested in the subject, required a substantial knowledge of organizational and structural aspects of the railway network both in the UK and Japan.

Mr Olcott's business experience and personal background made him the best person to take on this task, and I count myself extremely fortunate to have secured his assistance. Mr Olcott's dedication and professionalism were so central to the production of the English edition that I would even go as far as saying that this book bears his seal at least as much as it bears mine. Of course, all remaining errors are entirely my own. I would like to express my sincerest gratitude to him for his enormous contribution.

There are many other people who contributed to this project, including those who assisted me in writing the original Japanese volume. I especially wish to thank Mr Nozomu Nakaoka and Dr Christopher P. Hood, who produced the first English translation, and Christian Bell, who helped me in managing the production of the English edition of this book.

YOSHIYUKI KASAI
Tokyo, March 2003

EDITOR'S NOTE

Throughout the main text, Japanese names are quoted according to the Japanese convention of putting the family name first.

Central Japan Railway Company, the company operating the Tokaido Shinkansen and the former JNR network in the region surrounding Nagoya, is referred to as JR Central throughout the text, the name under which it is commonly known in Japan.

TRANSLATORS

Nozomu Nakaoka
Mr Nakaoka translated numerous materials on economic issues while serving as chief editor for several Japanese economic journals. He currently teaches a course on the Japanese and Asian economies at Washington University in Saint Louis (Missouri, United States of America).

Dr Christopher P. Hood
Dr Hood is the director of the Cardiff Japanese Studies Centre at Cardiff University. He is currently involved in research on the Shinkansen.

▶ *Chapter 1*

Merits and demerits of Japanese National Railways and its inherent defects

[1]   *Yu fa zi* ('There is a way')

I joined Japanese National Railways (JNR) in 1963, fifteen years after it was established as a public corporation.

On 1 April 1963, the ceremony to welcome new employees was held at the company's newly-built headquarters in Marunouchi, Tokyo's central business district. The ceremony followed the traditional pattern with the then president, Sogo Shinji, handing over a letter of appointment to each new employee, and then delivering a welcome speech. Immediately before the ceremony, I was summoned to the office of the recruitment manager who had been responsible for bringing me into the firm. He advised me that 'Mr Sogo is very old-fashioned, so when you receive your letter of appointment, look him straight in the eyes. Otherwise you will give him the impression of weakness'. Although I recall strictly following this advice, after handing over the letters to the sixty or so new employees, Sogo said to us:

> Having now handed each of you your letters of appointment in person and having had the opportunity of taking a good look at you all, I cannot conceal my disappointment. You certainly do not seem to be the kind to join me in battle to 'fight to the death, with a rail as a pillow'.[1] I would therefore like to explain my motto to all of you,

---

[1] Re-phrased version of the ancient Japanese expression 'Fight to the death with the castle as your pillow', i.e., fighting up to the last man.

who are about to become members of our firm in the hope that you will also make it your own. This motto is the Chinese expression '*Yu fa zi*'. When I was stationed in Manchuria before and during the last war I happened to befriend Chiang Kai Shek and some of his staff. They told me the following: 'The Chinese are lagging behind the great powers. One grave weakness of the Chinese is that we tend to give up too easily. In doing so we shrug our shoulders and say, '*Mei fa zi*', which means 'There is no way,' or 'It cannot be helped'. China won't get anywhere with this kind of attitude. If only we were able to develop a spirit of '*Yu fa zi*' ('There *is* a way'), whatever the difficulties we encountered, China would surely develop into a world leader.' I was deeply impressed by this comment, and have adopted '*Yu fai zi*' as my motto ever since. Please bear it in mind throughout your career at JNR.

I can still see Sogo's calligraphy depicting his motto hanging on the wall of the training school where I stayed as a freshman during my first three months at the company.

The performance of JNR for the eight years from 1955 to 1963 while president Sogo was in office might at first sight seem satisfactory. JNR had a predominant share of the total passenger and cargo markets in Japan at 45% and 30%, respectively. The Japanese economy was at the peak of its post-war economic boom and with demand for transport increasing steadily there was a chronic shortage in capacity. In order to cope with the constant increase in demand, the First Long-Term Plan was launched in 1957 and the Second Long-Term Plan was implemented in 1961 with the particular goal of modernizing rail infrastructure through investment in the double-tracking and electrification of trunk lines. Of particular significance was the Tokaido Shinkansen which was in the final stages of construction and which was expected to herald a new era in railway transportation. In the eyes of the public, JNR would have seemed a large company of great strength. It had a clear social mission, 450,000 employees working in a stably managed environment and operating a national rail network extending for more than 20,000 km (12,000 miles). This is certainly the impression we new recruits had of JNR and, not surprisingly, the president's speech, with its reference to 'fighting to the death with a rail as your pillow', left me feeling somewhat unsettled.

Looking back at the developments at JNR, however, President Sogo's motto was a clear indication of what was to come. JNR fell into the red the following year – 1964. Retained earnings, which amounted to around ¥160 billon ($1.3 bn)[2] in 1963, would be completely wiped out and by 1967 JNR found itself with accumulated net losses of ¥150 billion ($1.2 bn). Despite launching the First Reorganization Plan in 1969, JNR was virtually bankrupt by 1971 when it posted net losses before depreciation, meaning that the company had to finance operating expenses through borrowings. Thereafter, JNR suffered from chronic losses and steadily expanding debt until 1987, when it was broken up and privatized. Looking back now, I can see that Sogo must already have grasped the essence of the problems confronting JNR and my own twenty-four-year career at the company was a desperate struggle to resolve these problems. For me it was literally a case of 'fighting to the death with a rail as my pillow'. At the time of the break-up and privatization, '*Yu fa zi*' was far from being an empty slogan and had much practical meaning for me.

2   Electrification of long-distance passenger trains

JNR was created in 1949, at the initiative of General MacArthur's administration, by transferring direct control of railway operations from the government to a financially self-sufficient public corporation. Japan at that time was in the throes of the chaotic post-war period. Staff who had been in managerial positions during the war were summarily removed; the *Zaibatsu* were disbanded: Japan as a nation had effectively ceased to function. At that time, JNR was almost the only national organization that had the capacity to operate in a well-organized and orderly basis. In 1946, industrial production was still at 30–40% of 1936 levels, whereas transport capacity (i.e., rail miles) had recovered to 74%.

JNR was established with two key missions: firstly, as the only properly functioning element within the domestic infrastructure,

---

[2] Throughout the text, for the convenience of English readers, a current exemplary exchange rate of US$1 = ¥120 is used to provide the equivalent US dollar values, which are given in brackets.

to contribute to economic reconstruction through effective utilization of its national railway network; secondly, to modernize and streamline the railway infrastructure which had become degraded during the war, to strengthen transport capacity and capability in anticipation of an expected increase in demand for transport services. The rationale for the conversion of JNR into a financially self-sufficient public corporation was to ensure that JNR not only operated efficiently, but also financed the necessary investments to modernize and strengthen the railway network through passenger revenues. But as became increasingly apparent, this framework was essentially defective in terms of enabling JNR to raise sufficient capital to carry out its mission. However, it is also true to say that the history of JNR between its inception and 1965 was one of extraordinary achievements, particularly during the period of Sogo's presidency (1955–63).

The fact of the matter is that Japan has the world's largest and most advanced railway network, accounting for more than half of the world's share in terms of both the number of passengers and passenger kilometres. Triggered by the success of the Tokaido Shinkansen,[3] eight countries have already introduced a high-speed train system. However, total passenger numbers of high-speed rail services in those eight countries put together is only just equal to that of the Tokaido Shinkansen. Japan's geography, comprising major cities concentrated on a narrow strip of coastal plain, is undoubtedly a major factor in its success. However, it is also the tangible result of JNR's farsighted policies to modernize the railway system after its establishment in 1949.

Of major significance was JNR's effort to promote the electrification of trunk lines. Prior to and during the war, military considerations dictated that only steam locomotives were used on trunk lines, as it was believed that an electrified train system would be vulnerable to enemy attack. After the war, however, coal, which was then Japan's most important energy source, was strate-

---

[3] The 'Tokaido' refers to the ancient road connecting Kyoto, the former capital of Japan, and Tokyo. 'Shinkansen' means 'new trunk line' and refers to the so-called 'bullet' train which started operations between Tokyo and Osaka (located just to the west of Kyoto) in 1964.

gically allocated to the reconstruction of other basic industries such as steel. The government's adopted policy, therefore, was to encourage extensive electrification utilizing electricity generated by hydroelectric power stations. The United States opposed this policy, and with MacArthur introducing austerity measures to subdue the hyperinflation in the immediate post-war period, the Japanese government was ordered to cease expenditure for electrification in favour of diesel trains on cost grounds. After the signing of the San Francisco Peace Treaty and the recovery of sovereignty, the electrification of trunk lines once again became the main pillar of JNR's modernization policy. Subsequent developments showed this to have been the correct decision, as the railway systems of those countries that opted for electrification over diesel have performed significantly better.

Alongside electrification of trunk lines, policy also provided for long-distance passenger trains to be converted to the so-called Electric Multiple Unit (EMU) system which distributes traction over the entire train. This idea originated with Shima Hideo, the Director General of the Rolling Stock & Mechanical Engineering Department of JNR. At the time, the EMU system was used only in trams or underground trains in urban areas for short-distance commuting. Given that nowhere in the world was the EMU system used to provide mid- and long-distance transport, JNR took a big risk in adopting long-distance EMU trains. The EMU system was first used by JNR on the Shonan Line in Greater Tokyo to test its suitability for middle distance transport (i.e. about 100 km – 62 mph). Subsequently, the Odakyu Electric Railway, a private railway company also operating in the Tokyo metropolitan area, converted their trains to EMU. This laid the groundwork for the introduction of long-distance EMU trains. In 1958, the express train 'Kodama' ('Echo') was brought in and connected Tokyo and Osaka (about 560 km) in seven hours at a speed of 100 km/h. This revolutionary breakthrough was eventually to lead directly to the construction of the Tokaido Shinkansen.

The advantage of the EMU system is that by employing multiple motors, the number of driving axles can be increased, leading to a corresponding increase in adhesive power and providing lightweight trains with greater pulling power.[4] As a train with a locomotive system has fewer driving axles, the axle loads need to be greater in order to obtain sufficient pulling power. Trains therefore require large, heavy locomotives with greater horsepower, which inevitably cause a larger degree of wear and tear to the track than the lighter EMU trains. Furthermore, in spite of its light weight, an electric train has greater pulling power, improved ability to accelerate and decelerate, and to stop and start on slopes, giving them a relative advantage in a mountainous environment such as Japan. The adoption of EMU enabled the railway system to cope safely with a more intensive time table and spurred the development of Japan's long-distance high-speed train network. Of all the decisions taken by JNR in the 1950s and 1960s, electrification and EMU had the most far-reaching consequences: they led to the birth of the Tokaido Shinkansen and enabled Japan to gain a significant lead over other countries.

3 Construction of the Tokaido Shinkansen

By the mid-1950s, there was a growing feeling that something had to be done about the Tokaido Line[5] which had clearly reached its saturation point and was becoming a a bottleneck for the Japanese economy. Three plans were considered. The first was to expand the Tokaido Line with the construction of another narrow-gauge railway line running parallel to it. This plan maximized efficiency insofar as JNR could operate parts of the railway almost as soon as the track was laid, without waiting for the construction of the entire line. The partial operation of the railway in this way would enable JNR to recover some of the large investment required for construction more quickly. The second plan was to construct a new narrow-gauge railway, but on an entirely new route. In this case, it was expected that both line length and journey time could be shortened as the route would not be

---

[4] A train's traction can be determined by the following equation: (pulling power) = (adhesive coefficient) × (number of driving axles) × (axle load of each driving axle).

[5] The Tokyo-Osaka trunk line.

restricted to the Tokaido Line and advantage would be taken of advances in civil engineering technology. Moreover, as the new line could be connected to the existing line at major stations, the operation of through trains would be possible. The third plan was to construct a standard-gauge[6] railway on a separate track. This plan would eventually become the 'Tokaido Shinkansen plan'. Though transport time between Tokyo and Osaka would be dramatically shortened, the drawbacks to this plan were that, as there would be no interconnectivity, network efficiency would not be improved and that operations could not start until the construction of the whole line was completed. The enormous investment of capital and JNR's human resources into the construction of the Shinkansen would present a very large risk to the company.

With the benefit of hindsight, it is obvious that the Shinkansen plan was superior, although it did not necessarily seem so at the time. The majority of the management favoured the first plan, i.e., the construction of an additional narrow-gauge railway running parallel to the existing line. In 1963, just one year before the Tokaido Shinkansen started operations, the Director General of the Construction Department made the following comment in a lecture to new company employees: 'The Tokaido Shinkansen is the height of madness. As the gauge of the Tokaido Shinkansen is different from existing lines, track sharing is not possible. Even if the journey time between Tokyo and Osaka is shortened, passengers have to change trains at Osaka in order to travel further west. A railway system which lacks smooth connections and networks with other lines is meaningless and destined to fail.'

There had even been considerable opposition to the introduction of EMU trains proposed by Shima. Shima was an engineer in the Rolling Stock & Mechanical Engineering Department, which was assigned to design and manufacture trains. There was intense rivalry between Shima's department and the Train Operation

---

[6] The worldwide 'standard gauge' (i.e. the distance between both rails) is 1,435 mm. This gauge is used for the Shinkansen tracks. The conventional lines in Japan, originally developed under the mentorship of Great Britain, use the 1,067 mm narrow-gauge standard, which has been adopted by railways in British colonies.

Department, whose responsibility was train operation and driver scheduling. This department was also staffed by a number of mechanical engineers, many of whom strongly supported the locomotive system. They argued that it would be quieter for passengers, more fuel-efficient and less costly to manufacture than the EMU train, which had a motor in each car. Moreover, France and Germany both used the locomotive system. At the beginning of the twenty-first century, the argument seems finally to have been settled. Germany has already launched a programme to introduce EMU trains on its rapid-transit railway (ICE), and France is reported to be moving in the same direction. Developments in electrical engineering enabled us to manufacture compact, high-performance motors at remarkably low cost and any advantages that the locomotive system might have had have now disappeared altogether.

True Tokaido Shinkansen enthusiasts were very few in number. A small group comprising President Sogo, Shima (the Vice President responsible for Engineering), and several other engineers who were directly involved in its construction. They were referred to as 'the crazy gang' and generally sneered at by others in the organization. To be sure, when the age of the car and aeroplane was said to have arrived, pouring a large amount of money into the construction of the Tokaido Shinkansen may have been regarded as foolhardy. Many compared the construction of a specially designed high-speed railway such as the Shinkansen, which would operate only on the route between Tokyo and Osaka, to the construction of the Great Wall of China, i.e., a complete white elephant.

Although the parallel track plan had originally been favoured by many, this proved not to be feasible as much of the land adjacent to the existing track had already been developed and difficult to expropriate. People therefore started to promote the construction of a separate narrow-gauge railway as the second best option. Shima, however, showed great foresight in rejecting this plan. He had already formed his own idea about how to increase the transport capacity to alleviate the crowded Tokaido Line. The main barrier to efficiency is the operation of various types of trains such as local trains, long-distance express trains, and freight trains, all of which operate at different speed, have different weights, different lengths, stop at different stations, but operate on the same track. Shima clearly saw the answer as the Tokaido Shinkansen: a high-speed passenger train operating on an exclusive track. A station would be built about every 30 km (18.5 miles), connected to the existing lines to enable easy transfer. While the result of this was for physical capacity to be doubled, actual transport capacity would increase by considerably more. By removing high-speed trains from the Tokaido Line, capacity for slow trains would increase by a far greater degree than the reduction in the volume of express trains, resulting in much greater efficiency. Moreover, if the trains operating the Tokaido Shinkansen were lightweight EMU trains, wear and tear on rail would be reduced and the design of more economical track structures would be possible. Since there would be a freer hand in route design compared to the construction of a parallel track, construction costs would be lower and land appropriation would be easier. However, the most startling feature of the wide-gauged railway was the operation of trains that would run at more than 200 km/h (124 mph), and this meant that rail travel would have a relative advantage over cars and aeroplanes over the 500 km (310 m) Tokyo-Osaka route. Shima's plan, coupled with the passion of president Sogo, enabled them to overcome the many obstacles that confronted them: without the close cooperation between these two men the Tokaido Shinkansen may well not have become a reality.

Many years later, in 1994, when he was 93 years old, Shima was awarded the Order of Culture. A group of people connected with the Tokaido Shinkansen project held a small congratulatory party. Shima was asked to give a 'brief address'. He rose from his wheelchair, walked unsteadily to the podium, and proceeded to speak for almost an hour using the microphone stand to prop himself up. This was the last speech he ever made in public and could be regarded as rather like a valedictory.

I would like to take this opportunity to explain something of what he said that day. It was in 1903 that a train first recorded a speed of more than 200 km/h (124 mph) on a test run in Germany. An EMU train with a three-phase alternating current motor was used, reaching a speed of 210.2 km/h (130.6 mph).

Shima's father, who had joined the Railways Bureau of the Ministry of Telecommunications after leaving the Kansai Railway Company, had been sent by the Ministry to France to study. He had the opportunity to observe the test in 1903 and, taking detailed notes, began to dream of the possibility of high-speed transport in Japan. While in this particular test a speed of 200km/h was achieved, the persistence of resonance phenomena in the rolling stock prevented further development. Although the German team firmly believed that trains of the future would be able to travel at speeds in excess of 200 km/h, they concluded from the test that considerable progress in mechanical and electrical engineering would be needed before that dream was realized.

It was in 1939 that Japan launched its first 200 km/h train project. The plan was to run a 'bullet train' ('*dangan ressha*') at the speed of 200 km/h on standard-gauge track from Tokyo to Osaka, and on to Shimonoseki at the western end of the island of Honshu. The Imperial Diet approved the budget for this project in 1940, and partial construction of the railway started. Many of the standards that had been decided upon for the '*dangan ressha*' project were eventually adopted by the Tokaido Shinkansen; for example, the same radius of 2,500 metres (yards) for curves. While there were many differences, the main one being that the former would use steam locomotives whereas the latter used EMU trains, the fact that it took only five years for the Tokaido Shinkansen to start operations in 1964 from the start of construction in 1959 can be partially explained by the large amount of planning that had already taken place for the original '*dangan ressha*' project.

The fact that it took sixty-one years from its first experimental run in 1903 to the start of the business operation of the Tokaido Shinkansen in 1964, to bring a 200 km/h-plus high-speed train into service is an indication of both the massive technological input required and the long life-cycles involved in the railway industry. To take on such a challenge required a level of courage on the part of the JNR management that is perhaps not sufficiently recognized. If they had decided not to proceed with the Tokaido Shinkansen, the position of railways in the Japanese transportation system would be much weaker. It would have also been impossible to break up and privatize JNR, given that the earnings of the Tokaido Shinkansen supported a substantial amount of debt which had been transferred from other JR companies as part of the so-called 'profit adjustment' scheme.

President Sogo resigned in May 1963, soon after the welcome speech to us new employees. He was succeeded by Ishida Reisuke, who was the former head of the New York branch of Mitsui & Co. and had for a long time served as the chairman of JNR's Audit Committee. Isozaki Satoshi, a former member of the board of directors of JNR who had moved to the private sector for a short time, returned to JNR as deputy president. A new era had begun.

It was said that president Sogo resigned to take responsibility for two things: one was the ballooning cost of the construction of the Tokaido Shinkansen from the initial budget of ¥190 billion ($1.6 bn) to ¥380 billion ($3.2 bn); the other was the Mikawashima train accident in May 1962, which caused a large number of casualties when passengers evacuating from a derailed train were struck by an oncoming train. The tragedy was blamed largely on the congested train schedule. President Sogo's management was criticized for putting too much emphasis on profits over safety. President Sogo was indeed the last president to defend vigorously the principle of profitability within the framework of the financially self-supporting accounting system. Following the Railway Construction Law passed in 1922, JNR had always faced intense political pressure, which demanded the construction of local lines. Once JNR submitted to this pressure, a sharp negative impact on earnings was inevitable. President Sogo firmly refused to bow to pressures to construct local lines, which would inevitably weaken JNR's financial position still further. A number of politicians were evidently keen to get rid of him and it is quite possible that the construction cost overrun for the Shinkansen and the Mikawashima accident were used as an excuse to oust him. The words I heard him utter a month before his resignation 'Fight until you die with a rail as a pillow' may well have reflected his reaction to such pressures. After Sogo's resignation, the Railway Construction Corporation was established in 1964, which explicitly promoted the construction of local lines, but had been lagging behind schedule.

The hostility towards the Shinkansen project that had permeated JNR became more tangible after Sogo resigned and Isozaki re-joined as Executive Vice President. The newly-appointed President Ishida evidently commented that he was extremely unhappy to take responsibility for the risky and extravagant Tokaido Shinkansen project. With the embers of the Mikawashima and Tsurumi accidents still smouldering in the public's mind, there was widespread concern that high-speed trains operating at more than 200 km/h would naturally cause large accidents sooner or later. It was even reported that the newspapers had already prepared articles in anticipation of such an accident. Ishida's remark undoubtedly reflected the prevailing attitudes towards the Shinkansen project within JNR at the time.

Ultimately, of course, the Tokaido Shinkansen was a tremendous success. Some 3.8 billion passengers have travelled on the Tokaido Shinkansen over its first 38 years, and there has not been a single fatality caused by an accident, a superb record that the Tokaido Shinkansen still continues to maintain every year. It was in all probability the only profitable project among the many new lines and line extension projects undertaken by JNR.

Under normal conditions, the huge investment required would make a project as big as the Tokaido Shinkansen difficult to justify from a business point of view. Typically, investment in infrastructure, such as railways, tends to lead to large increases in capacity upon completion. Hence, to make such a large investment profitable, intensive utilization of new capacity is required. This helps spread the costs resulting from the initial investment over a large number of passengers, which in turn keeps fares at acceptable levels. In reality, however, demand does not build up over a short period of time. The establishment of the infrastructure itself has a positive impact on local economic activity and this gradually leads to a corresponding increase in passenger numbers. Typically, it takes decades until the utilization rate reaches the break-even point.

The Tokaido Shinkansen, however, together with the existing Tokaido Line, achieved profitability in the first year of operation enabling the amortization of the initial Tokaido Shinkansen investment within ten years. The key to this success was a combination of the high population density between Tokyo and Osaka and high economic growth rates during that period. The extraordinary improvement in transportation services brought about a new wave of regional economic activity, which in turn led to a rapid increase in overall transport volumes. Moreover, as the plan to construct a high-speed railway had been formulated before the war, part of the land had already been secured and work was partially under way. All these factors worked positively for the Shinkansen project, and enabled it to become profitable despite the inherently unprofitable nature of such large-scale projects. Throughout the JNR period the Tokaido Shinkansen continued to provide 'subsidies' to support the national railway network, which consisted in large part of loss-making lines. At the time of the regional break-up and privatization of JNR, the Tokaido Shinkansen assumed ¥5 trillion ($41.7 bn) of debt from JNR, a sum ten times greater than its book value of ¥470 billion ($3.9 bn). In doing so it shouldered the construction cost of other Shinkansen lines to the tune of about ¥2 trillion ($16.7 bn) and thereby reduced the interest payments of JR East and JR West, which suffered from a large number of unprofitable local lines. Currently the Tokaido Shinkansen is profitable despite shouldering 20% higher expenses than are intrinsic to its operation (based on ¥3 trillion ($25 bn) repurchase value).

There is a stereotypical pattern to the response of bureaucratic organizations to large, high-risk projects such as the Tokaido Shinkansen. In an organization where the emphasis of personnel evaluation is more on avoiding mistakes than on actual achievement, those deemed capable are those who skilfully avoid taking risk and stay out of trouble. They tend to take ambiguous positions on contentious issues. If a policy is successful they naturally supported it from the beginning. If it proves a failure, they naturally always disagreed with it. It came as no surprise that many people who had been withholding their opinions on the construction of the Tokaido Shinkansen quietly became promoters of the plan when the plan proved a big success. However, none of the subsequent Shinkansen projects, the Sanyo Shinkansen (which operates in the western part of Honshu), the Tohoku Shinkansen, and the Joetsu Shinkansen (both of which operate in the northern part of Honshu) is close to the profitability of the Tokaido Shinkansen.

It is worth stressing that had JNR not been run as a directly managed public corporation[7] the Tokaido Shinkansen project would never have got off the ground. Had it operated, for example, as a government agency, the process for the approval of JNR's budget by the Diet would have been very rigid, with agreement required on a project-by-project basis. Even with some authority to do external funding, it would not have been allowed to divert funds from one project to another according to its own judgement in the way that JNR did, enabling them to cope with the spiralling costs of the Tokaido Shinkansen. This would have been particularly true in an environment where mainstream public opinion argued that the age of airlines and cars was just around the corner. Therefore, with powerful politicians in the *zoku*[8] in the Diet comparing the construction of the Tokaido Shinkansen with the Great Wall of China, to decide to proceed with the project was a political decision with tremendous risk. In an environment where a decision to raise fares by the smallest amount would cause an enormous fuss, if JNR had been a government agency, it is unthinkable that the government would have been able to push through a project like the Tokaido Shinkansen. By comparison, private railway companies controlled their own destinies and the management was free to make decisions about fare increases,[9] funding and capital expenditure. However, a private company would have generally preferred safer investments in railway-related projects such as hotels, department stores, housing developments and amusement parks, which were adjacent to stations, where the scale of investments would be much smaller, and the amortization period much shorter than for a large-scale construction project

---

[7] There are several types of public enterprises in Japan which enjoy different degrees of managerial freedom. While JNR had always been an independently managed public corporation regulated by the former Ministry of Transport, the Postal Services, to take one example, have been operating as a government-affiliated agency under the auspices of the former Ministry of Posts and Telecommunication.

[8] A clique or group of politicians supporting a certain cause. For most causes, a *zoku* developed and many become highly influential within the LDP.

[9] Fare increases by private railway companies had to be approved by the minister of Transport, however JNR needed the approval of the Diet.

such as the Tokaido Shinkansen. Even in the private sector, investment in a Shinkansen-type project would have been inconceivable.

In the case of JNR, as a public corporation, investments in railway-related businesses were strictly regulated under the Japanese National Railways Law, and the process for approval of JNR's capital expenditure budget was the same as for the national budget, i.e. through Diet deliberations. But once the total budget for capital expenditure was approved, the JNR president was granted discretionary authority to decide how to spend it. This was what enabled President Sogo to exercise his leadership and get the Tokaido Shinkansen built. Knowing that the Diet would never approve the ¥400 billion ($3.3 bn) budget, which was the estimated construction cost of the Tokaido Shinkansen, President Sogo ordered the estimate to be reduced to ¥190 billion ($1.6 bn). From the outset, he intended to divert money from other projects to the construction of the Tokaido Shinkansen. The main reason for borrowing $80 million (about ¥28.8 billion at that time) from the International Bank of Reconstruction and Development was to cut off the Japanese government's escape route from the project. The securing of this loan was apparently the idea of the then Minister of Finance, Sato Eisaku (who later became Prime Minister), who had been Sogo's junior at the Railway Ministry. Those in JNR who were strongly opposed to the Tokaido Shinkansen project apparently cooked up a plan to use the Council of Railway Construction, an advisory body to the Minister of Transport to determine the approval of new lines, as a device to reject the plan. Sogo skilfully side-stepped the Council arguing successfully that the Tokaido Shinkansen was not a new line, but the expansion of the existing Tokaido Line to quadruple-track.

Some people are under the impression that the construction of the Tokaido Shinkansen used up enormous public funds and, as JNR started to post deficits around the time the Tokaido Shinkansen began operations, that it was this project that triggered JNR's losses. These two arguments are totally misguided. The construction of the Tokaido Shinkansen was financed with debt and funds accumulated through internal reserves. Investment costs were recovered only through passenger revenues. The two main reasons for JNR's deteriorating operating position after 1964 were first, the large investments in constructing commuter railways in urban areas, which were vital for the national economy, but also tremendously unprofitable, and second, that fare increases were strictly constrained.

After its break-up and privatization, JNR was often criticized for being a 'totally irresponsible and inefficient organization'. However, for a certain period, it functioned very efficiently. The construction of the Tokaido Shinkansen is one of the great legacies of the JNR era and the history of JNR should be seen in that light.

4 'A Train Ticket to Heaven'

When Ishida Reisuke inherited the presidency of JNR from Sogo he described his feelings about the assumption of the presidency of JNR as follows: 'Having achieved all I could in the private sector for Mitsui & Co, I would now like to dedicate myself to serving my country and the general public and thereby earn my train ticket to heaven.' This phrase summed up the period of Ishida's presidency. Having served first as a member, then as the Chairman of JNR's auditing committee, Ishida was requested to assume the office of JNR president. His appointment drew a favourable response from the public because of his background in the private sector. He was also popular with JNR's employees, because he expressed openly what many employees of JNR felt themselves but were unable to say in public because of the sensitive nature of the issues concerned. For example, he said in the Diet that it was 'not at all reasonable that the salaries of JNR employees should be the same as those of the Japan Tobacco and Salt Corporation (now privatized as Japan Tobacco) as JNR's employees carried the full responsibility for passengers' lives whereas all the staff of the Japan Tobacco and Salt Corporation did was to make cigarettes.' In reality, however, it is fair to assume that he entrusted the responsibility for running the day-to-day business to Executive Vice-President Isozaki, a career JNR man.

There was an interesting and slightly ironic contrast between Sogo, a career bureaucrat at the Railway Ministry prior to the war

16

but who also strongly emphasized profitability, and Ishida, after a career in the private sector who proclaimed unselfish devotion to the public interest. The former exhorted his employees to 'prepare to die in battle' while the latter talked about his 'train ticket to heaven'. Sogo's basic policy was to make investments only if there was a prospect that they would be profitable. However, just before the end of Sogo's presidency, the Mikawashima train accident occurred involving 160 fatalities. In November 1963, six months after Ishida took office, another tragic train accident, at Tsurumi, killed 161 people. These two train accidents were the most serious in terms of casualties in the post-war period. Investigations were carried out into the causes of the accidents, but were inconclusive. Although a number of factors were highlighted, in particular in the case of the Mikawashima accident, even in the event of a derailment, if a train had not been running on the opposite track, serious casualties could have been avoided. Sufficient capacity and proper scheduling could have avoided almost all the fatalities. Eventually, overcrowded scheduling was blamed and the tide of public opinion was moving irresistibly towards JNR taking responsibility to alleviate congested train schedules.

As a result, the conversion of congested metropolitan lines to four-track lines became an urgent issue. It was not clear, however, how much investment was required to procure the necessary land and build the extra line and how it would be financed, especially as fares had to be kept low for political reasons. Commuter passes were discounted by nearly 70% while student passes were discounted by nearly 90%. In reality, the transport of students and business people reached its peak during the morning and evening rush-hours, with low usage during the day. This, inevitably, led to low efficiency. As many of the trains were out of operation during the day, much greater space for rolling stock and train depots was required. Additional train drivers also had to be kept on to prepare for peak demand. Therefore, the common perception was that the business of rail transport, particularly for commuting, was inherently unprofitable because of low fares and poor efficiency.

Hitherto, JNR had been striving to meet the constantly increasing transport demands by increasing frequency, extending the length of platforms, and adding extra carriages, but after the two tragic accidents, JNR was forced to commit itself to the construction of four-track lines. The Third Long-Term Plan was agreed upon (with a budget for capital expenditure totalling ¥2.9 trillion – $24.2 bn) which would run from fiscal 1965 to fiscal 1971. It incorporated the so-called 'Five-Directions Strategy', a project to convert major rail arteries out of Tokyo – the Tokaido Line, the Chuo Line, the Tohoku Line, the Joban Line, and the Sobu Line – into four-track lines. The problem of congested train schedules persists to this day. If anything, it is now worse than ever. However, we no longer hear criticism from any quarters of society.

As the Third Long-Term Plan would require enormous expenditures, way beyond the budget of JNR at the time, JNR could not afford to implement the plan within the framework of the financially self-sufficient accounting system. Thus, a vital part of the plan was the provision by the government of direct grants or interest-free loans to JNR. While the First and Second Long-Term Plan were created and implemented by JNR's themselves, JNR decided to turn the Third Long-Term Plan into a national project by requesting approval of the Cabinet for the provision of such funding from the government.

Although the cabinet approved their overall plan, JNR failed to obtain direct government funding and were compelled to borrow the required funds. While most of it came from the government's Financial Investment and Loan Programme (FILP), JNR was forced for the first time to borrow from the private sector by issuing special bonds. Hitherto, bonds had been issued mainly in the form of private placements subscribed by corporations and close affiliates, such as JNR contractors. Henceforth, however, private financial institutions were expected to subscribe to the newly-issued bonds. Special bonds issued in fiscal 1965 amounted to ¥68.8 billion ($0.6 bn). After that, however, issuance increased sharply, and JNR's dependence on external debts to fund its investments, grew exponentially.

Recently, the view is widespread that everything should be determined by the market mechanism. However, the effectiveness of the market mechanism varies greatly according to the nature of the business. One of the characteristics of infrastructure businesses, such as railway and power-generation businesses, is the enormous initial investment that is required. Companies in these industries can only become profitable through the concentrated use of invested capital and strict cost-control. 'Natural monopolies' tend to form in these industries as the existence of direct competition will tend to drive down prices until one company is left remaining. In order to ensure the long-term stability of supply, the licensing system is used, with regulatory mechanisms to protect the benefits of consumers in return for allowing businesses to monopolize the market. Withdrawal from the market is not an easy process.

Needless to say, it is not just the passengers who enjoy the benefits of train transportation. The economy as a whole, including industry which relies on the rail system to enable workers to go to and from work, is highly dependent on rail transportation, which could thus be said to serve the 'public interest'. Economics defines this resulting wealth effect as an 'external benefit' or an 'external economy'. In the case of a railway business, the 'external benefit' which society enjoys far exceeds the 'internal benefit' enjoyed directly by passengers. These external benefits, which cannot be recovered through fares paid by passengers, are a critical consideration. In the planning, construction and maintenance of a railway system, therefore, the market mechanism can play only a limited role, and there is a strong argument that the funding of these projects should be done by the government through taxation in the same way that roads are financed. In the past, railways were owned and directly operated by the government. However, on completion of the construction of a railway network, as focus shifts to the challenge of enhancing operating efficiency, privatization is a highly effective alternative. The privatization of JNR was a typical case in point. During its development phase, however, it is difficult to conceive of a profitable railway business that was able to fund construction and maintenance of the railways on its own. In this sense, the establishment and collapse of JNR was quite predictable. The self-sufficient accounting system was based on the premise that all the railway operations, including investment for new or improved facilities, should be covered only by passenger and freight revenues. There clearly existed a large gap between the goals set for JNR and the means provided for JNR to achieve them. JNR became aware of this gap at an early stage, and recognized that it would need government investment to improve the railway infrastructure. However, the government resolutely denied JNR's persistent requests for capital. Instead, JNR was told to depend mainly on interest-bearing funds borrowed from the FILP and private financial institutions. Thus began JNR's heavy dependency on external debt, a growing problem that only came to the surface when the Third Long-Term Plan was launched.

Everyone at JNR, the Ministry of Transport and the Ministry of Finance had to be aware of the strong possibility of JNR's bankruptcy should things continue as they were. However, the proverb 'Look before you leap' never did apply very strongly in the world of politics. Understanding perfectly the consequences of massive increases in indebtedness, there being no alternative, the management of JNR continued down this road. They must have suffered a great sense of frustration as their increasing dependency on borrowed money from FILP and private financial institutions, funds which in reality should have come from the government. This was obvious even to a relative newcomer like me. At the time, having been at JNR for two or three years, I was working at the Budget Section of the Headquarters Finance & Accounting Department. I recall expressing my concerns to a director of the Budget Section about the level of JNR's increasing indebtedness. He replied: 'You are right. Our capital expenditures should essentially be funded by the government, but we have to shoulder this burden instead. So why not borrow as much as possible? When we can't borrow any more, let JNR go bankrupt. In any case, it's the government that will have to pick up the pieces.' I recall his remarks vividly to this day. JNR could have maintained the self-supporting accounting system for some time by resisting capital expenditure as long as the government declined to fund it. If Sogo had been president at the time, he might have tried to go down this route. However, since JNR's budget constituted an integral part of the government budget, any discrepancies between JNR and the Ministry of Finance would have delayed the submission of the proposed budget to the Diet, which would have had a tremendous impact and would have been unacceptable. Therefore, even though they were aware of the probable eventual outcome, JNR launched the Third Long-Term Plan.

Inevitably, as interest payments increased and fare increases continued to be restricted, JNR posted deficits in 1964 and 1965, and finally in 1966, retained earnings turned negative for the first time in JNR's history. It should be pointed out that much of the capital expenditure carried out under the Third Long-Term Plan was critical to the future of Japan's rail system. A number of major projects, such as the electrification and double-tracking of trunk lines, were still under way at the time. The Sanyo Shinkansen plan was added to these projects. Furthermore, the Five-Direction Strategy for commuting, to convert double-track lines in the Tokyo area into four-track lines, was also being implemented. One by one, these projects were completed from the mid-1960s to the early 1980s. These are now all trunk lines of great importance to JR. Strategic priorities between projects were very clearly defined and rigidly adhered to, with little scope for political intervention. Even though profitability was no longer a realistic objective, there still existed a consciousness among the management that the company's finances should be restored to a healthy state as soon as possible, and efforts were made to minimize construction costs to the greatest extent possible. The consequences of the government's refusal to help fund the Third Long-term Plan was that the bill, which the government eventually had to pay, ran up to ¥37 trillion ($308.3 bn). A total of ¥28 trillion ($233.3 bn) of this was shouldered by taxpayers in 1998 as part of the disposal of JNR-related debts. In that sense, the perspective of the then director of the Budget Section of the Finance & Accounting Department seems perfectly correct.

▶ *Chapter 2*

JNR's collapse

1 The first reorganization plan

Between 1967 and 1968, the JNR Financial Reorganization Committee considered how JNR should be reorganized and eventually issued its report in November 1968. The Special Measures Law for JNR Financial Reorganization, which was passed by the ordinary session of the Diet in 1969, was the embodiment of this report. As laid out in the Special Measures Law, JNR submitted a reorganization plan to the Minister of Transport. His approval of the plan, therefore, represented a consensus of all parties concerned, namely JNR, the government, the ruling party and the Diet, as to the future direction of JNR.

Coinciding with the start of the 'First Reorganization Plan', came the resignation of President Ishida Reisuke. He was succeeded by Executive Vice-President Isozaki Satoshi. As he was himself a former JNR employee, I can well imagine that President Isozaki would have been determined personally to put the management of JNR back on an even kneel. His philosophy was very much that the three interested parties, that is the passengers, the tax payers and the employees of JNR, should equally share the pain in the process of the rebuilding the company. The First Reorganization Plan was a ten-year plan, going through to fiscal 1978. In sharp contrast to the previous three Long-Term Plans, which were project-based and which focused on capital expenditure, the Reorganization Plan was a long-term management plan, the primary objective of which was to restore financial stability, concentrating on measures to increase revenues and restrain expenditure.

It was a good opportunity to look squarely at the inherent defects of the public corporation concept and to take radical measures to correct them. The major issues confronting JNR at the time were very clear to the eyes of everyone: i.e., the ability to raise fares in a proper and timely fashion; the provision of government funds for capital expenditure; dealing with the excessive debt that had accumulated; the thorough streamlining of employees; closing down from unprofitable lines, etc. The pain of surgery might not have been so unbearable if appropriate treatment had been administered at the time.

Unfortunately, the measures actually taken turned out to be only stop-gap solutions that postponed the real solution to the problems. This is clearly reflected in the long-term financial forecasts which were approved by the Minister of Transport at the time. For fiscal 1969, the first year of the Plan, accumulated losses were forecast to reach around ¥140 billion ($1.2 bn). For fiscal 1976, the eighth year of the Plan, this figure was expected to exceed ¥200 billion ($1.7 bn). However, by 1977, the deficit would suddenly shrink to ¥17.5 billion ($146 mn) with the benefits of increases in both fares and passenger numbers, and for fiscal 1978, the final year of the Plan, a surplus of slightly more than ¥20 billion ($167 mn) was expected to accumulate. Fare increases were expected to be quite restrained, going up three times every four years by about ten per cent each time. This was a much lower increase than the prevailing inflation rate. On the other hand, in the last year of the Plan, both transport volume and revenues were forecast to increase sharply, leading to a dramatic improvement in JNR's financial position. Even if these forecasts proved to be accurate, if one subtracted government subsidies, which were running at ¥25 billion ($208 mn) per annum, losses of ¥2 billion ($17 mn) would still be left. Considering all this, few actually believed that the reorganization would have the desired effects, or that the estimates were anything but fantasy. By 1978, accumulated losses had actually reached ¥890 billion ($7.4 bn), as opposed to the slight surplus forecast by the plan.

JNR's accumulated debt, which stood at ¥2.2 trillion ($18.3 bn) at beginning of the Plan, was expected to increase to ¥4.6 trillion ($38.3 bn) in the tenth and final year: the result of continuous borrowing to cover construction costs. According to the plan, the completion of major projects combined with the effect of other investments would result in increases of the transport volumes and revenues. However, even in that scenario, debt would still be more than double operating revenues by the tenth year, with no improvement on the first year. As it turned out, by the end of fiscal 1978, accumulated debts exceeded ¥11 trillion ($91.7 bn) indicating clearly how optimistic the plan was. The principle of financial self-sufficiency would be as good as dead.

I studied in America for two years from 1967 to 1969 and returned to Japan several months after the launch of the Reorganization Plan. When I returned, I was told by a senior member of staff who had been involved in the drafting of the Plan that it would only survive for another two years after which another more radical plan would be drawn up. As the first year of the ten-year plan was an integral part of the national budget, the only option was to use the figures in the national budget as the starting point. No major changes in the second year were allowed as the figures had to be consistent with those of the first year. The deficit, however, could not be left as it was, and a rosy scenario was needed to reduce it. From year three, improvement in the quality and quantity of services due to the full operation of newly-built facilities would result in the increase of both transport volumes and revenues. At the same time, operating efficiencies would ensure that the rate of growth in operating expenses would diminish. The First Reorganization Plan, therefore, had JNR's financial position attaining stability in year 10. This was all against the background of the high economic growth that Japan was enjoying at the time. Rapid growth in transport volumes, correlated to GDP, gave the reorganization and its targets a degree of plausibility.

The plan was a typical example of a refusal to face up to reality: taking inadequate measures on the one hand, making overly optimistic long-term forecasts on the other, and making the figures add up at some distant point in the future. The gap between the optimistic forecasts and reality would be filled by the 'indomitable resolve' of the employees, from the president downwards. Doubtless all of the employees who were engaged in the creation of the Plan realized that it could only survive for two years. If the true state of affairs had been revealed, much more radical measures, in some form or another, would have been required. Accountability and responsibility for JNR's losses would have to be clarified, and passengers and taxpayers would have to be asked to share the financial burden. Borrowing long-term funds would be the easiest way to avoid the issue of trying to ascertain who was actually responsible for this sorry state of affairs. Although money was to be borrowed from FILP, it was a government condition that any loan from FILP should be made on a 'safe and favourable' basis, i.e., that repayment would be guaranteed. Seeking a 'gimmick' to give the appearance of guaranteed repayment, it was decided that the Ten-Year Reorganization Plan should be drawn up as a law. Consequently, the Reorganization Plan became the Special Measures Law for JNR Financial Reorganization, and was granted approval by the Minister of Transport. Even if there was a common understanding among those concerned that the plan would be a 'busted flush' within three years, there would be no problem receiving a loan from the FILP, given that the plan had been officially approved and had the force of law. Even if the plan did not work out, responsibility for its failure would be widely dispersed among the various parties that were involved in drawing it up: no one would be held accountable. Borrowing money from the FILP would provide the Reorganization Plan with legitimacy in the eyes of the people. Using this impression of legitimacy as 'collateral', JNR were able to borrow from the private sector, which regarded JNR and an arm of the government, just as FILP was. However, anyone who cared to examine the Reorganization Plan in detail would have realized that it was a sham, patched together by members of the government, the ruling party and JNR to conceal the collapse of JNR and to postpone the confrontation of the real problems.

As many experts anticipated, the Reorganization Plan collapsed totally in fiscal 1971, in its third year. JNR suffered negative operating cash-flow for fiscal 1971, meaning that even operating expenses had to be funded by borrowing money. If JNR had been a private company, it would certainly have had to file for bankruptcy in such a desperate financial situation.

This was really the last opportunity for JNR to take proper action to save itself: to make its serious financial situation known, to raise fares to a proper level, to retreat from unprofitable lines, and to restrain capital expenditure for which it was totally dependent on borrowed money. If these measures had been taken at that time, the amount of debt JNR eventually had to pay back would have been much smaller: accumulated debt exceeded a little more than ¥3 trillion ($25 bn) at the end of fiscal 1971.

It was inconceivable, however, for JNR to cease providing transportation services on which the public was so dependent: JNR simply could not be allowed to go bankrupt. Furthermore, the bankruptcy of JNR would force not only the management of JNR but also the government and the LDP, both deeply complicit in directing JNR to its current situation, to take responsibility. A small lie inevitably leads to more and even bigger lies to conceal the first one: the quicksand will swallow you up in the end. The actions of the government, the ruling party and JNR in dealing with the reorganization of JNR were a case in point. Although they may have recognized deep down that 'Good medicine tastes bitter', the people concerned all agreed that the drug available in the form of 'Zaito' (abridged term in Japanese for the Fiscal Investment and Loan Programme (FILP)) tasted much better. By avoiding the acknowledgement of the debt problem at the time, all those concerned including the management of JNR, the Ministry of Transport, the Ministry of Finance and the ruling and opposition parties, finally lost any remnants of mental discipline to deal with the debt problem and became shameless and irresponsible in their approach: there was now no way back.

Thereafter, five reorganization plans were presented to the Diet. While the first, a ten-year plan (1972–1981), was stalled in the Diet and eventually abandoned, four plans (1973–1977, 1976–1977, 1977–1979 and 1981–1985) were approved and the necessary legislation put in place. However, it was more of the same. The last law, passed in fiscal 1981, was a true vintage: a comprehensive compilation of all of the patch-up measures of the previous plans. By then, it was far too late to save JNR.

It is perhaps an appropriate moment to review the events of that ten-year period.

[2] Restraining fare rises and compensation with loans from the Fiscal Investment and Loan Programme (Window-dressing by the Nation)

Setting the price for a company's goods and services is clearly one of the most important decisions that the management has to make. Since its establishment, all of JNR's fares were regulated by the Fare Act: the ability to raise fares would only be possible if the Fare Law were to be revised. Moreover, it was not just fares: the annual expenditure, budget of JNR, including wages and capital expenditure as well as borrowing plans from FILP were subject to the approval of the Diet as it was all regarded as an integral part of the national budget. It was the fate of public corporations such as JNR to suffer the intervention of government that had its own political agenda.

As far as fares were concerned, if JNR had had the flexibility to raise fares during the reconstruction and high-growth phases of the post-war period when JNR monopolized the transport market, it would have secured ample funds even operating within the framework of the nationally uniform fare system. JNR thus could have financed a considerable portion of its capital expenditure programme on its own instead of resorting to borrowing.

Unfortunately, throughout the 1950s the government consistently resisted JNR's repeated calls for proper and timely fare increases. While the issue of fare increases was critical for JNR, the objective was to keep fares as low as possible in order to assist other industries. Thus, while JNR helped plant the seeds for economic recovery in the post-war period, it did so by hindering its own development. This became clear with the accident tragedies at Mikawashima and Tsurumi in the early 1960's, which, in turn, forced JNR to borrow large sums to meet safety requirements.

I was assigned to the Corporate Planning Department in March 1971, and was involved in the putting together of the Second Reorganization Plan. This was a ten-year plan starting in fiscal 1972. It contained nothing new, being nothing more than a slightly more elaborate rehash of the failed First Reorganization Plan. The first step of this Plan was to raise fares by 20% in nominal terms from 1 April 1972. However, the proposal to raise fares caused a bitter political confrontation between the ruling party, the Liberal Democratic Party (LDP), and the opposition party, the Japan Socialist Party (JSP). At the time, the cold war was at its height and the JSP actively sought to steer Japan down the path of socialism and endeavoured to take advantage of any issues to rattle the LDP. It was just at this time that Prime Minister Sato publicly announced his intention to retire having successfully concluded the treaty with the US which returned Okinawa to Japan. Sato immediately became a lame duck and a bitter power struggle ensued among the LDP leadership as the selection process of Sato's successor got underway. As a result of strong resistance from the opposition parties and disunity within the LDP, the bill to raise fares was shelved and was finally abandoned. The chairman of the Diet Affairs Committee of the Socialist Party was reported to have boasted that they had spent three times longer killing the bill in the Diet than had been spent debating the entire Japanese Constitution. Immediately thereafter, Sato retired and Tanaka Kakuei became Prime Minister.

After the Second Financial Reorganization Plan had been aborted, a Third Reorganization Plan was presented to the Diet at the initiative of the Tanaka Cabinet. It was a revised version of the Second Plan and was due to be implemented from fiscal 1973. However, it quickly ran into difficulties in the Diet . Initially the bill was expected to become law on 1 April 1973, but its passage actually dragged on until the end of September. Moreover, as part of the compromise between the LDP and the JSP, it was agreed that fare increases would be implemented on 1 April 1974, six months after the passage of the bill. There was no rationale at all for this compromise other than to save the face of the opposition party.

To make matters worse, the Arab-Israeli War broke out on 6 October 1973, sparking off the first oil crisis. Just at that time, the 'Plan for Remodelling the Japanese Archipelago', Tanaka's grand idea to accelerate Japan's development through a series of huge public works programmes, ignited a speculative property boom. These two factors combined to cause a hyper-inflationary situation. Under such circumstances, the government decided to postpone the implementation of fare increases another six months, until October 1974.

The Third Reorganization Plan consisted of just another set of patch-up measures which ignored JNR's fundamental problems. Even if it had been implemented smoothly according to the original timetable, there would have been no meaningful impact on JNR. Instead, the two-and-a-half-year delay in fare hikes dealt a fatal blow to JNR's finances, producing a revenue shortfall of more than ¥1 trillion ($8.3 bn) compared to the original plan. The Third Reorganization Plan was already dead before it was implemented.

Suffering from negative operating cash-flow from fiscal 1971, JNR was already virtually bankrupt. As no tangible measures to tackle deficits had been taken in the intervening three years, the financial situation in fiscal 1975 had reached truly devastating proportions. It is said that once you start taking drugs, it is impossible to stop. For JNR, borrowed money was the drug, and they could not kick the habit. Operating costs financed by borrowing amounted to around ¥33 billion ($275 mn) for fiscal 1971, but by fiscal 1975 it had expanded to ¥630 billion ($5.3 bn). The government, however, continued to lend money to JNR by using FILP funds as if nothing was amiss, and by fiscal 1975, accumulated debts reached ¥6.8 trillion ($56.7 bn). The management of JNR was filled with a sense of powerlessness and resignation and it was around this time that the perception of JNR as an 'unsinkable ship' began to permeate visibly among both the management and the labour unions. President Isozaki had resigned at the end of 1973 and Fujii Matsutaro, a former employee of JNR, became President for a short period. In March 1976, he was succeeded by Takagi Fumio, former Administrative Vice-Minister at the Ministry of Finance (MOF).

During the Fujii and Takagi presidencies, there was finally a growing recognition that JNR could not continue to postpone dealing with its financial problems by borrowing money. The period of high economic growth had come to an end and in the environment of stable growth, the policy of subsidizing industry through low fares no longer made any sense. Opinion grew within the government and the ruling and opposition parties that fares should be increased, instead of pouring tax money directly into JNR. In this changing environment, JNR management began to focus more on short-term measures to fix the company's tattered finances, rather than through ten-year plans, and as part of this new strategy aimed to double fares in fiscal 1976 and 1977.

While it was certainly true that JNR's fares had been kept low compared with the prices of other services, the doubling of fares was going from one extreme to the other. The revenues from passengers and freight were ¥1.32 trillion ($11 bn) and ¥0.24 trillion ($2 bn), respectively, for fiscal 1975. If passenger fares were to double in nominal terms, it was estimated that revenues should increase by more than ¥1 trillion, even allowing for the expected decline in demand caused by the fare hikes, and the fact that JNR's poor competitive position *vis-à-vis* road transportation meant that freight rates could not be raised. In addition, it was decided to remove ¥2.5 trillion ($20.8 bn) of debt that had resulted from delayed fare increases at the end of fiscal 1975. The idea was to establish a special account for this portion of debt, which would be managed separately from JNR's total debts of ¥6.8 billion ($57 mn). Interest payments for that portion of debt would be made with subsidies from the General Account Budget of the government and the principal would be repaid with interest-free loans from the General Account.

Something also needed to be done about unprofitable lines and for fiscal 1976, the government provided a grant of ¥17.2 billion ($143 mn) to compensate for losses incurred from 11,000 km of loss-making lines that JNR operated nationwide. Based on expert analysis, JNR estimated that in the special geographic conditions in which JNR operated, a section traffic volume of 8,000 persons per day was required to achieve a break-even position. Accordingly, a network comprising 10,000 km of trunk lines was categorized as 'profitable' if taken as a whole. The idea was that these trunk lines should form a network that, through a rational system of cross-subsidies based on a uniform set of fares, would form the foundations of a sound business. Not all of these trunk lines were actually profitable and the number of profitable lines was declining every year with the result that the source of any cross-subsidies was getting smaller. According to the accounts for fiscal 1975, the only profitable lines were the Tokaido-Sanyo Shinkansen, the Yamanote Line and the Takasaki Line. The combined distance of these three lines was only 1,300 km. But it was thought that if proper measures were taken, the 10,000 km network of trunk lines would operate profitably within the framework of a rational system of cross-subsidies.

For JNR to maintain unprofitable, low-density lines through cross-subsidies, high-density lines with low overheads such as the Tokaido Shinkansen Line and commuter lines in the metropolitan area would inevitably have to shoulder costs over and above their inherent costs. As a result, even profitable lines would be uncompetitive against other forms of transport, trapping JNR in its entirety in a vicious circle of increasing fares, loss-making routes skimming off the cream from profitable lines, further fare increases, and so on. The fact that the number of profitable lines and therefore the extent of the rail network that they effectively could cross-subsidize was decreasing meant that this vicious circle had already been put in motion. JNR continued to ask for permission from the government to withdraw from chronically loss-making lines, or for compensation if withdrawal was not possible from a political point of view. While the amount was paltry, the government grant of ¥17.2 billion ($143mn) to make up for the losses of such lines indicated a partial acceptance of JNR's arguments. As the MOF had feared, the compensation for loss-making local lines increased sharply for fiscal 1981, to ¥120 billion ($1 bn).

These events occurred during my time at the Headquarters Corporate Planning Department from 1971 to the spring of 1977, when I was engaged in the budgeting and long-term planning process. Although there was remarkable progress it was insufficient to revive the fortunes of the JNR Reorganization Plans. By transferring debt of ¥2.5 trillion ($20.8 bn) into a separate account, JNR's debt temporarily decreased for fiscal 1976, but bounced back to its previous size within only two years due to growing losses and increasing capital expenditure.

As expected, the proposal for a 50% fare increase in 1976 ran into difficulties in the Diet, and the bill was shelved in the ordinary session. The bill was finally passed during the extraordinary session in autumn, and fare increases were implemented on 6 November. But the drastic nature of the increases had an impact on passenger demand: total passenger kilometres for fiscal 1976 declined 2%, and a further 5% in fiscal 1977.

31

With the 1976 fare hike ending so disastrously, the Fourth Reorganization Plan, with its stated objective of doubling fares within two years, naturally collapsed also. The Fifth (three-year) Plan was subsequently approved by the Minister of Transport on 1 April 1977.

A major component of the new plan was a new law allowing more flexibility in the setting of fares. Hitherto, fares were determined by a set fare rate per kilometre as stipulated by the Fare Law. Therefore, every time JNR wanted to raise fares, the Diet had to approve a revision of the Fare Law: the critical issue of fares was therefore subject to the prevailing political climate and JNR were never able to make flexible and timely changes in their fare structure. The new law permitted JNR to change fares according to a predetermined formula simply with the approval of the Transport Minister. The maximum increase permitted under the formula was related to the expected rise in operating expenses arising from increases in consumer prices and labour costs. It was clear that the primary purpose any fare increase was not to bring about any fundamental improvement in the financial position but merely to stem any further deterioration. The lesson learnt from the substantial fare hike in 1976 was that a large one-off rise would have a dramatic impact upon passenger demand and that a system of *ad hoc*, but frequent, increases would produce better results. The new law enabled remarkable progress to be made in the flexible setting of fares well beyond what could have been imagined only a few years earlier. The scale of the crisis facing the management of JNR was of such magnitude that on this issue there could not be any possibility of a political confrontation between the ruling and opposition parties, and the bill was enacted in December 1977.

Thereafter, piecemeal fare increases were implemented annually between 1978 and 1982 resulting in JNR fares being much higher than those of the private railway companies, a total reversal of the previous situation. Revenues of the Tokaido Shinkansen Line were now double actual operating costs. Similarly, JNR's commuter fares in urban areas in some cases were double those of the private railway companies whose tracks ran parallel to JNR's. It therefore became impossible for JNR to consider any further increases.

Notwithstanding this, the financial situation had not improved in any fundamental way.

③ Penny wise and pound foolish

If you were to encapsulate the attitude of the fiscal authorities towards JNR's problems in one phrase, it would be 'Penny wise and pound foolish'.

From the beginning, the management of JNR recognized the inherent problem facing it as a public corporation. Accordingly, the company repeatedly requested state funding to strengthen its operating infrastructure, but these requests were simply ignored. Furthermore, JNR had hitherto calculated depreciation on a historic cost basis. In the high inflationary environment of the era, depreciation reserves generated on this basis inevitably resulted in a shortfall against replacement costs. To alleviate this structural problem JNR proposed a revaluation in the book value of its assets, as practised by the private railway operators. This was also rejected by the government on the grounds that it would lead eventually to fare hikes, which the government feared might provoke public criticism. If fares had been appropriately raised while JNR monopolized the transport market, it would have been able to create reserves sufficient to maintain an adequate capital structure. As JNR was forced to borrow money and thereby accumulate debt in order to maintain the value of its fixed assets, the company requested the government to allow it at least to make provisions for debt repayment, but this again was refused by the authorities.

When President Sogo was urging us to 'fight to the death' he was undoubtedly thinking of the struggle to maintain the fundamental principle on which JNR was founded, namely as a financially independent stand-alone entity. JNR was trying to abolish local lines which were becoming increasingly unprofitable as more roads were constructed. Far from shutting down unprofitable lines, political pressure from all parties was for JNR to build still more local lines. This pressure was firmly resisted by President Sogo. In their efforts to dismiss President Sogo, politicians resorted to a 1922 law on railway construction passed by the then ruling party, Seiyukai, which promoted the construction of local lines for purely political ends. In 1964, one year after Sogo's resignation, the Railway Construction Corporation was established at the initiative of the increasingly influential Tanaka Kakuei. This opened the door to the construction of local lines at the behest of self-seeking politicians who wanted railways in their constituencies regardless of the judgement of JNR's management and irrespective of commercial considerations.

Thus, while local lines were becoming increasingly unprofitable, a policy of constructing additional local lines in underpopulated areas was being implemented with disastrous consequences for JNR. The bureaucratic élite is trapped in the belief of its own infallibility. Therefore, when confronted with difficult situations they either look to shift the responsibility onto others, or to defer a definitive solution by adopting temporary relief measures. This predisposition to evade responsibility is a universal characteristic of bureaucrats and was greatly nurtured during the Cold War. JNR went from bad to worse as a direct result of this bureaucratic predisposition. The root causes of Japan's current financial crisis are the same as those which eventually brought about the downfall of JNR.

The authorities continued to bury their heads in the sand and refused to confront the real issues facing JNR. No one was prepared to take responsibility for a decision to increase government subsidies to JNR and in the meantime FILP loans were used to provide temporary relief. Looking back, it is clear that the piecemeal response to subsidy requests and a steadfast refusal to face up to reality brought about the very situation the bureaucrats wanted to avoid, where tough decisions could no longer be postponed.

In fiscal 1969, the first year of the First Reorganization Plan, the government subsidy was only ¥8.3 billion ($69 mn). Interest payments on JNR debt for which the government was responsible was funded by the issuance of 'JNR Reorganization Bonds'. Interest payments on those bonds was funded in turn by yet another subsidy, amounting to ¥1.3 billion ($11 mn). An additional ¥7.0 billion ($58 mn) of 'Construction Cost Subsidies' was appropriated to fund interest payments on borrowings for construction purposes over and above a pre-agreed level. Since then, year after year, similar measures that were 'too little, too late' have been repeatedly taken. Pretexts for subsidies multiplied giving rise to many different types and the total amount grew to intolerable levels.

It was under the presidency of former MOF Vice Minister Takagi, from January 1976, when subsidies really started to surge. His career had given him strong personal contacts with both the ruling and the opposition parties and he used these to gather support for increased government subsidies. The issue of subsidies, or what Takagi called compensation for 'structural losses', was his top priority. While explaining that the internal restructuring and tightening of discipline were in progress, and that the unhealthy labour-management relations that had plagued JNR were gradually being improved, in reality the management adopted a policy of concealing the actual situation from outsiders.

'Structural losses' meant costs with which JNR was burdened for political reasons, costs which no amount of management effort could reduce. A typical example was the distorted demographic structure of the employees. During World War II, a large number of railway employees were drafted into the armed forces and in order to continue railway operations JNR hired young boys under conscription age and young girls as regular employees. After the War, former employees were demobilized and sent back home. In addition to having to re-hire former JNR employees, JNR had to hire those from railway companies outside Japan such as the Manchurian Railway Company and the Korean Railway Company as well as army engineers. As a result, the total number of JNR employees exceeded 600,000 for a while and there was inevitably chronic over-manning. On the order of the General Headquarters of the Occupation Army JNR reduced employees by 100,000 by mainly culling the young employees hired during the war. But the strongly distorted demographic structure of the employees remained. As the generation of employees who swelled JNR's ranks immediately after the War reached retirement age towards end of the 1970s, JNR entered a period when between 20,000 and 25,000 employees were retiring every year. Ageing and retiring employees inevitably meant increasing unit labour costs, increasing severance payments for retirees and sharply increasing corporate pension liabilities. Costs accruing to JNR from these problems were regarded as a typical case of 'structural losses'. The interest burden from the ever-accumulating debt due to JNR's inability to increase fares and the maintenance of unprofitable local lines, were another example. Even unprofitable investments in safety and disaster prevention were regarded as structural losses.

The main categories of 'structural losses' for which subsidies were provided under the Takagi regime were construction costs, local transportation costs and the special account for extraordinary debt settlement. For fiscal 1976, the subsidy to cover construction costs amounted to ¥97.6 billion ($0.8 bn). The provision of subsidies for interest payments on loans for construction over and above a fixed rate (6.5%) started during the time of the First Reorganization Plan. However, the threshold above which interest subsidies could be provided was gradually reduced, first to 5.5%, then to 4.5% and finally to 3.5%. At the same time, the length of time for which the subsidy would be paid was extended from seven to ten years. Total construction costs for fiscal 1981 exceeded ¥1 trillion ($8.3 bn) as the construction of the Tohoku and the Joetsu Shinkansen Lines reached its peak, and construction cost subsidies correspondingly grew, reaching ¥164.3 billion ($1.4 bn). However, if one accepts, as has been argued above, that the Shinkansen Line should, in principle, be constructed with government money, measures to reduce the interest payment burden should have been applied to the entire life of the loans: the ten-year period was certainly not sufficient.

The special subsidy for the operation of loss-making local lines started from fiscal 1976. In the first year, the subsidy amounted to ¥17.2 billion ($143 mn), but by fiscal 1981, it had increased sharply to ¥126.4 billion ($1.0 bn). As mentioned above, the subsidy to cover interest payments for debt in the Special Account for Extraordinary Debt Settlement was instituted in fiscal 1976. Originally the subsidy was applicable to ¥2.5 trillion ($20.8 bn) of debt and for 1976 totalled ¥244.1 billion ($2.0 bn). But from fiscal 1980, the applicable amount of debt increased to ¥5 trillion ($41.7 bn), and the total subsidy increased to ¥345.7 billion ($2.9 bn).

For fiscal 1976, these three major categories accounted for all subsidies paid to JNR. Many other subsidies were introduced at the initiative of President Takagi thereafter to cover other 'structural costs'. However, even by 1981, when the system of subsidies was fully established, these three major categories still accounted for 87% of the total subsidies paid.

'Penny wise and pound foolish' adequately sums up the government's attitude, particularly that of the MoF, towards subsidies. It amounted to nothing more than throwing money at a problem rather than trying to tackle it at its roots. Eventually, subsidies reached truly irrational levels at more than ¥700 billion annually.

4 Runaway capital expenditure

If one examines the trend of JNR capital expenditure, it shows a consistently upward trend, which shows scant regard for the company's financial situation. Since JNR registered cumulative losses for the first time in fiscal 1964, and as losses grew thereafter, so did the levels of capital expenditure.

The construction costs of the Shinkansen lines were obviously the major component of capital expenditure. For fiscal 1963 when the construction of the Tokaido Shinkansen Line reached its peak, construction costs amounted to ¥291.4 billion ($2.4 bn). Until then, financial self-sufficiency was clearly the JNR management's guiding principle: profitability was the key goal and operating and capital expenditures were coordinated with this goal in mind. JNR therefore made strenuous efforts to keep construction costs as low as possible. In the construction of the Tokaido Shinkansen Line, for example, creativity in structural designs, such as adjusting the diameter of support columns for raised track, helped to reduce costs greatly, within, of course, the bands of safety standards. Where safety was not directly a factor, even the smallest opportunity to save costs was not overlooked. For example, roofs over platforms were constructed to cover the length of 12 instead of all 16 carriages at major stations, and 8 carriages at smaller stations.

However, financial self-sufficiency gradually lost its relevance and by 1969 when the First Reorganization Plan was launched, losing money was regarded as a matter of course, and did not seem to cause the slightest concerns to the management. In 1971, JNR suffered from negative operating cash-flow and funding of capital expenditure depended totally on borrowings. Despite this, construction costs for the Sanyo Shinkansen Line continued to increase, reaching ¥800 billion ($6.7 bn) annually by the start of full operations between Okayama and Hakata in March 1975. When full-scale construction of the Tohoku-Joetsu Shinkansen Line neared completion in 1982, annual construction costs reached ¥1 trillion.

By the time the construction of the Tohoku Shinkansen Line started, the notion of profitability and cost control in the construction process had lost all meaning. Rather, with the prospect of plum posts in the construction industry for retiring JNR officials, especially those in the Construction Department, the ability to maintain or even increase the construction budget was vital to preserving the influence of those awarding lucrative construction contracts. This is clearly illustrated by making a comparison of specifications for support columns, platform size, etc. between the Tohoku-Joetsu Shinkansen Line and the Tokaido Shinkansen Line. There is clear over-specification for such construction in the case of the former, leading to significantly higher construction costs.

While the construction cost per kilometre of the Tokyo-Osaka Tokaido Shinkansen Line was ¥640 million ($5 mn), the cost for the Sanyo Shinkansen Line was much higher, i.e., ¥1.37 billion ($11 mn) between Osaka and Okayama and ¥1.76 billion ($15 mn) between Okayama and Hakata. Construction cost for the Tohoku Shinkansen Line was ¥5.36 billion ($45 mn) per kilometre, and reached ¥6.05 billion ($50 mn) in the case of the Joetsu Shinkansen Line. These figures eloquently illustrate the increasing trend of construction costs during that time.

It was always going to be difficult for the Sanyo, Tohoku and Joetsu Shinkansen Lines to be profitable in the same way that the Tokaido Shinkansen was. The fact of the matter was that the transport volume of these lines was much lower. Despite all concerned recognizing this at the outset, however, specifications for equipment on these lines were unnecessarily extravagant. This led to the Tokaido Shinkansen Line having to shoulder part of the ¥5 trillion ($41.7 bn) of debt held by the Sanyo, Tohoku and Joetsu Shinkansen Lines, corresponding to their construction costs at the time of JNR's privatization.

The collapse of JNR between 1981 and 1982 coincided with the completion of the construction of the Tohoku and Joetsu Shinkansen Lines. If we interpret JNR's mission as having been to construct Japan's comprehensive post-war rail network it could be argued that the company collapsed due to sheer exhaustion, having had to complete its job taking on ever-increasing amounts of debt within the irreconcilable framework of financial self-sufficiency. As this contradiction became ever more apparent, so did the apathy and lack of discipline of the company's management.

► *Chapter 3*

Collapse of labour relations

1 Characteristics of labour relations in public corporations

From the outset, the central issue for JNR's management was industrial relations. When JNR operated as a monopoly, strikes resulted in serious disruption to the economy and people's lives and industrial action became a major concern to all. As the financial position of JNR started to deteriorate from the beginning of the 1970s improving labour productivity became the most pressing concern. The labour unions, however proved to be the biggest obstacle to JNR's management's attempts to implement change.

At the time, JNR had three major labour unions to deal with: the National Railway Workers' Union (Kokuro), the National Railway Locomotive Union (Doro) and the Railway Labour Union (Tetsuro). By far the largest union was Kokoro which represented 70% of the work-force, compared to Doro and Tetsuro's share of 12–13% each. Doro was set up in 1951 as a splinter group from Kokuro and in 1962, a moderate group of Kokuro members broke away to form Tetsuro. Whereas the membership of Kokuro and Tetsuro encompassed a broad cross-section of JNR's work-force, membership of Doro was restricted to train drivers and inspectors.

These unions were a precise reflection of Japan's political landscape during the Cold War. Kokuro and Doro were members of the General Council of Trade Unions of Japan (Sohyo), whose major members were public sector unions, and which regarded the labour movement as a means to establishing a socialist government in Japan. They supported the Japan Socialist Party (JSP) and the Japan Communist Party (JCP). Tetsuro, on the other hand, pursued a policy of 'economism' emphasizing the economic benefits for their members over political goals, and sought to improve working conditions under a liberal regime. Tetsuro belonged to the Japanese Confederation of Labour (Domei), whose membership comprised primarily of private sector unions and supported the more moderate Democratic Socialist Party. Domei and Sohyo competed in the public arena at the time of the Cold War by promoting slogans which respectively reflected the perspectives of the Western and Eastern blocs. They have now merged to form the Japanese Trade Union Confederation (Rengo).

Doro was a union for the more skilled employees, with drivers enjoying relatively high job classification within the hierarchy of JNR's work-force. No one could be promoted to driver without previous work experience as an inspector or in maintenance. The union had difficulty in expanding its membership base as there was a limited number of the more highly skilled jobs relating to train operations compounded by the fact that many potential members had already joined Kokuro and Tetsuro prior to their promotion. To compensate for this weakness, Doro was obliged to impose a strict discipline to ensure the unity of its members. Thus, notwithstanding its moderate and élitist origins, Doro became intensely radical and militant, earning it the nickname '*Oni no Doro*', roughly translated as 'reckless Doro'.

Industrial relations at JNR suffered from two major problems. The first had its origins in the 'Public Sector Labour Relations Law'. JNR's company structure was similar to that of other major public corporations such as Nippon Telegraph and Telephone (now NTT) and the Japan Tobacco & Salt Corporation (now Japan Tobacco). Regulations governing the labour-management relations of public corporations were different from those of private companies. In particular, the Japanese Constitution stipulated that individual rights should be restricted when they impinged upon public welfare. Thus, while the labour-management law granted public sector unions both the right to organize and the right of collective bargaining, Article 16 of the Public Labour Law denied employees the right to collective action, i.e., the right to strike. Kokuro and Doro repeatedly carried out illegal political acts in their struggle to 'Gain the Right to Strike'. While the Public Labour Law stipulated that illegal strikers could be fired, it was not an effective deterrent as it was unrealistic to fire all workers who joined strikes. In reality, the authorities could only fire the leaders and impose minor penalties on their followers for violations of the regulations of the Japanese National Railways Law. At first, the possibility of enforcing the right to fire strikers under the Public Labour Law did act as a psychological deterrent, but as the number of strikes grew, the hollowness of the threat was revealed.

The other major problem was the budget system of JNR. As discussed above, the annual budgets of public corporations such as JNR were regarded as part of the national budget, and had to be approved by the Diet. In JNR's budget plan, total expenses, including personal expenses, capital expenditure, and the amount of money to be borrowed from FILP all had to be clearly itemized. While the most important issue in industrial relations is the determination of wages, the management of JNR was not granted any authority to set them. The management of JNR was in a position to divert general expenses for various purposes within the totality of the budget, but not for wages. Wages were calculated according to historic wages, and the inability of the management to ensure that there was adequate compensation for rising inflation during the high-growth period was therefore a major drawback. To make up for the management's lack of authority to determine wages and for the labour union's lack of striking rights, the Public Labour Law stipulated the use of arbitration by the Public Sector Labour Relations Commission, which consisted of members representing the interests of the public, employers and workers. The Commission could make legally-binding decisions in response to the request of either the employers or the labour unions. The Ministry of Finance could then permit changes in personnel expenses for that particular public corporation. With wage rates of the private sector usually being used as the standard, the system of arbitration was an indispensable part of the determination of wage rates during JNR's life as a public corporation.

While JNR's business performance was favourable, the management of JNR sought the authority to determine wage rates on its own. However, once the business performance started to deteriorate, both the management and the labour unions were quite happy to rely on arbitration to protect their wage levels. It is not surprising, therefore, that the management of Nippon Telegraph and Telephone and the Japan Tobacco and Salt Public Corporation, whose businesses prospered, strove consistently for the right to determine wage rates until the very moment of their privatization.

These two problems did considerable damage to the credibility of the JNR management in the eyes of the employees, and pushed Kokuro and Doro further towards greater militancy. Furthermore, awareness of the fact that wage rates had nothing to do with business performance and were in any event determined by a third party led Kokuro and Doro naturally to focus their efforts away from wages and towards the 'relaxation of working conditions'. The more undisciplined workers became, and the less effort they made, the more efficiency fell and the more the payroll would have to swell. This in turn increased union membership and union dues. JNR was an 'unsinkable battleship', no matter how far the business performance deteriorated, wages would never go down: the greater the inefficiency, the better it was for the unions. Numbers were what mattered and the prevailing attitude that 'numbers mean power' poisoned the minds of the union members.

Industrial relations started to deteriorate drastically after JNR's rationalization programme was carried out between 1967 and 1968. Engine stokers, indispensable for operating steam locomotives, and steam locomotive depots, which were located every 50 km or 100 km (31 m or 62 m) to supply water for boilers and coal, were no longer needed as lines were electrified or diesel locomotives introduced. Kokuro and Doro fiercely resisted their abolition, and resorted not only to strikes but also to frequent acts of sabotage. Incidents such as putting stones on tracks happened frequently. As a result, management was forced to make substantial compromises in setting standards for crew allocation, which varied according to type of carriage and type of train, and in limiting the distance for one crew duty. These compromises effectively nullified any efficiency increases derived from modernizing train operations,

e.g. through the introduction of diesel locomotives or electrification. As the business environment became more hostile, so too did
the industrial relations climate.

☐2☐ The fate of the productivity movement

When he became president of JNR in 1969, Isozaki Satoshi was
instructed by Prime Minister Sato to introduce proper management to the company: to instil rigorous discipline at the work-site,
and to carry out thorough rationalization. Following this the
training of employees on the importance of productivity began in
earnest. During the 1950s and 1960s the focus of industrial relations in the private sector had shifted from the class struggle to
one based more on the principle of 'economism'. The Japan
Productivity Centre, which had led the movement to democratize
the private sector unions was asked by JNR to lead this training
programme.

Once training began in April 1970, many of the employees,
who were critical of Kokuro and Doro's anti-rationalization
agenda and wilful attempts to paralyse the command-chain of the
company, gradually became sympathetic to the company's
attempts to raise awareness of the importance of productivity.
Many of them withdrew from Kokuro and Doro and it seemed
that an industrial relations environment similar to that of the
private sector could be established with one final push.

Kokuro and Doro, gravely threatened by this development,
counter-attacked through the mass media, using the political
power of the JSP and JCP. The unions brought a number of suits
against JNR accusing them of unfair labour practices and this set
off a campaign to undermine the productivity training
programme itself. The dispute even became an issue in the Diet,
then in the midst of discussing the return by the US of Okinawa.
President Isozaki was forced to apologize in the Diet for
conducting unfair labour practices in October 1971 and publicly
announced that productivity training would cease forthwith. In
doing this, Isozaki was probably concerned, firstly, that the labour
issue should not derail the Okinawa discussions and, second, that
the deliberations on the Second Reorganization Plan of JNR,

which were about to start, would progress smoothly in the Diet with a minimum of resistance from the media and the opposition parties.

Committed employees and middle managers, who had embraced the productivity training programme and had taken a critical stand against Kokuro and Doro, were left completely isolated by Isozaki's climbdown. Kokuro and Doro proceeded to victimize and intimidate this group, threatening them with psychological and physical violence at the work-site and pressuring management to remove them.

The attitude of senior management at the headquarters and the Railway Operating Division changed completely to one of appeasement towards Kokuro and Doro, leaving reform-minded workers even more isolated at their work-sites. These workers were forced to pay a heavy price for the failings of management; they lost confidence in the senior managers at both the headquarters and at a local level, and any sense of unity was lost.

Meanwhile, within Kokuro and Doro, crowing over their victory over management, a power struggle developed between the existing leadership and the next generation, resulting in the union leadership losing control. Within Kokuro, the Socialist Association and the Communist Party gained grass-root support and within Doro, the radical Seiken Group ousted the more moderate Rounken leadership, and established complete control. The failure of the productivity movement led to a weakening of the union leadership's authority over its members and a radicalization of the JNR labour movement. Strikes against rationalization and for political purposes became commonplace with scant regard for the impact on the travelling public.

As a result of the failure of the productivity movement and the steady deterioration in the business performance of JNR, the management lost confidence in what had hitherto been regarded as a positive and resolute industrial relations strategy. At the headquarters and at the thirty Railway Operating Divisions, as all pretence of an industrial relations policy crumbled, a cosy, mutually dependent relationship between management and the unions developed. This policy of appeasement was led by the Headquarters Personnel Department and the Administrative

Department of the regional Railway Operating Divisions where an accommodative and deeply anti-confrontational attitude took root. Needless to say, the official policy of firmness towards the unions was nominally unchanged, but in practice local managers were instructed to do whatever was necessary to avoid conflict. This left responsibility for labour relations completely in the hands of the local managers who were therefore personally accountable in the event of dispute breaking out. Naturally, the chain of command within JNR and any attempt of rationalization were paralysed. In spite of this, other than during prolonged strikes trains were operated more safely and reliably than might have been expected. Receiving contradictory and confusing orders from above, the non-union managers on the ground strove valiantly to manage the situation the best they could. These foremen had to fill in when union members staged walk-outs, were late for work, or thoughtlessly absented themselves without notice. For a time these men managed to uphold the hundred-year-old tradition of JNR but were ultimately unable to stem the tide. Local management positions could not be filled as rewards failed to match the responsibility that had to be shouldered. The spirit of JNR was gradually crumbling.

⟨3⟩ The strike for the right to strike: the collapse of the JNR myth (November–December 1975)

In line with the management's new strategy of appeasement, the Personnel Department started at around this time to reconsider its opposition to the unions being granted the right to strike. The law prohibiting industrial action by public sector unions had already become meaningless and the Personnel Department saw advantage in granting the right to strike to the labour unions in return for union concessions on such issues as the right of lockout. Nonetheless, within both the company and the government there were those who argued that to concede the right would be seen as a surrender to the illegal intimidation by the labour unions. The exchange of the right to strike for the right of lock-out was misdirected and misguided, as it conceded too much to the labour unions. It is clear that stable labour relations in the private sector were not due to the deterrent created by the right of lock-out. As criticisms of the cosy relationship between the management of JNR and the unions became stronger and voices demanding a reversion to a firmer attitude towards the unions became louder, so the sympathy of the Personnel Department towards the labour unions became stronger. There were even some opinions expressed that strong labour unions could provide a bulwark to protect the interests of JNR. The attitude of some JNR managers when pressed by outsiders on the need for management reform was 'So I suppose you're going to take full responsibility if Kokuro and Doro paralyse the country with their strikes as a result of us antagonising them?' The Personnel Department, sympathetic to Doro and Kokuro's campaign for the right to strike, worked on the government, the ruling party and the opposition parties. In response, a government committee was set up to look into fundamental issues relating to public sector corporations, including the matter of strike rights. It was a matter of some irony for JNR and the unions that it was in this committee that the issue of JNR's privatization was brought up for the first time, with the argument being made that if the union were to be given the right to strike, JNR should be broken up and privatized.

Anticipating that the committee would not come to a quick conclusion, but recognizing that the doveish Miki Cabinet would cave in to their demands (a view also shared by the Personnel Department), Kokuro and Doro decided to force the agenda and resort to industrial action. 'The strike for the right to strike' started on 26 November 1975 and was quickly joined by other public corporation labour unions. Just before the strike, the Personnel Department had convened an emergency national meeting of the Directors in charge of personnel, labour and general affairs, and agreed a resolution that the conditional right to strike should be granted to the labour unions. President Fujii and the Executive Vice-President at the time were opposed to the idea of giving unions the right to strike and this was evidently a move to pressure them to change their attitude. It certainly had an effect on Inoue, who expressed his intention of agreeing to the unions' demands.

However, when the strike actually started, public opinion hardened against it. Within the ruling party, there was uproar against the compromising attitude of the Miki Cabinet. The general consensus was that the unions were holding the public to ransom in order to achieve political, rather than economic, ends. Feelings ran high that the government should not give in to labour intimidation. Moreover, with the Miki Cabinet nearing the end of its term, its influence was on the wane. Sensing the anger of the public towards the irresolute attitude of the Cabinet, the majority of the ruling party was leaning towards the idea of letting the strike continue, and use it as a pretext to force Prime Minister Miki to take responsibility and resign. The attitude of the public mass media and politicians stood in stark contrast to the events that led to the collapse of the productivity movement at the end of the Sato government.

There were no signs of a government cave-in during the first days of the strike. On the contrary, there appeared to be a great degree of unity among the travelling public, the public at large as well as the LDP against the strikers. By coincidence, the fiscal 1976 budget was in the pipeline at that time. This was seeking to implement a 50% fare hike and to suspend the repayment of accumulated debt of ¥2.5 trillion. This caused people to become even more critical, arguing that tax payers and passengers were on the one hand being asked to shoulder an unfair financial burden to prop up JNR while having to put up with a totally illegal strike on the other. The management of JNR had no authority to give away the right to strike and the unions' attempts to seize this right through illegal means was an outrage, to be strongly resisted by the management. With little hope of a successful outcome, and against a background of mounting criticism the Secretary-General of Kokuro, Tomizuka Mitsuo, was forced to order a halt to the strike on the eighth day having won no concessions at all.

The success with which Kokuro and Doro had crushed the productivity movement had given them an arrogance that would lead to their ruin. While the entire JNR network had been brought to a standstill for eight days, there was virtually no disruption in economic activity, thus exploding the myth that chaos would result if JNR were to stop operating.

The 'Strike for the Right to Strike' clearly revealed that alternatives to JNR existed and this turned passengers and the general public against the labour unions. The mass media, which had been sympathetic to the labour unions because of their status as underdog, did a complete about-turn sensing the change in the public mood. In addition to criticizing the unions, they also blamed the JNR management for having spoilt the labour unions so much. A further problem was that in giving their approval to the right to strike to the unions, the Personnel Department had made absolutely no effort to develop a consensus with other key departments such as Corporate Planning and Finance & Accounting. While one part of the firm was requesting a substantial fare hike and the suspension of ¥2.5 trillion ($20.8 bn) of accumulated debt, another was alienating the public by supporting an illegal strike. Each department pursued its own self-interest with no attempt at coordination with other departments. Any sense of unity was lost: these were typical symptoms of an organization that was losing its way.

In March 1976, both the president and executive vice-president resigned, and Takagi Fumio, former administrative vice-minister of the MOF became the new president of JNR. The senior management of the Personnel Department was also replaced. There was little discussion within the labour unions, however, as to who should assume the responsibility for the failure of the strike. The union leadership patted each other on the back for having demonstrated their power by having 'put up a good fight for eight days and the withdrawing in an orderly manner'. Nobody was fooled by such bravado, however.

The LDP and the government put further pressure on the JNR management by demanding that the labour unions compensate taxpayers for the damage caused by the illegal strike. Though the JNR management shrank from a further confrontation with the labour unions there was little room to argue and a suit demanding ¥20.2 billion in compensation from Kokuro and Doro was filed in 1976. This marked the beginning of the decline of Kokuro and Doro.

While the new president, Takagi, was a clever and able bureaucrat, he was far from being a popular leader or a man of strong will. He had a reputation for having excellent connections with politicians of both the ruling and opposition parties, but he lacked clear ideas on how to deal with industrial relation issues. President Takagi apparently preferred to see his main mission as being to secure subsidies from his former colleagues at the MOF, rather than getting immersed in painful negotiations with the labour unions. If he had taken a firmer stance, he might have won over the hearts and minds of the managers and employees at the front line where resentment about the Strike for the Right to Strike still simmered. Craving a disciplined and dedicated organization, public opinion would have strongly supported him. However, senior management including the president, and particularly the Personnel Department, decided to do precisely the opposite: to obfuscate and conceal the real situation. This may have been because they did not want to repeat the mistakes of the failure of the productivity movement, or simply because they had got so far into bed with the unions in the right to strike dispute. In any event, the President's character and the agenda of the Personnel Department complemented each other and determined JNR's course of action.

The president continued to claim to people outside of JNR that the company was entering a honeymoon period for industrial relations. This was to pull the wool over the eyes of the MoF, who would otherwise have insisted that a thorough rationalization take place before handing over any subsidies. The president's tactics were successful and JNR continued to receive subsidies. Given this, and with the benefit of hindsight, the argument could be made that the fact that a complete settlement of the industrial relations problems was put off until such time as a fundamental reform of JNR could be completed, including the establishment of a timetable for privatization, may not have been a bad thing. This argument would not, however, have found much sympathy with the site managers, who had to work under increasingly difficult circumstances with discipline continuing to deteriorate.

For four years from March 1977, one year after Takagi became president, I was assigned as Director of the Administration Department, for two years at the Shizuoka Railway Operating Division, followed by two years at the Sendai Railway Operating

Division. During this period, as manager in charge of personnel and labour relations matters, I sought to re-impose management control over labour relations and work-place discipline. This proved to be an invaluable experience subsequently in carrying out the break-up and privatization of JNR.

4 The era of restructuring begins

Faced with the strong demand of the government that, in return for a substantial fare hike and the suspension of debt, JNR should carry out a major rationalization, the management turned their attention to the freight business. Over the years, freight capacity had considerably outstripped demand. The management persuaded the government that it would take at least two years, until October 1978, for a new timetable, reflecting a reduction in freight capacity, to be put in place. By contrast, in the more flexible labour relations environment we had after JNR's privatization, a revised timetable could be put in place within one year.

JNR's freight business was already in desperate straits, reflecting in part changes in Japan's industrial structure and its geographical situation. The history of freight transportation since the mid-1930s was one of seeking ever faster and more timely deliveries, with the focus of freight shifting from bulk cargo to finished industrial products. In order to meet this changing demand, it was necessary for JNR to consolidate the freight loading stations thereby bypassing the marshalling yards, to provide non-stop operation of longer freight trains, and to rationalize the loading and unloading process through containerization. While these changes would greatly enhance speed and punctuality of deliveries, the reduced number of stops made by freight trains would lead to a considerable reduction in flexibility.

Had the industrial structure of the 1960s, dominated by petrochemicals, machinery and home appliances sectors, remained unchanged, this reconfiguration might have been effective. Nonetheless, the longer term trend was for truck freight, which could provide a higher standard of customer service, in terms of guaranteed and prompt delivery and faster responses to customer requirements, to become more competitive than the rail alternative.

While truck transportation could guarantee delivery to within the nearest one hour or even thirty minutes, the best that JNR could promise was delivery to the nearest half-day period. As Japan's industrial base became more highly developed the distribution process involved much smaller units of delivery and inventory management became much more critical relative to transportation, so the advantage of truck transport became even more apparent. Even in the case of bulk cargo, whereas in Europe and the US railway transportation enjoys a relative advantage over truck transportation, in Japan, due to its geographical situation, the advantage is with marine transportation. In the end, therefore, rail freight lost out on all fronts.

Notwithstanding the worsening competitive situation, Kokuro and Doro frequently resorted to targeting freight trains through illegal strikes, at least until the 'Strike for the Right to Strike'. They misguidedly argued that high passenger fares subsidized low freight rates for monopoly capital. Targeting freight operations through strike action was, therefore, the optimal way of inflicting damage to monopoly capital and promoting the cause of socialism.

Frequent strikes affecting freight operations had the effect of accelerating the shift towards truck transportation. Too late, the labour unions, particularly Doro, many of whose members were freight train drivers, became aware of freight's weakening position. In a panic, fearing they would lose their membership base, they changed their tactics and decided to exempt freight trains from strike actions since they carried daily necessities such as fresh vegetables, meat and fish. After the 1975 'Strike for the Right to Strike', freight trains were exempted from strike action. This, however, had no impact on halting the long-term decline of rail freight in favour of truck transportation.

As freight services were only reduced in proportion to decline in demand, and no reduction in staff levels and freight carriages had taken place, JNR's measures could not be called a rationalization in a real sense. While the public would have supported proper measures to increase efficiency, JNR was still concerned about a union rebellion and sought to give them a 'sweetener' to accept even these modest measures. The deal they reached was to re-hire fired union members. As a result of the series of illegal strikes and other industrial action designed to paralyse the organizational hierarchy, many members of Kokuro and Doro had been fired, or had been subject to disciplinary actions such as a suspension from work. There were great numbers of union members whose wage increases had been reduced. Fired union members were hired by the union to work as full-time officials, and compensation was paid out of union funds to those whose salary increases had been reduced on the pretext that they had suffered as targets of 'victimization'. The resulting financial burden on the labour unions was considerable. It was particularly heavy for Doro, which was smaller and more militant. Doro's dues were by far the highest among the labour unions.

Personnel reduction meant a decline in union members and therefore, a decline in union dues. Still bearing the scars of the failure in the productivity movement, the management shied away from confronting the unions: like a cornered rat, they might take desperate action. One way of softening the blow would be to hire fired union members. This would alleviate some of the unions' financial difficulties and hopefully encourage them to accept the rationalization measures.

Soon after taking up my position in Shizuoka, I hired two full-time union officials, one a Kokuro member who had been fired for joining strikes, while the other was a Doro member who had been fired for a criminal assault on a member of the management. While the Shizuoka Railway Operating Division had been against this arrangement, such deals were conducted directly between JNR headquarters and union leaders on a country-wide basis as compensation for personnel rationalization, with the detailed implementation being left to each regional Railway Operating Division. This process of the company abandoning its prerogatives in personnel management in exchange for the union cooperation in rationalization continued unabated: once your sense of pride is lost, there is little left to lose. The JNR headquarters and the labour unions reached agreement that reductions in wage increases for those punished for company rule violations would be made up within three years. Previously, wages would only be made up either through the enthusiastic commitment and hard work of the employee which would lead to productivity bonuses on top of their basic pay, or when they passed tests for promotion and were assigned to a more senior position. While the automatic restoration of wages within three years was passed off as a humane gesture to avert 'permanent punishment' the real objective was to render financial assistance to the unions.

Once the management agreed to this, they were also forced to concede restoration of wages within three years for those that had been subject to disciplinary action due to poor work performance, a clearly lesser offence than illegal or even criminal actions. In this way, the management ceded, step by step, their authority over personnel issues and displayed the extent to which they were prepared shamelessly to undermine the prerogatives of management in their dealings with the unions. Their only interest was to be seen by the public to be moving forward with the rationalization programme. The rationale put forward to the unions was that any rationalization in cargo operations and personnel would be purely temporary and that following the expected 'V-shaped' recovery, the process of recovery and expansion would be back on track. No one, however, took this explanation seriously.

In the end, all the fuss made about the timetable revisions was soon forgotten and negotiations progressed quite smoothly and the changes were implemented on schedule in October 1978. It is true to say, however, that the revision to the freight schedules was an important turning point in JNR's history. Firstly, it represented a major strategic change in policy. Hitherto, notwithstanding the downward trend in rail freight, capital expenditures, mainly on containers and bulk cargo, were justified on the grounds of a strengthening of JNR's competitive edge and thereby as a means of recovering market share. Moreover, capital expenditure would help to maintain the morale of workers engaged in the freight business. Now, with the revision of the freight timetable, this strategy was abandoned, and any talk of a 'V-shaped recovery' was not taken seriously by anyone.

Secondly, the rationalization of the work-force, stalled for so long, had actually commenced. It was no more than a tentative one, with a small 'recovery' in efficiency which had been in such long decline. Nonetheless, it did mark somewhat of a turning point. At the same time the company represented the success of these negotiations to the government in such a way as to extract the maximum possible subsidy. The company's tactic was to provide a continuous stream of minor successes. Once the system of financial self-sufficiency was implicitly abandoned, JNR's management was under no illusion that their future lay in extracting maximum advantage in their dealings with the government and the ruling party. The government for its part responded with a series of minimalist measures designed merely to prevent catastrophes during their term in office. The situation offered little prospect of improvement as, irrespective of JNR's management's efforts, the government seemed incapable of focusing on a long-term solution. Thus a strong, mutual distrust developed, with each being as guilty as the other. It was very much a case of 'like father, like son'.

While the revision of the freight timetable was held up as a remarkable achievement, it was nothing more than what the management should have been doing as a matter of course. It did absolutely nothing to stem the downward spiral in the freight business.

5 The start of the reform process

In March 1979, soon after the revision of the freight trains timetable, I was transferred to the Sendai Railway Operating Division as Director of the Administration Department. The most pressing task for the Sendai Division was to ensure the smooth inauguration of the Tohoku Shinkansen due to start three years hence.

Soon after my transfer and just prior to the 'Spring labour offensive' in April the national conference of Directors of regional Administration Departments was convened. After the conference, the Personnel Department sponsored an informal social gathering of the Directors of the major regional Divisions (Sapporo, Sendai, Niigata, Tokyo South, Tokyo North, Tokyo West, Nagoya, Osaka, and Moji), and the leaders of Kokuro. The gathering was held at an old Japanese-style restaurant standing by the Sumida River in Tokyo. The participants from Kokuro were Tomizuka Mitsuo plus a group of senior union officials. Tomizuka had been director of the planning department of Kokuro at the time of the failure of the productivity movement, and had led the 'Strike for the Right to Strike' as the secretary-general of Kokuro. He was also secretary-general of Sohyo at the time of the gathering. The banquet was progressing in a friendly and informal atmosphere when I was approached by Hosoi Soichi, a member of the central executive committee of Kokuro and the leader of the union's Communist group. He said:

> Kasai-san, we have had to give a lot of thought to your assignment. Kokuro doesn't have good people in Sendai, but there's a lot to be done there, particularly with the inauguration of the Tohoku Shinkansen in 1982. Labour-management relations is a difficult issue and after a lot of thinking we came to the conclusion that you were the only person to do the job. However, while I am sure you can manage the hopeless Kokuro members in Sendai, my big concern is the response of Doro. While you worked in Shizuoka, you seem to have incurred the wrath of the mainstream faction of Doro. The biggest headache for the Tohoku Shinkansen is going to be the issue of train drivers. Doro's central headquarters' hostility towards you would cause you a problem in handling the drivers. Fortunately, the Sendai chapter is dominated by Rounken, who are anti-headquarters, so they will follow you. That's why you were chosen for the position. It's going to be a tough job, but give it your best shot.

I had long heard rumours that no personnel matters regarding the management of the regional Administration Departments could be decided without the consent of the labour unions, but I never expected to witness it first hand. I replied politely that I would do my best. I mention this conversation because it is quite an accurate reflection of the way labour-management relations were carried out at the time. After assuming my new position in Sendai, I discovered that Kokuro had much less power there than they did in other Railway Operating Divisions such as that in Shizuoka. Doro competed furiously with Kokuro for members among drivers and train depot workers, while at other sites, competition was between Kokuro and Tetsuro.

In this kind of competitive situation, labour unions tended to stick more rigidly to their principles and to behave more militantly. Kokuro in Sendai were part of the dogmatic Socialist Association and were forever talking openly about the 'destruction' of the JNR management and how such a blow to monopoly capital would eventually lead to the establishment of a socialist regime. Persistently harassing the site managers and assistant managers as well as the members of the moderate Tetsuro, and demonstrating its power by causing paralysis at the work-sites, Kokuro strove to expand its organization. Doro's Sendai chapter, the majority of whom belonged to the moderate Rounken group, was extremely concerned about the radical Seiken group in Tokyo taking advantage of the opening of the Tohoku Shinkansen to penetrate the Sendai organization and this made them lean towards the JNR management.

Thanks to the support of the Tetsuro members, the morale of the site managers and assistant managers remained quite high and they were as determined as they had been prior to the collapse of the productivity movement to re-instil and maintain discipline at the work-place. However, to the management in JNR's headquarters who had capitulated to Doro and Kokuro, special situations as that in Sendai were awkward: for senior managers in the Railway Operating Divisions who could be transferred at any time to almost anywhere in the country the last thing they wanted to do was make themselves unpopular with Kokuro, which was the dominant force at almost every work-site. Although there were frequent disputes between the site managers and assistant managers and local Kokuro members, former senior management of the Sendai Railway Operating Division would ignore them out of consideration for Kokuro. Even when disputes got out of hand, it was usual practice to appease Kokuro and to ignore the site managers. While in Sendai, Tetsuro's membership was exceptionally high, being nearly equal to that of Kokuro, the senior management no doubt wished deep down that Tetsuro's membership would fall to the same levels as in other regions.

With this kind of interference from headquarters and the Railway Operating Divisions, the site management were filled with a sense of frustration and failure. Since as Director of the Administration Department I was also in charge of personnel and labour relations issues, I fully intended to give the local and site management my full support. Given my long involvement in drawing up JNR's restructuring plans and budgets, I had a thorough grasp of the desperate plight of the performance of JNR and given that there was by now clearly no value in trying to raise my stock with headquarters or the labour unions, the thought of a confrontation with Kokuro did not cause me great concern.

At the time, nothing could be done without discussion with and the consent of the labour unions. If we really wanted to establish a strong and independent management, this was obviously an absurd situation. Decision-making should be the prerogative of those who were responsible for running the company and accountable for its performance, i.e., the management. The only responsibilities of the management towards the unions should be the issuance of clear work instructions, to ensure the fair treatment of workers and the proper application of reward and punishment. However, those who held such views were a tiny minority. It was clear I would face strong opposition from Kokuro and cause not a little concern within JNR's headquarters, but I felt strongly that I should restore common sense at the work-sites at least in Sendai. I therefore spent the whole of my two years in Sendai rescinding unauthorized agreements and trying to rectify bad practices which had resulted from previous labour-management consultations. A typical example of the sort of situation I had to deal with, and which symbolized the environment at the work-place occurred in August 1979.

One day, a train which had pulled out from Aizu-Wakamatsu Station separated in two en route to the next station as the carriages had not been properly coupled. This was a serious incident which could have resulted in human casualties, and it was clear that the workers responsible should be punished. After an investigation, it was revealed that an assistant manager had filled in for a job normally carried out by subordinates. It had occurred during the lunch break, when all the workers responsible for such work were absent. On this particular day it so happened that there were even fewer workers than usual as Tetsuro had organized a camping expedition while Kokuro had sponsored a softball tournament. The station-master had been unwilling to ask Tetsuro to cancel the camping trip programme as he had asked Tetsuro on numerous occasions to fill in for work at very short notice when Kokuro members suddenly absented themselves or had resorted to the tactic of taking holidays collectively. Knowing of Tetsuro's camping event, Kokuro intentionally sponsored the softball competition to coincide with it. However, in a labour-management environment where Kokuro was able to get away with almost anything, the assistant manager had no option but to do the work himself and was blamed for the accident.

Examining the assistant manager's work record, it transpired that he had not had one day's rest, including Saturdays and Sundays, in the two-month period prior to the accident. He had had to fill in for other workers almost every day, and was clearly quite exhausted. I even heard that some Kokuro members, standing idly by puffing away at cigarettes watching him work, commented that the assistant manager looked half asleep and was likely to cause an accident. I felt very sorry for him. Determined to seize this opportunity, I drew up a list of 19 improper practices at Aizu-Wakamatsu Station which required change. I told the station-master that he was henceforth to give work instructions without being bound by any improper historic work practices.

A typical example of such practices was the notion that 'a work timetable is a labour contract'. A 'work timetable' was merely a work plan drawn up for each worker at the various work-sites to help him prepare for the working day taking into account such factors as train arrival and departure times. This plan was certainly never a labour contract, which is used to define more general and universal working conditions such wage rates, working hours, and so on. However, the radical groups within Kokuro allied to the JCP and the Socialist Association, continued to press the site managers at labour-management consultation meetings to confirm that the 'work timetable' was in effect a labour contract which defines working conditions at particular work-sites. As train operations were inevitably influenced by various external factors such as the weather, the working day would rarely progress exactly according to plan. Therefore, to accept the argument that the work timetable was the same as a labour contract would be to accept that one's labour contract changed according to whatever happened on a particular day. Whenever conditions change, there would have to be a work-site meeting to discuss changes to the contents of the labour contract and it would become impossible to plan work flexibly to anticipate unexpected occurrences. Thus, the power to make scheduling decisions for train operations would shift to the local chapters of the labour union, which of course was precisely the aim of this radical Kokuro faction. The basic framework of management, which permitted work-site management to issue instructions flexibly to workers within the limitations of specified working hours, was being undermined by JNR in its attempts to implement its rationalization programme.

In order to put an end to these improper practices, there existed both a necessary and sufficient condition. The necessary condition was that site managers had both the power and the guts to supervise workers uncompromisingly and to apply the principle of punishment and reward. The sufficient condition was that senior management in the Sendai Railway Operating Division and others would back them up. The suggestion, made by some at Headquarters, that inappropriate work practices were rectified by some sort of joint consultation between regional management and the local Kokuro leadership was without foundation. Whatever might have been agreed between the senior managers of the Railway Operating Division and union leadership, new bad practices would replace the old unless the work-site management had the determination to stamp them out. The local chapter of Kokuro at Aizu-Wakamatsu Station, adherents to the dogmatism of the Socialist Association, never missed an opportunity to press site managers with unreasonable demands. Although the site managers wanted a firm stand to be taken towards these demands, the Railway Operating Division management, nervous to maintain a good relationship with regional and central Kokuro leadership, would instruct them to maintain a low profile and grin and bear it. I was more than prepared to provide the sufficient condition in order to put an end to the practices that had been built up in this way.

The first step in this process was for the Railway Operating Division to demonstrate sufficient determination in order to regain the site management's confidence. In order to sweep away the distrust that had accumulated over the years, working level management in the Railway Operating Division in Sendai, below the Section Manager level, from general affairs, personnel, labour and marketing were obliged to negotiate with the work-site managers face to face on frequent occasions. At the final stage of these negotiations, the Directors of Administration and Marketing participated in order to show their resolve. At the end of November, site managers were told to expect a directive from the Director of the Administration Department instructing them to propose to the local chapter of Kokuro that improper practices be corrected by a certain date. When the deadline arrived, the work order would be issued in accordance with formal labour regulations. If violations of these regulations took place, which would be expected as a matter of course, each of the violations would be recorded and punishment and wage cuts would be handed out. Neither the site management nor the Railway Operating Division were to make even the slightest compromise to the unions.

As soon as work orders were issued at the beginning of December, I telephoned the station-master to give him encouragement. While union members, clearly sensing an usurpation of their vested rights, put up some resistance, they were charged with a violation of the work order and their wages were cut and the operation of the station continued smoothly. Frustration mounted for the members of the local chapter and they put strong pressure on the local headquarters of Kokuro to do something. The local headquarters of Kokuro in Sendai responded by proposing a collective bargaining session, threatening a strike at the end of March. There was obviously no scope for us to recognize unreasonable special privileges, especially against the threat of illegal strikes. A collective bargaining session was held, which lasted for four days, watched carefully by both the site management and the members of the local chapter. The result was that Kokuro's local headquarters were forced to accept the order to correct improper practices in its entirety. Agreements reached previously between the site management and the unions where site managers did not have the authority to make such concessions, were not legally binding and were declared invalid. Kokuro gained nothing. The trouble at Aizu-Wakamatsu Station was settled with seventy members of Kokuro being punished. Within two years in Sendai, the self-confidence of the site manager and assistant managers of the Railway Operating Division in Sendai had grown out of all recognition.

Kokuro were evidently imploring the headquarters Personnel Department to transfer me to another position. At the work-site, Kokuro tried to frighten management staff by dragging up the spectre of the failed productivity movement. When I heard that, I made it a rule to say, 'JNR's disastrous financial position is now our ally. Fares are twice those of private railway companies. In spite of the injection of ¥700 billion ($5.8 bn) of tax money every year, JNR still posts a ¥1 trillion ($8.3 bn) deficit. Who is going to tolerate JNR in its present state? Anyone in my position has no alternative. Don't worry and follow my lead.'

The local headquarters of Kokuro put pressure on the central headquarters of Kokuro to have me replaced. The Personnel Department at JNR headquarters, perplexed at Kokuro's request, consulted with the Director-General of Sendai Railway Operating Division as to how to handle it. As a last resort, they decided to transfer me to headquarters. They could save Kokuro's face and their own, by transferring me with a promotion. By appointing as my successor, Otsuka Mutsutake (now the president of JR East), who had already succeeded me on two other occasions, they tried to maintain management consistency and allay the concerns of the local management in Sendai.

Although I was initially told to stay in Sendai until the construction of the Tohoku Shinkansen was completed, one year before that in April 1981, I returned to Tokyo as Deputy Director-General of the Corporate Planning Department. I was also assigned to the President's Office as Deputy Director-General in charge of matters relating to the Second Administrative Reform Committee (SARC).

The launch of the movement to improve discipline at the work-site in Sendai was treated with hostility by both JNR headquarters and Kokuro: it was the only such initiative among thirty Railway Operating Divisions across the country. Within two years, however, the actions of the Sendai Division came to be regarded as a model for local management to follow. Looking back on those days, I believe that what happened in Sendai marked the first steps towards the reform of JNR.

▶ *Chapter 4*

The Second Administrative Reform Committee (SARC)*

☐1 The management improvement programme (nothing left to sell)

When it became apparent to everyone that the Fifth Reform Programme to restore financial health to JNR by fiscal 1979 was doomed to failure, the government, the LDP and the company immediately started to consider new measures, which were drafted into the 'Special Law for the Promotion of the Reorganization of JNR'. It became law on 28 November 1980 and marked the start of what came to be called 'the last resort programme'. The then Minister of Transport Moriyama Kinji, who was regarded within the ruling LDP as an expert on labour policy, was critical of JNR's measures regarding the labour unions. While the government and the LDP had tended, in a rather tentative way, to get involved in some JNR-related issues, labour had always been regarded as something of a sacred cow, and left entirely to the management of JNR. Raising this issue now was an excellent opportunity for the Ministry of Transport to make it clear that they could assume no responsibility for the failure of the previous reform programmes: JNR was entirely to blame.

As a sign of responsibility for the failure of the reform programme, the Minister 'suggested' the bonuses for the Board Members of JNR to be cut by 50% from fiscal 1979 with

---

* Advisory body to the Prime Minister established in March 1981 to suggest measures to solve Japan's fiscal crisis, including the privatization of public-sector corporations.

management in JNR headquarters above Section Director having theirs cut by 10%. As it was not legally permitted to impose mandatory bonus reductions on employees, they were voluntarily refused. However, as there were many other issues on which JNR needed the minister's goodwill, JNR was forced to cooperate. In exchange for this, permission was granted for JNR to hire new college graduates. As the Minister of Transport was in any case not in a position to interfere in the hiring policy of JNR, this was a somewhat illogical intervention on his part. Past measures to deal with JNR's problems, as poorly conceived as they had been, had been arrived at with the consensus of JNR, the government, the LDP and ministries such as Transport and Finance. JNR itself had frequently had to make compromises in accepting the cosmetic solutions proposed by the government and the LDP. While JNR, the government and the LDP were, therefore, jointly responsible for the failures of the past measures, the minister's instruction concerning the bonuses indicated clearly that JNR management was to be held entirely responsible. Realizing that JNR was beyond repair, the government started to prepare for a complete break with JNR, and having the President of JNR taking the blame for everything. The criticism that JNR was 'spoiling the labour unions' was used as the platform to make that break, although quite frankly, no one could have expected any other result from such an inadequate series of measures from the very beginning.

The new reform programme came into force from fiscal 1981 and was due to run until fiscal 1985. Despite its dramatic nick-name there was in reality nothing 'last resort' about it. It was just more of the same; just designed to buy more time by pushing problems out into the future. In fact it was, if anything, even more irresponsible than previous programmes.

The main points of the programme were as follows:

1. Of the ¥16 trillion accumulated debts as of fiscal 1981, ¥2.5 trillion ($20.8 bn) would be moved to a separate account from JNR's general account. This was on top of the ¥2.5 trillion which had previously been moved to that account. Thus, the government would be sharing a financial

burden totalling ¥5 trillion. Total subsidies to be paid to JNR for fiscal 1981 would be around ¥730 billion ($6.1 bn).

2. Based on the Flexible Fare Revision Law already in effect, fares could now be raised when necessary in line with changes in the consumer price index.

3. The work-force would be reduced by 70,000 to 350,000 by 1985 through natural attrition with only half of the vacancies created by retirees being filled.

4. Capital expenditure was set at a minimum level of ¥1 trillion ($8.3 bn) per annum for the duration of the programme.

Through these measures, the programme aimed 'to establish the foundation of a well-managed and healthy company on a firm financial footing'. The most significant aspect of the programme was that JNR would temporarily abandon the objective of restoring the financial health to the whole firm. Only Shinkansen and other trunk lines were expected to be in the black on a recurring profit[1] basis. For the whole of JNR, delivering a positive operating result[2] was seen as a sufficient for the time being. The goal of 'establishing a well-managed company' was a sham: the goals laid out were no more than intermediate steps before something drastic really needed to be done.

The other striking characteristic of the programme was its use of exaggerated and eloquent words to gloss over its inadequacy. It was peppered with slogans such as 'a thorough effort to improve management', 'a change of thinking', 'to foster a sense of entrepreneurship', 'to go forward undaunted with the employees united', 'the ultimate programme', 'management's readiness to assume total responsibility', and 'the major mission shared by all JNR's employees to achieve the programme's targets'. The reality was so obvious that we were greatly embarrassed. 'The last resort' was supposed to mean that if the programme were to fail, the only choice left would be the break-up and privatization of JNR. But no one took this seriously.

---

[1] Recurring profit: net income before corporate tax and extra-ordinary items.
[2] Operating result, i.e. not including JNR's substantial interest payments.

This programme contained only one new measure – to reduce the work-force by 70,000. A large number of the employees who were hired immediately after the end of the War had reached retirement age and with more than 20,000 employees retiring every year, JNR could reduce the head-count without having to lay off anyone. The plan not to fill half of the vacancies was included in the programme, but the Personnel Department, petrified of a major confrontation with Kokuro and Doro, was vehemently opposed to it from the outset. When the law was enacted, the first thing the personnel department considered was how it could appease Kokuro and Doro. It had very little to bargain with, having relinquished much of its authority in favour of the labour unions in order to have them accept the reduction in freight capacity in 1978. As a last resort, they worked out a deal with the labour unions that in return for accepting the workforce reduction and cooperating with its implementation, they would drop the ¥20.2 billion ($168 mn) damages suit against the labour unions following the 'Strike for the Right to Strike'. Deep down, JNR had never wanted to sue Kokuro and Doro in the first place. It had only done so under strong pressure from Nakasone Yasuhiro, chairman of the Executive Council of the LDP, and other influential LDP politicians.

For JNR dropping the case was therefore very much a case of 'killing two birds with one stone'. It was clear that the Personnel Department and Kokuro had been negotiating secretly on this. As early as 1981, Hosoi Soichi of Kokuro made reference to this idea in a speech at the local union headquarters in Morioka. Shortly thereafter, at the national conference of the regional Administration Department Directors, it was explained that the suit would be dropped when the head-count was successfully reduced to 350,000. Around that time, the management of the Personnel Department requested to the Legal Affairs Department, who were acting as internal counsel on the case to put the matter on the 'back burner'. Kokuro was in fact predicting that the case would continue for a hundred years and would finally be forgotten without a ruling being reached.

In JNR's fiscal 1981 budget, total personnel expenses accounted for around 84% of the total railway operating revenues of ¥2.9 trillion ($24 bn). In order to reach the levels of the private railway companies, around 30% to 40%, JNR would have to reduce its workforce by at least 200,000. A reduction of 70,000 was therefore entirely insufficient. For those in charge of labour relations at JNR, however, it was earth-shattering.

JNR fares were already twice as high as those of private railways running in parallel with JNR lines.[3] Increasing revenues by raising fares was clearly difficult. The programme stipulated that 'decisions on fare increases should be made based on the independent judgement of the management at the appropriate time, within the legal limits – taking into account the competitive situation, JNR's financial situation, trends in inflation and so on'. This wording was highly ambiguous, but the phrase 'independent judgement of the management' ensured that the government would not be held responsible, whatever happened to JNR. It was indeed highly unusual for the real intention of bureaucrats to be crudely exposed by a public statement of this kind. The expected increase in transport volume was set relatively modestly for the first one or two years of the programme, but rose sharply to an unrealistic degree towards the end. Bureaucrats usually spend one, maximum two years in one post and in the case of ministers it is even shorter. Tenure for the JNR board members was three years. The programme was clearly designed to collapse, but not before all the people who were involved in its creation had moved on.

The programme limited construction expenses to ¥1 trillion ($8.3 bn): no one expected that they could be further reduced. Given that construction expenses for fiscal 1981 exceeded ¥1 trillion, it was as good as saying that they would not be less than ¥1 trillion. New debt for fiscal 1981 amounted to ¥2.3 trillion ($19.2 bn), ¥0.3 trillion ($2.5 bn) of which was for the repayment of past debt, ¥0.9 trillion ($7.5 bn) for interest payments, and ¥1.1 trillion ($9.2 bn) for construction-related expenses (including ¥0.1 trillion ($0.8 bn) for interest payments relating to construction in progress). According to the plan, the net debt was expected to increase by ¥2 trillion ($16.7 bn) in fiscal 1981. Even with the

---

[3] Although this may seem unthinkable in many European countries, two, or more, railway lines would frequently run between the same destinations in urban areas in Japan, sometimes alongside each other for part of the journey.

removal of the ¥2.5 trillion ($20.8 bn) of debt, JNR's indebtedness would return to previous levels within two years. As with all its predecessors, the 'Last Resort Programme' was doomed to fail from the very start.

[2] Assigned to Deputy Director-General of the President's Secretariat in charge of SARC

In April 1981 I returned to headquarters as Deputy Director-General in the Corporate Planning Department and Deputy Director-General responsible for the Second Administrative Reform Committee (SARC) within the President's Secretariat. With SARC having been established in March, public support for administrative reform was growing. Although the Japanese economy had successfully weathered the second oil crisis, the appreciation of the Yen had caused the economy to slow again and a siege mentality was gripping the country. Down-sizing government became a popular theme. The shortfall in tax revenues could only be covered with the increasing issuance of government bonds and without thorough reforms the future tax burden would inevitably increase with serious consequences for the competitiveness of Japanese companies.

This change of mood presented the ideal opportunity for JNR to start with a clean slate: to separate accumulated debt completely from its balance sheet, to work out a thorough solution for the problem of local lines, to implement a meaningful personnel rationalization, and to put the brakes on new construction. On my return to headquarters, I thought that in my new position in the Corporate Planning Department, and as Deputy Director-General of the President's Secretariat, I was well positioned.

My predecessor at the Corporate Planning Department, Ide Masataka (currently the chairman of JR West), had finished drafting the management improvement plan and was about to present it for approval to the Ministry of Transport ('MOT'). Many of the senior executives in headquarters appeared unmotivated, but Ide was proceeding with his management improvement plan full of zest. Ide had been Deputy Director in the Personnel Department at the time of the collapse of the productivity movement and was keen to settle old scores with Kokuro and Doro: the planned 70,000 head-count reduction offered the ideal opportunity.

Despite its defects, those at JNR and the MOT who had been involved in the 'Management Improvement Programme' thought that it might provide breathing space for at least two years. There was, however, very strong resistance within JNR and the MOT to any interference by SARC in their affairs: a typical response of any bureaucrat to third party interference. JNR and MOT regarded SARC as an intruder, who would try to rearrange their own house in any way it pleased. Indeed, the relationship between SARC and the other ministries was much the same. Even the railway *zoku* of the LDP felt the same way. Only the media and business world were supportive of SARC.

At this point, JNR, the MOT and the Transport Division of the Policy Deliberation Committee of the LDP were all prepared to reject any involvement by SARC, arguing that they had already formulated their own improvement programme. Certainly the authority of the 'Last Resort Programme', with its basis in law, resulting from deliberations in the Diet and the consensus of JNR, the government and the LDP, having been authorized by the Minister of Transport after the establishment of SARC, would be interpreted as being higher than that of SARC. When the 'Last Resort Programme' was approved in May, SARC had still not started to function.

Although there was almost no one who seriously believed that the Programme was sufficient to reform JNR, once it was implemented, it gave the Ministry and JNR the excuse to stop thinking any further about the issue. As far as they were concerned the targets had been set and JNR needed to achieve them. What they meant, of course, was the programme had bought them another two years. Meanwhile, SARC was having to find its own feet: selecting what themes to focus on and how to set about tackling them. It was rumoured that Sejima Ryuzo, chairman of Itochu, one of Japan's largest trading firms, might become an adviser to Doko Toshio, chairman of SARC, to facilitate coordination among politicians, bureaucrats and business people. It was in early May that I visited Sejima through the introduction of a friend.

Sejima emphasized two points in particular: 'The old JNR was an excellent organization, but discipline has collapsed. It must regain the discipline of old.' He added: 'I have been hearing that there are a lot of dubious practices in the area of procurement. JNR deliberately sets specifications at a level so that nothing can be bought in the open market. The point is to secure plum jobs for retiring JNR executives. If you relaxed these specifications, JNR could greatly reduce costs.' This was my first encounter with Sejima. Subsequently, there were a number of important occasions when he gave me invaluable advice and support.

In the middle of May, SARC started interviewing a great number of people as part of its information-gathering process. We were also brought in on a number of occasions. A Deputy Director of the Finance Section of the MOT's Railway Supervision Bureau provided the explanation and I supplemented where necessary. If I implied any deficiency in the Management Improvement Programme, the Deputy Director would kick me on the leg under the table. On receiving this signal, I would hurriedly conclude my explanation and keep silent. However, as we were seated side by side, the movement of our legs under the table was quite transparent to our interviewers. Tanaka Kazuaki, chief examiner of SARC in charge of JNR issues, evidently observed our behaviour, and concluded that the Management Improvement Programme was not entirely free of problems. At that point, SARC's questions covered only the broad outline of the Programme.

On 10 July, SARC issued its first report, in which JNR was just one of a number of issues covered. Comments about JNR in the report were moderate in tone. For example: 'We expect the steady implementation of the Management Improvement Programme.' In any case, as the Programme had been approved by the Minister of Transport only in May, it was perhaps too early to make any strongly critical comments.

However, a year later, in July 1982, a dramatic event was about to unfold that would greatly alter the landscape: the publication by SARC recommending the break-up and privatization of JNR. This marked a fundamental turning point in the reform process of JNR and it is perhaps worth reassessing briefly the major milestones in the road to the company's eventual privatization. If one accepts the argument that the history of JNR reform is the gradual awareness of the fundamental structural problems with which JNR was saddled and how these defects should be addressed, then it could be said that the reform process started with the birth of JNR itself. Another interpretation is that the process of reform started in 1964 when problems actually came to the surface and JNR's operating performance started its rapid deterioration. However, the establishment of SARC could be regarded as the starting point of reform of JNR because it was the first time that fundamental discussions took place as to the future of the 'self-supporting' public corporation.

Similar arguments can be made about when the reform process was completed. It was generally believed to have ended with the establishment of the JR companies in 1987. Other interpretations as to when it was completed were when the listing of the three Honshu JR companies took place in the early and late 1990s, or when the JR law was revised in 2001 so that regulations governing the three Honshu JR companies were harmonized with those for the private railway companies. Others might argue that it will only be completed when all the shares held by the government are sold off to the public, while an argument could also be made that, since the structure of JR companies contains many of the same defects as JNR, the actual reform process is still far from complete.

③ Simulation of the break-up of JNR

In July 1981, immediately after the release of the first SARC report, I initiated my own research into the radical reform of JNR. As I would be exploring options to which there would be great opposition within JNR and the MOT, I had to start it on an informal basis. However, I secured the understanding of my seniors, the Director of the General Affairs Section in the President's Secretariat, the Director-General of the Corporate Planning Department and the board member in charge of the Personnel Department. I had worked closely with both of them in the past and they both understood and acknowledged how serious the situation at JNR was. A study group was set up consisting of seven members from various departments including Personnel (Matsuda Masatake, now Chairman of JR East), the President's Secretariat, the Corporate Planning Department and the Finance & Accounting Department. The membership was limited to middle-ranking managers like me and those who had worked together and had developed a high degree of mutual trust. We all agreed that our goal should be to take advantage of the rising tide in public support for administrative reform to seek a fundamental solution to JNR's problems.

While the time horizon of the top executives of JNR was two or three years, the time left until retirement, the members of our study group were all aged around 30. We quickly came to the conclusion that the break-up and privatization of JNR was the only solution, a quite different judgement from that the top executives would have made.

The starting point of the study was to discover, from the viewpoint of economic rationality, what JNR might achieve if all the constraints under which it had operated were lifted. Industrial relations was one of the most important problems which JNR faced. There were two separate but inter-linked issues, both of which could be resolved internally: discipline at the workplace and head-count rationalization. To raise productivity to the level of the private railway companies meant simply to stop hiring and to reduce the number of the employees to the appropriate level. We thought that if we could, through the break-up of JNR, reduce unit labour costs in regional areas to levels of other workers in the region, tremendous savings could be made in personnel costs. Something also had to be done about JNR's debt, which had grown to ¥16 trillion ($133.3 bn) (including the suspended amount of ¥5 trillion ($41.7 bn) for fiscal 1981). Debt had accumulated as a result of a number of non-management factors, such as political constraints on JNR's ability to increase fares, uneconomic capital expenditures, the maintenance of unprofitable lines, and so on. The company was already sinking through the weight of interest payments, which would only get worse if nothing was done. Debt would have to be separated from JNR's balance sheet to a manageable level where interest payments could be funded from operating revenues. No JNR rebirth would be possible without breaking down the mechanism whereby the company's future would persistently be undermined by actions of the past.

To achieve the transfer of JNR's accumulated debt to the government, there would need to be a guarantee that there would be absolutely no new debt in the future and for this, privatization was the only solution. A privatized JNR could only survive by stopping all new construction work and reducing the work-force and wages as far as possible. With the construction of the Tohoku and the Joetsu Shinkansen Lines nearing completion, we believed that new railway construction could be restrained.

If JNR were to be privatized, the concept of a single national railway operation would clearly be unworkable. The huge regional variability in passenger volumes, combined with the need to maintain a nationally uniform fare system had given rise to the inefficient system of cross-subsidies. The Tokaido Shinkansen, which was profitable, was obliged to charge fares double the level of its intrinsic costs in order to subsidize loss-making local lines. Commuter trains in the Tokyo area also charged fares double those of the private railway operators. Ordinarily, no form of transport could possibly compete with the Shinkansen on a route such as Tokyo-Osaka-Okayama. However, the high fare level that JNR was obliged to set meant that it was profitable for other modes of transport, such as airlines, to enter this market, skimming off JNR's most profitable passenger base. This would weaken JNR's competitive position on its key trunk lines, necessitating a further set of fare increases, perpetuating the vicious circle.

This situation would not only have a harmful influence on the management of JNR but also on the national economy and peoples' lives. If the Tokaido Shinkansen, in which all the favourable characteristics of railway transportation were combined, was allowed to set competitive fares based on its inherent cost structure, other transportation modes would have been kept out of the market. As things were, passengers had to pay unreasonably high fares, enabling inefficient transportation modes to enter the market. This undermined the basis for an efficient railway transportation system and increased costs for many sectors of the national economy. On the other hand, railways in local areas, which would otherwise have lost out to road transportation, continued to survive, and the high cost structure of the railway network was therefore firmly established, creating inefficiency and economic distortions in many parts of the economy.

The only way to break this vicious circle was to do away with loss-making local lines. As we have seen, this proved impossible politically and the government had resorted to compensating JNR for the operation of these lines and for this purpose more than ¥120 billion ($1 bn) of public money was spent in fiscal 1981. These subsidies proved to be neither sufficient nor even the right way to tackle the issue.

The only conclusion, therefore, was to break up JNR into regional operating companies. Take Hokkaido, for example, where the traffic density was low, resulting in a high cost base per passenger. If Hokkaido fares reflected this cost structure, they would naturally be higher than those on Honshu after the break-up of JNR and if fares exceeded the value of services which the local lines provided, no one would take trains and these lines would be abolished. The ending of this dependency on a few profitable routes would force local railway companies, local passengers, local governments and tax-payers to manage their own local transportation affairs and in doing so examine their own priorities. One way of cutting down on costs would be to recognize that living costs were not uniform across the nation and that wages would be reduced in local areas to reflect this.

We attempted to create simulations of the various scenarios of the break-up of JNR. In these simulations, one constant was that we excluded the possibility of a 'functional break-up'. In other words, the management of the infrastructure (stations, track, power supply, signalling facilities etc) and the operation of the trains would be done by the same company. In the past, whenever the MOT considered the reconstruction of JNR, they were inclined to separate infrastructure and train operations, in their expectation of managing the infrastructure themselves. In our view, uniform management of both was essential for efficiency and safety: there would be no question about the possibility of multiple companies operating their trains on the same track. We decided to regard each route as one unit of management, and considered a combination of these units, or a network, as constituting one company.

JNR had made a detailed analysis of transport volume, revenue and cost structures by route for the purpose of calculating cross-subsidies, and this data proved invaluable for our simulations. One of the objectives of the simulation was to study regional passenger flows in order to determine a logical way to break up JNR, with the principle that the majority of passengers should move within the business region of one company. Not surprisingly, Hokkaido, Shikoku and Kyushu emerged as discreet business entities, as in excess of 90% of traffic within those areas was local. There was, however, some debate on how to divide Honshu. In the end, we reached the conclusion that the most realistic way of looking at this issue was by thinking in terms of the Shinkansen lines.

Most passengers on the Tohoku and Joetsu Shinkansen lines that went north from Tokyo were moving from one station to another on those lines. Only one to two per cent transferred to the Tokaido Shinkansen. It was therefore quite practical to separate the Tohoku and Joetsu Shinkansens from the Tokaido Shinkansen. Besides, the Tohoku and Joetsu Shinkansen lines operated the same rolling stock. As the Sanyo Shinkansen was an extension westwards from Osaka of the Tokaido Shinkansen the same rolling stock obviously operated on both lines and it would be natural to combine them as one unit. In this case, however, Honshu would be divided into two regions, i.e., north and south, which were considered too large. By focusing attention on the fact that 80% of passengers of the Tokaido Shinkansen were travelling between Tokyo and Osaka, a separation of the Tokaido Shinkansen from the Sanyo Shinkansen appeared logical.

We concluded that three combinations should be created: one consisting of the Tohoku Shinkansen, the Joetsu Shinkansen and the conventional lines in the metropolitan area of Tokyo and the northern region of Honshu, another for the Sanyo Shinkansen and the conventional lines in the Kinki and Chugoku regions, and a third for the Tokaido Shinkansen and the conventional lines in the Chubu and Tokai regions. We examined each combination to see if they would stand up as separate businesses. As for freight transportation, we judged that there would not be any problem dividing it into various regional businesses in the same way as we had done for the passenger companies. We simulated various fare and wage levels, repeating these calculations excluding the particularly unprofitable lines, to examine at what wage and fare levels these combinations were sustainable.

By the autumn of 1981, the study group reached the conclusion that the passenger division of JNR could logically be divided into six more or less profitable companies, even if these remained integrated with the freight business. The study progressed to the point where a rough outline of revenues and expenditures of each company was outlined. The most important part of the analysis was to ascertain that the division of the passenger business into six companies reflected the geographic reality of the transportation situation and that each of them would be able to stand on its own two feet. I explained this scheme to Sejima, a member of SARC, in November 1981. SARC, whose core members were three men – Nakasone, Doko and Sejima – with strong personalities who were prone to top-down decision-making, was quite different from usual bureaucratic organizations. It was left entirely to Sejima to consider the scheme and we were to keep silent until such time as the scheme was widely accepted. When it became clear in April 1982 that SARC had made up its mind to break up and privatize JNR, we secretly explained the scheme to Tanaka Kazuaki, who was responsible for the fourth panel of SARC that was looking into JNR matters. Our scheme became the basis for the draft of SARC's Basic Report which was subsequently adopted in its entirety by the JNR Reorganization Advisory Panel (JNR RAP) in its report, resulting in the shape of the JR companies we see today. The logic and rationale of the scheme was such that anyone who attempted a simulation would have come up with the same result.

4 The reform of JNR: the main priority for SARC

SARC started full-scale deliberations in September 1981. SARC had established four panels, each of which was given a specific subject and to which members had been assigned. The panels were strengthened by the assignment of professional staff. The Fourth Panel was assigned to consider the future of the three public corporations. Kato Hiroshi, professor of Keio University, was appointed as Chairman of the panel and Tanaka Kazuaki, assistant director of the Administrative Management Agency (currently the Ministry of Public Management, Home Affairs, Posts and Telecommunications) was assigned as chief investigator.

SARC had not yet made public its recommendation that the three public corporations should be privatized. Nippon Telegraph and Telephone and the Japan Tobacco & Salt Corporation both had profitable monopolies and were soundly managed. The government would therefore not have to shoulder any financial burden if they were privatized and indeed the companies them-selves were keen to take advantage of SARC's formation to break free from the shackles of public corporation status. I felt in partic-ular that Nippon Telegraph & Telephone led by President Shinto Hisashi, who was himself from the private sector, would welcome the prospect of privatization.

JNR's situation was, of course, quite the opposite and in order to privatize it, the government would have to be prepared to shoulder a large share of the debt that the company had accumulated over the years. Furthermore, the executives of JNR and the MOT still clung to the Management Improvement Programme, and were unwilling to cooperate with SARC. However, through the process of hearings which were conducted through to the summer, SARC became convinced that radical measures would be needed to solve JNR's problems. SARC anticipated fierce resistance from both bureaucrats and politicians and saw that it needed to focus its atten-tion clearly on one outcome: the privatization of the three public corporations. Gradually, the direction was becoming clear.

On the other hand, the MOT clearly resented interference into its affairs by SARC's amateurs. This was perhaps justifiable, given the reputation of consultative organizations for coming in, making comments, create confusion and disorder and not assuming any responsibility for the outcome. Besides, if the Management Improvement Programme, which had been approved by the MOT, were terminated after just a few months, the MOT would lose face and would have some awkward explaining to do. In response, the MOT set up a private study group led by Tamura Hajime, former Minister of Transport, to work out a more detailed plan for the reform of JNR, and thereby hoped to neutralize SARC's deliberations which were scheduled to start in full after the autumn.

Tamura's study group was held once a week and was attended by Hayashi Junji, chief of the General Affairs Section of the Minister's Secretariat, Ide Masataka, Deputy Director-General of JNR's Corporate Planning Department, and several other select members from both of the Ministry and JNR. At this point, the Ministry believed that the break-up and privatization of JNR could not be achieved. Two years later, by an ironic coincidence, Hayashi was assigned to the Secretariat of JNR RAP, which was established in response to the Basic Report of SARC, and became a central figure in considering, drafting and promoting the plan to break-up and privatize JNR.

The conclusion of the study group was made public, as Tamura's private plan, in November. The main recommendations of the plan were for the provision of more generous government subsidies to JNR, to give greater definition to the Management Improvement Plan, and then to carefully watch the efforts of JNR. While the plan seemed at first glance to be full of good intentions, in reality it argued for the maintenance of the *status quo* and was without substance. Fearing that the plan would dampen the rising momentum for radical reform, a newspaper article by Professor Kato Hiroshi appeared immediately criticising Tamura's private plan, to which Tamura promptly made a counter argument. Tamura's private plan did manage to catch the temporary attention of the public, but failed to stem the tide. I had written Kato Hiroshi's article at the request of Tanaka, chief investigator of SARC's fourth panel, and it was not until many years had elapsed that I discovered that the person who had written Tamura's reply was Ide, who sat right next to me in the office.

SARC's deliberations on JNR started in early October and until the end of the year there was a frequent exchange of opinions with the management of JNR and hearings were conducted with executives of private railway companies, industry and other informed experts, and the union leadership. The SARC members attempted to steer the discussion in the direction of radical reform by suggesting restrictions on capital expenditure, a complete freeze on hiring, a review of fringe benefits for employees, the restoration of discipline at the work-place, and a much more substantive plan for reform. JNR and the MOT, however, only reiterated the need to put the existing Programme into practice. This failure of the two sides to communicate effectively led to a growing mutual distrust.

It was a little after mid-October that Takagi, the President of JNR, secretly told Kato Hiroshi, the fourth panel's Chairman that he agreed with the break-up and privatization plan and with the proposal to create nine operating companies. However, he could not make his views public as resistance within JNR was so intense and he suggested to Kato that SARC was ideally placed to peg JNR into a corner from which there should be no escape.

On 4 November, an article appeared in the *Asahi Shimbun*, one of Japan's largest and most influential newspapers, by Otani Ken, a senior reporter, arguing for the break-up and privatization of JNR. This was the first editorial article supportive of the plan. At the informal request of a Director in the Administration Section of the Railway Supervision Bureau of the MOT, I delivered a lecture on the issue. It was becoming more apparent that the Management Improvement Programme was effectively dead and that its prolongation would only increase the burden on the taxpayer to unbearable levels. The public, especially those that used JNR, was getting frustrated, and with JNR and the MOT apparently just playing for time, a satisfactory conclusion seemed a long way off. Kato Mutsuki, leader of the Transport Division of the LDP's Policy Deliberation Committee launched an open assault on SARC, which drew an immediate counterattack by SARC on the members of the LDP rail zoku. The situation seemed to be reaching deadlock, requiring some sort of external shock to get things moving again.

An important turning point came in January 1982, when it was sensationally reported by the press that locomotive inspectors at the Tokyo depot were paid allowances for bogus business trips despite not even being on duty. Thereafter, cases of corruption at the work-place, hitherto hidden, were revealed in a series of exposés and press criticism of JNR started to mount inexorably.

Those that had hitherto remained silent on JNR's financial problems and lack of work-place discipline started to speak out.

On 15 March 1982, a drunken locomotive driver failed to spot a worker signalling for him to stop and ran his locomotive into the rear of a sleeper train at Nagoya Station. Three carriages were totally destroyed and fourteen people were injured although miraculously no one was killed. There was a surge in momentum in favour of radical measures and this paved the way for SARC to proceed with its recommendation to break-up and privatize JNR. The privatization of the three public corporations thus became the main focus of discussion at SARC.

Ide, Senior Deputy Director-General of the Corporate Planning Department, had been against JNR's break-up and privatization, but came to recognize that clinging to the existing Programme was no longer tenable. In mid-November Ide and I discussed with Matsuda of the Personnel Department the need for some kind of breakthrough. We agreed that dealing with the problem of worker discipline would be a good place to start. We then decided to set up a liaison meeting, calling together twenty reliable deputy directors from various departments. This group would subsequently be referred to as 'the reformist' faction. This kind of movement was obviously not sufficient to transform the organization, especially with the Personnel Department still bent on appeasing the labour unions and seemingly unwilling to show any resolve. We, therefore, decided to work on the members of the Transport Division of the LDP Policy Deliberation Committee and to use them as a leverage to change the atmosphere within JNR.

As a first step, the three of us approached Mitsuzuka Hiroshi, Chairman of the Transport Division, and asked for the LDP's support. Mitsuzuka was from Sendai and I had become acquainted with him during my two-year stint there. We had a one-hour breakfast meeting with Mitsuzuka and we proceeded to give him a full explanation about the actual situation of discipline at the work-place. Mitsuzuka listened to us earnestly and sympathetically. Soon after the meeting, I ran into the board member in charge of the Personnel Department, who told me: 'When I saw Kato Mutsuki of the LDP's transport zoku, he told me of a group of rebellious young turks within JNR stirring up a '2/26 incident'.[4] I couldn't help thinking of you. Keep your head down and don't be so critical.' I supposed that Mitsuzuka told Kato Mutsuki about our breakfast meeting. I was aware of the hostile attitude of many people in the personnel department, and appreciated the board member's looking after my interests. He was a member of the recruiting team when I was offered a job at JNR and after entering the company, he gave me a lot of guidance, both official and private, and I greatly respected him. However, while I regretted being a worry to him, once the ball started to roll, there was no way to stop it. He warned me: 'You've got to be careful: someone was criticising you for violating the organization's rules.' I replied: 'Yes, I know. But while we are all members of this organization, we are also part of this country. Don't you think it's more of an offence to collude with the labour unions which repeatedly stage illegal and disruptive strikes?' He seemed to understand, but still ended the conversation, which took place privately in his office, by urging me to be careful.

5   The Mitsuzuka Committee

In February 1982, a sub-committee to look into matters relating to JNR was set up within the Transport Division of the LDP. It came to be called the 'Mitsuzuka Committee' after the chairman. Since January 1982, as media reports of corruption at the workplace spread, the feeling grew that not only did JNR's weak-kneed labour policy have to be changed, but also that the belief that whatever JNR did would be underwritten by the government, which many saw as the cause of the irresponsible management of JNR, needed to be wiped away. Given this shift in public opinion and SARC's focus on the privatization of the public corporations, the LDP could not stand by and let events take their course. The Mitsuzuka Committee was clearly conscious of the direction in which SARC was headed, started to review JNR issues more urgently, deciding as

---

[4] '2/26' incident refers to an attempted coup by young officers of the Japanese Imperial Army which took place on 26 February 1936, and is commonly used to refer to rebellious young members of an organization.

a first step to focus on the problem of discipline. The most significant figure in the Transport Division, Kato Mutsuki, was weighed down by his involvement in the Lockheed scandal and had chosen a man as his successor whom he could control and influence, Mitsuzuka Hiroshi, an honest but not well-known Diet member.

Mitsuzuka made a proposal to set up a committee, and received Kato Mutsuki's approval. I wonder to what extent the discussion the three of us – Ide, Matsuda and I had had with him – might have influenced him. I had heard that the manager, who had become the Director General of the Personnel Department after completing his assignment as Director General in Sendai (Mitsuzuka's birth-place), had also requested Mitsuzuka directly to take up the issue of JNR worker discipline within the LDP.

At first, there was much speculation about the role of the Mitsuzuka Committee, which made Kato Mutsuki feel uncomfortable. His comment, that 'It is sufficient for the committee merely to follow-up on the progress of the Management Improvement Programme', revealed his true feelings. Kato might have felt uneasy that Mitsuzuka, who was supposed to be his puppet, was starting to show a degree of independence. The Transport Division, under the leadership of Kato Mutsuki, had hitherto not interfered in matters relating to industrial relations as the issue of labour was regarded as the management's domain, and the LDP saw little benefit in antagonizing the powerful Kokuro and Doro unions. Not only did Kokuro have a leadership role in Japan's labour movement, they also had fourteen Diet members belonging to the JSP who had been Kokuro leaders and were elected with direct Kokuro support, and that gave it great sway over the opposition parties. The major interest of the transportation zoku was in such matters as construction, procurement and regulation governing who could do business within station precincts. Interference in matters of discipline would mean a lot of trouble for nothing.

Some JNR executives headed by President Takagi thought that the maintenance of a degree of mutual trust with the LDP was very important. They also thought that harmonious and friendly relations with the opposition parties, particularly the JSP, were also essential and, for that purpose, the policy of appeasement towards Kokuro was the most realistic. They therefore considered deep down that the actions of the Mitsuzuka Committee were no more than meddling. They wanted to reassure the LDP that the present labour policy was working, and by persuading them that discipline was gradually improving, they hoped to soften the criticism from within the LDP. They expected the LDP to resist the path of the break-up and privatization of JNR being advocated by SARC and the JNR executives were counting on Kato to direct Mitsuzuka accordingly.

Within JNR, a senior group of executives, led by the Executive Vice-President, the Director-General of the Personnel Department and the Director-General of the Finance & Accounting Department, intended to take advantage of the rising tide of criticism against the slack discipline in JNR. They would, with the help of the LDP, change the excessively placatory labour policy, restore discipline and promote personnel rationalization. In order to achieve this, they would have to seize control of the firm from the firm's mainstream, led by President Takagi. This group seemed to share our ambition in the sense that we both saw no future in the *status quo*. With the personnel department being responsible for the relationship and communication with the Mitsuzuka Committee, the Director-General of the Personnel Department decided on a duplicitous approach: on the one hand he instructed the Director in charge of the relationship with the committee to paint a positive picture of JNR's progress in public while on the other hand he secretly requested the Mitsuzuka Committee to expose the falsehood of JNR's public statements. Ide, Matsuda, myself and others, were assigned to the group's 'unofficial Secretariat'. But what the Director-General of the Personnel Department wanted to do most of all was to regain control over industrial relations, which meant a return to the situation before the productivity movement. The break-up and privatization of JNR was for him completely out of the question.

Most of us who served on the 'unofficial Secretariat' shared a common goal, i.e., the restoration of discipline, and were inclined to get SARC and the Mitsuzuka Committee to work together and use this cooperation to realize the ultimate goal of the break-up and privatization of JNR. Meanwhile, the MOT stood by impassively, waiting to see how the situation developed. They certainly had no interest in being involved in the issues of discipline: these were not their problems.

Having no direct vested interest in JNR, Mitsuzuka was in an excellent position to tackle the fundamental problems of JNR and in doing so further his career as a politician and as Chairman of the Transport Division. He was a man of great spirit and it was therefore not surprising that Kato Mutsuki, who was an old-style politician sensitive to issues of vested interest and patronage, was having an increasingly difficult job keeping him under control. The Mitsuzuka Committee exposed the falsehood of JNR's official statements one after another in accordance with the information we fed them. With the increasing media focus on JNR's poor record on discipline, the LDP started to pay more attention. A proposal to restore work-place discipline, which was incorporated in the interim report of the Mitsuzuka Committee, was supported unanimously at the LDP party conference. The proposal contained a set of corrective measures, the comprehensive nature of which would hitherto have been unthinkable from a Japanese industrial relations perspective.

When the Mitsuzuka Committee gave its official seal of approval to the Executive Vice-President and his group, the power base within JNR shifted away from President Takagi. The group feared that the Committee had been excessive in their demands and became defensive. They told us that the role of the Committee was over and that we should persuade Mitsuzuka not to get involved in management issues. They stressed that this was Kato Mutsuki's wish also. 'Getting involved in management issues' necessarily meant that capital expenditure would have to be restrained. Construction work, which had been steadily increasing, would be curtailed, and scope for patronage reduced. As Mitsuzuka's reputation grew, Kato Mutsuki came to regard him as a rival and they started to argue. This made the relationship between us and the Executive Vice-President and his group difficult, because while we supported in secret the Mitsuzuka Committee, their longer-term relationship was with Kato Mutsuki.

After successfully publishing its interim report in May, the Mitsuzuka Committee started to look into the reform of JNR in earnest. Over at SARC, the policy of the break-up and privatization of the public corporations was taking a much clearer shape. The main focus of the Mitsuzuka Committee shifted from matters relating to personnel to those relating to finance, under the jurisdiction of the Finance & Accounting Department. Kato Mutsuki and the Director-General of the Finance & Accounting Department looked at this development with unease. As for us, we continued to lead a double life, doing our normal jobs during the day and then working hard for the unofficial Secretariat at night and on holidays.

The proposal of the Mitsuzuka Committee called 'The Plan for the Reform of JNR' was ratified by the Party Conference on 2 July. In addition to the establishment of discipline and further efforts to improve operating performance, the report touched upon the company's structure itself: the 'Exit Theory', which referred to the plan to break-up and privatize JNR. 'Firstly, the company will have until 1985 to intensify the implementation of the existing Programme. If this does not bring about the desired results, JNR will be broken up and privatized: this will be accomplished by 1987. An organization will be immediately set up to consider the actual procedure to privatize JNR, while efforts to improve management will continue in parallel.'

SARC published its report at the end of July, and put forward something called the 'Entrance Theory.' Basically, SARC proposed break-up and privatization by 1987, with an organization being established to work out a plan by the end of 1985. Until the completion of break-up and privatization, further efforts to improve the company's management would be made. The difference between the two plans was that the 'entrance theory' started with the assumption that JNR would be broken up and privatized, whereas the 'exit theory' gave the management some breathing space, at least on paper, to put their house in order until a decision was taken. The Mitsuzuka Committee had conceived the 'exit theory' out of consideration for those within the LDP and JNR who were opposed to the break-up and privatization of JNR, and to minimize the confrontation between the Mitsuzuka Committee and SARC. There was sufficient commonality between the proposals and Committee and SARC made it easier for the LDP to agree to the Basic Report of SARC when it was presented. However, the JNR senior management and Kato Mutsuki's supporters at the Transport Division saw the possibility of the 'exit theory' sabotaging SARC's 'entrance theory'. This was a typical case of 'sleeping in the same bed, but having different dreams'.

6 The Basic Report of SARC

The Basic Report of SARC was presented on 30 July 1982. The privatization of the three public corporations was proposed, and all of them were eventually privatized. The break-up and privatization of JNR was also realized within five years in exactly the same way proposed in the Basic Report, enhancing greatly the reputation of SARC and its sponsors, Doko and Nakasone. There were a number of factors as to how the Basic Report led to the successful privatization of JNR, seemingly an impossibility only a short time before, but I would like to mention three points in particular.

The first key point was that the Basic Report's policies maintained consistency with those of the LDP. At the time of the establishment of the Mitsuzuka Committee, JNR's senior executives and the MOT fully expected the LDP to act as a check on SARC's evident desire to see the break-up and privatization of JNR. SARC itself initially considered the transportation *zoku* of the LDP, with its history of putting vested interests first, as the largest obstruction to the reform of JNR. Had the composition of the Transport Division remained as it was, SARC's fears may have been justified. However, Mitsuzuka becoming Chairman of the Transport Division changed all of this. Being a relative newcomer to the political world, he was less interested in patronage and more in establishing his reputation as a politician who was willing to confront difficult issues head on. The mutual distrust that had plagued SARC's relationship with the LDP gradually dissipated, and the relationship between Sejima, Kato Hiroshi of SARC, and Mitsuzuka became ever closer. They actively encouraged each other, and worked cooperatively to produce the final report.

Whilst the LDP's 'Exit' and SARC's 'Entrance' theories may have seemed at first sight to be working in opposite directions, they shared the common goals of establishing a professional organization and the processes outlined on how JNR should be privatized by 1985 were similar, as were the emergency measures to be taken. SARC argued for division into seven companies, while the LDP argued for four, according to the islands, but the differences were not of great substance.

The second key point was the establishment of the JNR Reorganization Advisory Panel (JNR RAP). It was between the end of 1981 to the beginning of 1982 that SARC made up its mind to set the direction for the break-up and privatization of JNR. As the other two public corporations, NTT and the Japan Tobacco & Salt Corporation, were in good shape, the privatization process for them would be relatively straightforward: there would be no financial burden on the government, and there would be no difficult break-up issues. Furthermore, these two public corporations were themselves promoting privatization and as a consequence, there would be no need for external pressure. This was obviously not the case for JNR. The huge financial burden that the state would have to assume removing the company's accumulated debt caused the MOF to be strongly opposed to the idea of privatization. There were also significant logistical challenges in dividing up the company in terms of where to draw boundaries between one company and another, how to divide assets and personnel, and so on. There was little confidence that the 'layman' at SARC would be able to put together the extraordinarily complex and detailed plan required in such a short time. The sceptics muttered to each other that the plan would be abstract and would eventually just fade away. Given the tight schedule for deliberation and SARC's limited human resources, their prediction would have come true if things had been left as they were.

In April I gave Tanaka Kazuaki of SARC's secretariat a full private briefing of our idea of dividing JNR into six regional companies. I also gave him an overview of the business environment and an estimate of revenue and expenses for each of the divided companies. I proposed to him that only a broad outline of the scheme for JNR's break-up and privatization and how it was to be achieved should be incorporated in the Basic Report, and that a professional organization should be established to work out the details after the Report's publication. An incomplete and incoherent report would play right into the hands of those opposed to the plan. It was therefore essential to set up a professional body which would work to establish firmly the link between the ideal and the reality. Tanaka instantly agreed to this, and we worked out a contingency plan. In the process, the plan to establish JNR RAP was incorporated into the Report. The original plan which Tanaka and I conceived was that JNR RAP should be established as an organization with full executive authority (based on Article 3 of the National Government Organization Law). This, however, would be a staggering blow to the MOT: giving JNR RAP executive powers to direct and implement the break-up and privatization of JNR would undermine the raison d'être of the MOT's National Railway Department.

The Ministry lobbied hard to have the status of JNR RAP as a mere consultative organization (based on Article 8 of the above Law). In the end, a compromise was reached whereby JNR RAP would be established as a consultative body reporting to the Prime Minister, but there would be an obligation to respect recommendations of the Report in much the same way as those of the Atomic Energy Board. Hitherto the MOT had been standing by and regarding SARC's deliberations with hostility. The proposal to establish JNR RAP with executive powers was in effect a vote of no-confidence in the Ministry. With little room for manoeuvre, the MOT would have no alternative but to change its stance and embrace the reform of JNR wholeheartedly. A significant development was the request by Hayashi Junji, a rising star in the Ministry who had long stood in opposition to SARC, to be transferred to the Secretariat of JNR RAP and to engage in the promotion of JNR's break-up and privatization. Hayashi's change of heart was a decisive factor in determining the fate of the reform. JNR RAP was therefore quite different from many consultative bodies that do nothing more then come up with interesting, but unworkable, concepts: it was a professional body with the necessary breathing space and resources to get the job done.

The third key point was the acceleration of emergency measures. It would take three years to get the Basic Report enacted into law: the first year getting the bill approved by the Diet and preparing for the establishment of JNR RAP, and the following two years for drafting a feasible plan for the implementation of the emergency measures. It was essential, however, not just to get the law passed, but to maintain political awareness of the terrible state JNR was in, and the need for continuous action, including major surgery. I proposed to Tanaka that a series of eleven emergency measures should be included in the Report. As I was also working at the unofficial Secretariat of the Mitsuzuka Committee, I felt it would increase the chances of action if the same momentum for urgent measures also came through that committee.

A freeze on new hiring and in construction investment (other than for safety enhancement) were particularly effective in improving the financial situation. At the end of July, when the basic report was presented, the government declared a state of emergency concerning the reform of JNR, and the emergency measures were implemented. In September, the 'JNR Emergency Measures Office' was established in the MOT, and in November, the bill for the establishment of JNR RAP was approved by the Cabinet. The curtain had fallen on Act One. The next act was about to begin.

Chapter 5

The JNR Reorganization Advisory Panel (JNR RAP)

1 Breakthrough in head-count rationalization

From July 1982 onwards, when the report of the Mitsuzuka Committee and the Basic Report of the SARC were released, JNR took advantage of the new atmosphere and concentrated its energies on improving worker discipline. Perhaps the most significant achievement in this process was the abolition of 'The Work-site Labour-Management Consultation System'.

'The Work-site Labour-Management Consultation System' was meant to enable collective bargaining to take place at the level of the work-sites, such as stations, the various types of depots and maintenance yards. *Ad hoc* consultations on a wide range of worker demands made separately across a large number of work-sites inevitably undermined the chain of command. In industries with a large network and variety of work-sites located nationwide, the railway industry being a typical example, it only requires confusion at a small number of them for it to have a ripple effect, spreading rapidly to a large number of other work-sites. The radical pro-Communist group 'Kakudo' within Kokuro had intended to have train operations put effectively under the control of the labour unions. In addition to demanding the institutionalization of a work-site consultation system, they would frequently violate work rules, for example by conducting unlawful 'negotiations' which, in effect, were a form of Kangaroo court where work-site managers were put on trial. The management clearly recognized the union's hidden agenda and refused its demands. In

90

1968, however, the management made concessions to the union regarding the institutionalization of a work-site consultation system in exchange for the union's acceptance of JNR's rationalization and modernization plans.

The management's pretext to the work-site managers for allowing the work-site labour-management consultation system was that JNR were being entrusted to carry out conciliation by the Public Sector Labout Relations Commission. However, the unions succeeded in confusing and dividing the management with a profusion of demands at each of the work-sites, resulting in a large increase in unauthorized holidays and payments, which were determined at work-site level. Kokuro effectively used the work-site labour-management consultation system as a means of increasing its influence at the expense of management's at a time prior to the productivity movement when the management held the upper hand. However, as management authority started to disintegrate, Kokuro found that they were increasingly unable to manage its local chapters at the work-site level. They became more independent and reckless in their behaviour, adding to the chaotic situation. Having been severely criticized by the public for their irresponsible behaviour during the Strike for the Right to Strike, the Kokuro leadership was trying to move in a more moderate direction. The local leadership, however, completely ignored the orders of Kokuro's headquarters and continued to wreak havoc at the work-sites. The work-site consultation system was ideally suited to their purposes.

The abolition of the work-site labour-management consultation system was therefore a remarkable step towards the restoration of work-site discipline, totally unimaginable just one year earlier. The management group led by JNR's Executive Vice-President had become convinced that appeasement was the only solution. This group evidently thought that they had done all they could and had achieved more than enough. Further provocation of Kokuro would only provoke a counter attack and threaten what had been gained. Public opinion was capricious: the issue of discipline had excited people for a while but they were now tired of it. If Kokuro were edged too much into a corner, public sympathy might again be with them.

These executives had presumed that unprecedented developments being contemplated, such as the break-up and privatization of JNR, would never materialize. The fact that the JNR Reorganization Advisory Panel (JNR RAP) was established as an article-eight organization based on the National Government Organization Law became a good excuse for them to cease attacking the labour unions. The then top management joined JNR between 1950 and 1955 when JNR was in its heyday. Many of their generation still saw JNR as an 'unsinkable battleship' and behaved accordingly. They strove to do nothing more than to maintain their influence and control internally. Incremental improvement within the framework of JNR was quite sufficient and from their point of view, they had already achieved unexpected results. It was time, therefore, for a reconciliation with Kokuro in order to put the relationship on a stable footing.

Although we say 'Kokuro and Doro' in the same breath, they were in reality treated quite differently by JNR management. While Kokuro had 300,000 members at the time and a large number of senior union leaders were elected as Diet members with Kokuro's support, Doro only had 50,000 members, and were strongly united but radical. Traditionally, the JNR management gave top priority to a stable relationship with Kokuro. To the Personnel Department, Doro was a 'problem child' while the more moderate Tetsuro was no more than a puppet. Doro, which was in a position to move much more quickly, saw the issue of discipline as an issue which they could use opportunistically to gain an advantage over Kokuro, whose decision-making process was much more tortuous and decided to cooperate with JNR management. For the JNR management, this was a decidedly mixed blessing. For the so-called 'reformists', the younger members of the firm below the director level, the thinking was quite different. For us, the process of reform had only just started. This zeal should be kept alive in order to achieve the break-up and privatization of JNR. While significant progress had been made in the last year, the management of the firm was still in a state of collapse. After a series of minor gains, senior executives appeared satisfied with the *status quo* and were bent on appeasing Kokuro. It appeared to many in the reformist group that the discipline issue was just an excuse to stir up an internal power struggle and decisive cracks appeared between top management and ourselves, although we once seemed to share the same ambition.

The abolition of the work-site labour-management consultation system in the autumn of 1982 was a watershed in the reform of JNR. I worked for the Corporate Planning Department until the end of April 1983. In May I was transferred to the Personnel Department as Director of the Staff Relations Section in charge of labour productivity. I was again working for the Director-General of the Personnel Department, who had been my superior in Sendai. There was a rumour circulated within JNR at the time that the Mitsuzuka Committee was being supported by Ide, Matsuda and Kasai. As there were only three people, the Executive Vice-president, the Director-General of the Personnel Department, and the Director-General of the Finance & Accounting Department, who knew that we were working as the unofficial Secretariat to the Committee, it was obvious who the source of this rumour was. Under such circumstances, it was difficult to understand why I had been appointed as Director of the Staff Relations Section. I thought perhaps that they might have explained to Kokuro that it was better to have me directly under the supervision of the Director General rather than creating havoc from the outside. This became clear to me soon after I arrived at the office, when he told me: 'You have been working on various strategic matters for the Secretariat of the Mitsuzuka Committee, but from now on you are to devote yourself totally to your new assignment as Director of the Staff Relations Section.'

My confrontation with the Director-General of the Personnel Department started on the very first day over the revision of train drivers' work rules.

On the day I assumed my post as Director of the Staff Relations Section, the Director-General of the Personnel Department, the Director of the Labour Section and the Director of the Remuneration Section held a welcome party for me. The party was held in a room on the second floor of a small Japanese restaurant located in Akasaka, one of Tokyo's lively entertainment areas. On that occasion, the Director-General told me that my first task as Director of the Staff Relations Section would be to withdraw the proposal to revise the work rules for train drivers, which had just been negotiated eighteen months ago. He criticized the 'half-baked' proposal, which he claimed was put together by the Staff Relations Section on its own authority and with inadequate explanation. There was no consensus on the proposal within the Personnel Department: he was personally far from convinced by it and did not wish to risk provoking the unions with such a 'trifling matter'. I made a non-committal reply, undertaking to study the matter carefully.

During our hand-over, my predecessor told me that a year-and-a-half had passed since the proposal had been made and that within one month an agreement would be reached with the labour unions. As I was newly assigned to this post, I did not need to get involved as everything could be left to the staff. I didn't know what to think. When I explained to my staff that the Director-General had told me to shelve the proposal, they advised me in a most serious tone that I should do nothing of the sort. Far from being 'half baked', the Staff Relations Section had been working on the plan for ten years, and it had been meticulously prepared. The revisions would lead to tremendous improvements in efficiency and if it were withdrawn now, the opportunity to make such fundamental changes would never present itself again. Furthermore, the proposal had been made after a full explanation to a department meeting where approval had been given. It would be totally irresponsible to withdraw it now. This opinion was shared by all of the staff.

What was 'the revision of train drivers' work rules'? Work rules for train drivers were based on the rules laid out in 'the First Internal Ordinance', issued in 1949. This system was built around the operation of steam locomotives, which were in their heyday at that time. These required depots to be located every 50 to 100 km, where locomotives were changed as fresh coal and water needed to be supplied. As a result, there were a large number of locomotive and inspection depots.

With the modernization of railway infrastructure, and the introduction of EMU, diesel engines and increasingly long distances travelled, locomotive depots were no longer required at such short intervals. There were great opportunities to increase efficiency by consolidating crew depots, by extending the distance of one ride duty, and by reducing the number of inspectors and other crew that manned the depots, many of whom were members of Doro and Kokuro. However, the labour unions strongly resisted such rationalization, and between 1967 and 1968 there was a fierce anti-modernization campaign waged by the unions. Management was forced to make a number of concessions to the unions on manning levels and rostering with strict limitations, such as minimum rest periods, according to train type. Even within the category of electric trains, different conditions were imposed for the various sub-groups, such as commuter train, limited express train, Shinkansen and similarly for the various types of diesel trains. As a result, JNR was forced to cope with a highly ineffi-cient rostering system. The Staff Relations Section had long been preparing to take advantage of the benefits of modernization to consolidate and simplify these rules and conditions.

At the time, contractual working hours for train drivers were set at 40 hours a week. If the contract had been interpreted to mean that 40 hours was the maximum amount drivers were allowed to work, the hours put in by some train drivers would be substantially less than 40 hours: in fact the actual hours locomo-tive crews spent driving would be less than three hours per day. The Labour Law stipulated that legal working time was 48 hours per week and the Staff Relations Sections' interpretation was that overtime in excess of 40 hours a week up to 48 hours could be regarded to be within the legal limit. The basic aim of the proposal was to reach agreement with the unions on working hours within the legal framework and on payment of an overtime allowance when necessary, and in so doing create an efficient work schedule.

By regarding 40 working hours not as the maximum but as the standard, actual working hours could vary, for example, between 39 hours and 41 hours per week, so long as the average was within 40 hours per week for the month and did not exceed 48 hours. Overtime would be paid for hours worked in excess of 40 during any given week, up to a maximum of 48. If a work schedule based on an average 40-hour week could be agreed, efficiency would be greatly improved. Another proposal was to consolidate the twenty-five standards which governed working conditions according to different train types into a single uniform standard.

When the proposal had been explained to me, I felt that it would certainly simplify the confusing drivers' work schedules that had resulted from the past intransigence of Kokuro and Doro. At the same time schedules would become substantially more efficient if they were designed on the assumption that crews would do overtime work. I realized that the proposal could represent a real breakthrough and decided to take it forward.

The Personnel Department used to hold a department meeting once a week, where the Director-General, Section Directors, and Senior Assistants got together for discussion. At one of these meetings, soon after I assumed my post, I spoke out strongly against the withdrawal of the proposal, arguing first that we would never get such an opportunity again, second that it would be revolutionary and greatly enhance efficiency and third that the Personnel Department had worked hard on the proposal and negotiations had already carried on for more than one year. A withdrawal now for no apparent reason would certainly undermine the Personnel Department. No one was able to voice a contrary opinion.

If the unions had been united in their opposition to the plan, it would have been impossible to implement it. The issue of increasing efficiency through revision of drivers' schedules had provoked fierce resistance from Kokuro and Doro between 1967 and 1968. Negotiations had run into numerous difficulties, resulting in the present extremely complex agreement. Under normal circumstances, Kokuro and Doro would doubtless have been expected to oppose strongly any new arrangement. It was reasonable that someone such as the Director-General of the Personnel Department, who had experienced the bitter negotiations of that time, would be cautious about the proposal. However, the decision to stop hiring new employees became a decisive factor in promoting the proposal. Hitherto, at the strong insistence from Doro, candidates for train drivers were selected from newly-recruited workers, and transferred to train-driver depots where local chapters of Doro were located. They would then have several years' experience as train inspectors before being assigned as drivers. This training course for drivers was created with the aim of perpetuating Doro's organization. With new recruitment coming to a halt, so did the supply of new drivers. The only possibilities now were either that positions opened up by retiring drivers would be left vacant as part of the rationalization process or that such posts were filled by other workers, such as retrained station staff or conductors, who themselves had become surplus as a result of rationalization.

The result was a conflict of interest between Kokuro and Doro: if members of Kokuro became drivers, Doro's share of driver membership would go into permanent decline. Therefore, it was Doro's judgement that they would benefit from accepting the proposal. On the other hand, Kokuro were naturally opposed to it as they expected the proportion of train drivers who were Kokuro members to increase. Therefore, however sincerely we negotiated, there was no way of gaining support from both unions. For staff such as myself and my colleagues in the Staff Relations Section, our objective was quite clear: to implement a complete and thorough personnel rationalization.

At the time, 70% of unionized locomotive crews belonged to Doro, and the remaining 30% to Kokuro. We therefore judged that it would be possible to gain the support of 70% of the total crew. We entered into negotiations with each of the labour unions separately. Though some members of the moderate Tetsuro were locomotive crew, the union was in favour of rationalization from the beginning. Previously, negotiations were carried out first with Kokuro, being the biggest and most important union, and Doro and Tetsuro would be kept waiting. Based on the result of the Kokuro discussions, negotiations would take place with the other two unions. On this occasion, we decided to hold negotiations simultaneously. The general thinking within the Staff Relations Section was that agreement could be reached with Doro and Tetsuro, but that negotiations with Kokuro would come to a standstill. We judged that once agreement was reached with Doro and Tetsuro, Kokuro would be isolated. By burning our own bridges, we would force Kokuro to compromise. Ironically, Doro was trapped in a paradoxical situation where it could only maintain its influence and bargaining power through a contraction of its own organization as the company reduced head-count.

We therefore toughened our stance in our negotiations with Doro. I explained that we had no choice other than to transfer and retrain other workers as train drivers unless the rationalization of train drivers was implemented, leading inevitably to an increase in Kokuro's share of driver membership. We advised them that from their point of view, it would be better to accept the proposal to increase efficiency. By the end of that summer, it seemed clear that Doro were beginning to accept this argument. As for the proposal to change the basis of shift-work to one premised on overtime, Doro appeared to have changed its slogan to 'the harder you work, the more you get!'. The message appeared to be getting through.

One day, a senior member of Doro's negotiating team told me that the Director of the Labour Section of the Personnel Department had visited Doro's headquarters and told them that there was no consensus on the proposal to revise the drivers' work rules. It was only the Staff Relations Section that was promoting the idea and it would not get off the ground. He therefore advised not to take the matter seriously.

The agreements related to the First Internal Ordinance laid out the conditions governing the wage and work systems, or more precisely what wages would be paid for what kind of work. Under normal circumstances, the Staff Relations and the Remuneration Sections had to cooperate closely and conduct tightly coordinated negotiations with the unions as the work and the wage systems were regarded as two sides of the same coin. However, as the senior executives of the Personnel Department were clearly against the timetable revision and were shying away from a quarrel with Kokuro, the Remuneration Section would do nothing, arguing, with rather bizarre logic, that unless the work system was sorted out, it did not make sense to discuss a wages structure.

I then asked the Director of the Remuneration Section: 'You said that we should first create the work system, and then you would come up with the wage structure. If that is the case, tell me how many days you need to conclude a wage agreement with the unions after we have come up with the work system.' He replied, 'One day is enough.' I said, 'Really? You can actually do this in one day? In that case, we will get on with our own job and fully expect the same from you.' And with that, we entered the final stages of our negotiations with Doro. We were conducting simultaneous negotiations with Kokuro, but there was predictably no progress.

As the end of March approached, the negotiations with Doro were nearing conclusion. Although the Director of the Remuneration Section had said, 'One day is enough,' I decided to hold the final negotiation with Doro at 8 pm on 29 March, two days before the end of the fiscal year. In order to prevent any disturbance from the outside, we did not disclose any information about the progress of the negotiations, which were carried out in secret between two parties, the Staff Relations Section and Doro. The Remuneration Section from the Director downwards felt sure that compromise was absolutely impossible, and the Director-General and the Director of the Labour Section clearly felt the same way. At 8 pm on the appointed day, I called all of the labour unions one by one and presented our final proposal. We were completely confident of reaching a compromise with Doro and Tetsuro, but we kept that to ourselves.

We stood by all night awaiting their response. Finally, at 9:30 the following morning we received a telephone call from the senior Doro negotiator. He said, 'We broadly accept the final proposal.' As Doro, whose members accounted for 70% of all of the train drivers, had broadly agreed to the proposal, we had passed the point of no return. We had no other choice than to pressure the other labour unions to accept. Tetsuro had quickly given their agreement: only Kokuro remained. We eventually decided to enforce the new rules from fiscal 1984. This meant that only 2 days were left to respond. Realizing the hopelessness of their position, Kokuro eventually capitulated just before the deadline.

The plan of the Director-General and the Directors of the Labour and Remuneration Sections to shelve the revision had collapsed. They were surprised at the unexpected development and could barely hide their irritation. It was not only the Staff Relations Section's path of retreat that was cut off: it applied to the whole of the Personnel Department. The Remuneration Section panicked and staff sat up for two solid nights from the 30th and 31st to put together their proposal. In this way, the revision of the train drivers' work rules was completed by the end of the fiscal year. The success of the work rules revision, which resulted in drastic work schedule rationalization, was in a sense the end of the fourth act of the drama that had started with a fierce struggle against the proposal 'one crew on duty' for electric and diesel loco-motives in 1967 and 1968. The second act was the failure of the productivity movement; the third was the period following the Strike for the Right to Strike when transport volumes dropped sharply; and this, the fourth act, was the conflict of interests that emerged between Kokuro and Doro as a result of the across-the-board halt in the hiring of new workers. The same 'devilish' Doro that would resort to anything in order to preserve and expand its power base in the battle against rationalization, was now taking the lead in promoting rationalization in order to keep itself alive. This ironic situation was very much a matter of 'what goes around, comes around'.

I believe that if the recruitment of new workers had not been suspended, we could not have reached any agreement with the unions on this issue, as both Kokuro and Doro would have strongly opposed any rationalization measures as they had done hitherto. The result of the suspension of new recruitment was to send these two unions in different directions. For the manage-ment, the logic of pursuing the traditional policy, that of appeasing Kokuro, suddenly collapsed. The confrontation between the top executives, who nonetheless still wanted to main-tain the *status quo*, and us, who sought drastic reform, clearly came to the surface.

[2] Mitsuzuka supports 'the Entrance Theory'

In June 1983, JNR RAP had been established as an advisory committee based on Article 8 of the National Government Organization Law. Nobody from JNR was permitted to become staff of the Secretariat. When there was an argument about whether its legal status should be based on either Article 3 or Article 8, JNR sided with the group which insisted on Article 3 (i.e., that it should have statutory powers). The Ministry of Transport took exception to this and obstructed JNR's participation. The leadership of JNR RAP centred mainly around its Chairman, Kamei Masao, and Kato Hiroshi, a professor at Keio University. Hayashi Junji, Director-General of the National Railway Department of the Railway Supervision Bureau of the Ministry of Transport, was dispatched as a Vice-Director of the Secretariat. In August 1983, immediately after its establishment, JNR RAP issued the 'Basic Policy Review' outlining emergency measures to improve the management of JNR. The guidance contained in the review was the same in nature as the Eleven Emergency Measures outlined by SARC. By obliging the management to carry out drastic emergency measures, the objective was to have the reform process already under way even while debate on reform was taking place. Other than the Corporate Planning Department, which served as the contact point with JNR RAP, JNR took a completely uncooperative attitude. JNR's thinking was that JNR RAP had no authority to act. Deep down, their feeling was still that the break-up and privatization of JNR was impossible. It was apparently the opinion of Tanahashi Yasushi, who had succeeded Hayashi as the new Director-General of the National Railway Department, that the Ministry of Finance was strongly opposed to the privatization of JNR on the grounds that enormous amounts of debt would have to be stripped from the company. Hayashi's future as a bureaucrat was as good as finished and he would never be able to return to the Ministry. This was the rumour being spread within JNR by a friend of Tanahashi's.

Within JNR, tension continued to mount through fiscal year 1983 between the top executive group who resisted JNR RAP, and our group who actively cooperated with it. We were concerned that if the momentum for reform were to stop and drastic measures were postponed, partial achievements, such as the correction of discipline, would soon come to nothing. It was vital that this opportunity should be seized. At this very moment, however, we got a message from Mitsuzuka to the effect that he would like to write a book about what his committee had achieved and what the future direction should be. Ide, Matsuda and I, who had once worked for the unofficial Secretariat, got together to help him write the book. It was an excellent opportunity to spread the message about reform as widely as possible.

Since working for the Mitsuzuka Committee, we had got accustomed to living a double life: one by day and the other at night. We prepared drafts which we discussed over a number of sessions with Mitsuzuka and afterwards we would revise and polish them. After the approval of the Mitsuzuka Committee proposal at the LDP party conference and the issue of SARC's report, the mood within JNR became even more conservative and any discussion about drastic reform gradually became taboo. It was essential that the flame of reform that had been kindled within the LDP be kept alive. I suppose that Mitsuzuka felt much the same. Though I only came to know of it later, Hayashi had developed a close relationship with Mitsuzuka around that time and it was probably he who had recommended Mitsuzuka to write a book. It was published, under the title 'The Only Way Forward for JNR', in the summer of 1984.

When we were drafting the last part of the book, in which Mitsuzuka touched upon the issue of break-up and privatization, we couched his thoughts more along the lines of the more conciliatory 'Exit Theory' which had been put forward by the Mitsuzuka Committee. However, Mitsuzuka, in a hand-written memorandum, told us to emphasize two points: firstly, that the basic premise should be that JNR should be broken up and privatized, and secondly, that the government make strenuous efforts to prevent JNR workers who lost their jobs as part of the rationalization process being 'thrown out into the street' including the setting up of a special office to deal with the re-employment of such workers. I recall thinking to myself: 'Can we really go that far?'

The most significant obstacle standing in the way of JNR RAP's ultimate mission, the privatization of JNR, was the fate of the workers who would lose their jobs. As I found out later, Hayashi had developed his own ideas on how to deal with this issue and he apparently hoped that Mitsuzuka would develop it in his book. In the process of their discussions, Mitsuzuka gradually came around to the idea of the 'Entrance Theory' and Hayashi's idea (i.e., JNR RAP's idea) thereby became incorporated into the conclusion of the book. The plan to establish a special organization to deal with the issue of the re-employment of surplus workers was included in JNR RAP's report, and was instrumental in the eventual success of the break-up and privatization of JNR. Perhaps Hayashi was expecting that as Mitsuzuka got away from the 'Exit Theory' and started to lean more towards the 'Entrance Theory', consensus within the LDP would also shift towards the ideas promoted by JNR RAP. At around that time, Ide finally came around to the idea of JNR's break-up and privatization. However, there were significant differences in our thinking until very late on in the process. Ide's idea was that JR East would act as a kind of hub, or parent company, and that fast-track career staff, hired by the headquarters, would move back and forth between JR East and other JR companies as they climbed the corporate ladder.

The book sold more than 90,000 copies, and served greatly to educate people as to the necessity of breaking up and privatizing JNR. There was also a strong reaction against the book, and the tension within JNR immediately intensified. It was obvious that members of the unofficial Secretariat had helped him write the book, and we were put under close scrutiny. The relationship between Hayashi and the reformists within JNR did not really become close until around the summer of 1984. JNR RAP had not yet commenced its investigation in earnest and as Mitsuzuka started to expound his own theories on JNR's privatization, the company stiffened its attitude against JNR RAP, and became even more uncooperative. As the work of JNR RAP progressed, so the need for close coordination with JNR increased. Therefore, the Secretariat started to seek the cooperation of the reformist group within JNR, and the reformists themselves began to look more to Hayashi for spiritual support. Matsuda was transferred to the Corporate Planning Department when I was assigned to Director of the Staff Relations Section in Spring 1983, and he became the formal contact point for JNR RAP, while I served in a similar, but informal, capacity as I had previous contact with Hayashi.

③ President Nisugi's comment on JNR's privatization

In December 1983, Nisugi was installed as the President of JNR as Takagi's successor. Nisugi was an engineer who had been engaged in the construction of Shinkansen, and had for a while been President of Seibu Railway Company, a private railway company operating in the Tokyo area. He subsequently became the President of the Railway Construction Corporation. At the request of Prime Minister Nakasone, he became President of JNR with the mission to 'break up and privatize the company'. Since he was an engineer, he had less experience in labour issues and he was not the sort of person who could be described as strong-willed. These factors inhibited Nisugi's ability to act effectively.

In June 1984, Nisugi delivered a speech at the Japan Press Club in which he outlined his support of JNR's break-up and privatization. The newspapers reported his remarks with big headlines. The President had expressed his thoughts candidly, but the other top executives and the labour unions, coordinating closely with each other, immediately rebelled against him. At the time, I was totally absorbed in the details of the surplus workers' problem, having not even had time to 'come up for air' after the matter of the revision of the train drivers' work rules had been settled. The Director-General of the Personnel Department, who had been promoted to the Board, and all of the other Section Directors excluding me, maintained their 'appease Kokuro' position and were inclined to be confrontational towards JNR RAP.

While the majority of the top executives of JNR were determined to maintain the *status quo*, the relationship between the reformist group and Hayashi was getting ever closer. Hayashi was isolated from the Ministry of Transport. Despite the fact that the Ministry of Transport had pledged its full commitment to the reform programme during the 'Article 3 or Article 8' debate, it did a complete about-turn after the establishment of JNR RAP and the transfer of Hayashi to the Secretariat.

Under such circumstances, the President's announcement of support for the break-up and privatization of JNR was definitely premature. However, once he made the announcement, it was imperative that he stuck to the same line. Expecting a sharp reaction from the anti-reform group, we met the President and advised him not to change his basic message. We also talked with people such as Hayashi, Kamei, chairman of JNR RAP, Kato Hiroshi, professor of Keio University, and others outside of JNR, and asked them to phone Nisugi and encourage him to stay firm. Faced with the unexpectedly fierce counter-attack, however, Nisugi offered an unreserved apology. He even went as far as having an extra issue of the in-house newsletter, '*Tsubame*'[1] brought out, in which he said: 'I was thoughtless. My explanation was inadequate.' He had been unable to resist the pressure to withdraw his comment from the Executive Vice-President and other top executives who reasoned that JNR should pay due attention to the labour unions. Clearly, if he was willing to apologize and withdraw his comment under such pressure, he should not have made such a statement in the first place. Being too affable, he was incautious: the conversations between us were immediately leaked out.

In another incident, some time after the Japan Press Club episode, Nisugi called Ide, Matsuda and me to his official residence to seek our opinion on various matters. One Saturday morning, we visited the President's residence. A forthcoming reshuffle of the top executives was the main topic on the agenda and we were asked how this, and other situations, shall be handled. We had not been at the President's house for more than thirty minutes when I received a call from one of the staff of the Staff Relations Section, who told me, 'the Director-General is rather angry and saying, 'Where did Kasai go?' He seems to know exactly where you are, what you are doing, who you are meeting, but I just replied, 'I will try to find him.' In any case, you'd better come back as quickly as possible.' Deciding to leave for the office immediately, I asked the President, whether he had told anyone of our visit. He replied: 'Oh yes. Before leaving the office, I told the Executive Vice-President that I had called Ide, Matsuda and Kasai to ask for their opinions on various matters.' He might as well have broadcast it on the television, I thought to myself as I returned to the office.

Without showing any sign that he knew where I had been, the Director-General said to me: 'There will be problems if you leave the office without saying anything.' I replied that I had made arrangements so that people could make contact with me at any

---

[1] '*Tsubame*' means 'Swallow'. This name has also been used for some high-speed trains in Japan.

time if necessary and that I should be able to leave the office at any time if it was a business matter. A rather emotional exchange followed, and he advised me sternly to 'carry a pager'. After letting his true feelings slip out on just one occasion and being attacked for it, the President appeared to have become extremely timid.

4 Dealing with the surplus workers problem

The pace of rationalization accelerated after fiscal 1982 with the tail wind of SARC's report and favourable public opinion behind it. In the case of train drivers, for example, once rationalization measures such as the schedule revisions were implemented, the number of surplus workers increased rapidly, in spite of the hiring freeze. As the lay-off of surplus workers was not allowed, and the existence of such workers posed a serious threat to discipline and safety at the work-sites, they had to be transferred to other companies or ordered to take a leave of absence. It was also necessary to have them earn some money, even if it was a small amount. Therefore, through fiscal 1983, we continued negotiations over train drivers' work rules on the one hand, and on the other, we sought practical measures to deal with the problem of surplus workers.

Having studied the case of the private companies and what JNR had done in the past, three solutions were found. The first was the dispatch of surplus workers to other companies. In the private sector, for example, steel companies had surplus workers, but auto-makers were faced with a labour shortage. Companies with surplus workers dispatched them to companies which lacked them. This was called 'dispatch for support'. There were two types of dispatch systems in private companies: one was 'a short-term dispatch' whereby workers would be dispatched to other companies for three months; and the other one was 'a long-term dispatch' whereby workers would be dispatched for two or three years as part of a personnel rotation programme. Personnel costs could obviously be reduced while workers were dispatched and we introduced a similar system by imitating private companies.

The second system was known as 'leave of absence on the condition of retirement'. If, at the beginning of a fiscal year, workers announced their intention to retire at the end of it, they would be paid a whole year's wages and would not have to work at all. They could then take advantage of this period by searching for new jobs or for receiving vocational training. This system was applied at the time of the closure of the Shime coal mine, which JNR took over from the Navy immediately after the end of World War II. We would apply it once more.

The third system was 'leave of absence on condition of rein-statement'. Workers would be allowed to take up to four years' leave of absence (the usual period was two years). During their period of leave, up to 60% of their wages would be paid and they would be allowed to work on a part-time basis for other companies or to study to gain some form of qualification. Some part-time jobs paid higher wages than jobs at JNR. When the leave of absence was over, they would return to their former post. While they were on leave, as no replacement would be hired, there would be some contribution to the problem of surplus workers and cost reduction.

The Director-General had gone so far as to suggest that 'there were no surplus workers'. He argued with the Staff Relations Section, including myself, that the existence and recognition of surplus workers would cause large problems with the unions as it would increase resistance towards rationalization programmes. The growth of surplus workers despite personnel rationalization was a peculiar feature of industrial relations in Japan, where compulsory redundancies were virtually impossible. A company can cope with a small number of surplus workers, but if the number increases to 30,000 or 40,000, they become highly visible. Discipline is undermined and if surplus workers remained at the same work-sites, the effect of rationalization is nullified.

The labour unions already regarded the problem of surplus workers as their top priority and although management pretended it did not exist, both Kokuro and Tetsuro demanded that they take prompt corrective action. Naturally the JSP and the Democratic Socialist Parties asked questions in the Diet about this issue and the mass media reported widely on it. In May 1984 the Director-General of the Personnel Department finally made up his mind to lay out the 'Three Pillars' proposal.

After a tortuous process, at the end of September we reached a compromise with Doro and Tetsuro. Kokuro itself was very divided over this issue and the size of the organization caused inordinate delays in a conclusion being reached. This was to be a growing problem in our dealings with Kokuro.

5 The last fruitless struggle: 'The Basic Plan for Management Reform'

Provoked by Mitsuzuka's espousal of the break-up and privatization of JNR, there was a growing sense of crisis within the management. With this came the belief that JNR RAP, and all those who supported JNR's privatization, were to be opposed. A series of counter-attacks started with the replacement of Ide, Director of the Secretariat Section. In September 1984 he was transferred to the position of Director-General of the West-Tokyo Railway Operating Division on the pretext that he had a poor reputation among the JNR 'old boys' and that he had instigated a power struggle with the Director-General of the Personnel Department.

Soon after Ide was transferred, the senior management set up a study group with the aim of producing their own plan for reconstructing JNR. Its membership was very restricted, and the content of the plan was kept confidential. Their intention was to make a more persuasive alternative plan than that of JNR RAP, and thereby obstruct the JNR privatization plans. President Nisugi's comments at the Press Club supporting privatization served only to deepen the management's sense of crisis. The senior management considered the members of JNR RAP as amateurs and that if JNR stopped providing material and information and halted all cooperation, JNR RAP's activities would come to a standstill. They also believed that JNR could win over public opinion, if they managed to put together a persuasive plan. Needless to say, Matsuda of the Corporate Planning Department and all those who had worked for the unofficial Secretariat of the Mitsuzuka Committee were excluded from this process. The majority of 'front office' staff were supporters of privatization and were also excluded, with the consequence that it was a very small group that started to consider the plan. It consisted of the President, the Executive Vice-President, and all members of the Board, plus, the Director-General of the Corporate Planning Department. However, the newly appointed Director-General of the Finance & Accounting Department was excluded because he was allegedly a supporter of privatization. The Directors of the Secretariat Section, the General Affairs Section, and the Budget Section became the Group's Secretariat. Ide's transfer from the Secretariat Section was designed specifically to exclude him from participating in the Group.

Study meetings involving a limited number of senior managers were held 35 times over five months from August to December 1984 but no attempt was made to consult those working on the 'front line'. The atmosphere of secrecy and lack of trust in which this working group operated was somehow typical of all that was wrong with JNR and illustrated why it was unable to find a solution to its problems. Minutes were prepared for each of the thirty-five meetings, but copies were strictly limited to one for each of the fifteen members. They realized that meaningful opposition to break-up and privatization meant they had to come up with a plan of their own. Without it, they were certainly in no position to do anything about the reformists in the Corporate Planning Department and the Staff Relations Section who cooperated with JNR RAP and who were supportive of the idea of privatization. Once they produced a plan, however, it would become the company's 'authorized' view, and those who opposed it could be punished for insubordination.

The media realized that JNR had been pegged into a corner and understood that JNR could not be left as it was: that would only result in a further waste of taxpayers' money. The press was therefore critical of JNR's management, accusing it of laziness and of sticking to the *status quo*, and urged it to support the reform process. The top executives of JNR were extremely nervous of the press as briefing materials were immediately passed to JNR RAP and comments they made to reporters invariably leaked out, followed by critical comments from the public. Therefore, the information about the study group was kept under strict control.

At the end of December, its work was finished, and the 'Basic Plan for Management Reform' was finalized.

Rather ironically, as Matsuda had made an arrangement beforehand with the company that had been engaged to print and bind the documents, it was delivered to Matsuda and us ahead of members of the Study Group.

The main points of the Basic Plan were summarized as follows:

- The plan was to cover the period from fiscal 1986 to fiscal 1990. During this period JNR would become profitable.
- Personnel would be reduced to 188,000.
- Land amounting to ¥3 trillion ($25 bn) to be sold.
- Subsidiaries (100% JNR-owned) to be set up to assume responsibility for loss-making local lines. Government to provide subsidies.
- Of the ¥26 trillion ($216.7 bn) outstanding debt at end of fiscal 1986, ¥16 trillion ($133.3 bn) to be suspended, with remaining ¥10 trillion ($83.3 bn) to be shouldered by JNR.
- JNR to be privatized and reorganized as a special company to operate nationwide (in fiscal 1986).
- Arbitration of labour disputes to be settled, as currently, by the Public Sector Labour Relations Committee; wage rates to be determined accordingly.
- Capital expenditure to be restrained and concentrated on specific priority projects.
- A review of company structure, including the issue of break-up, to be carried out in fiscal 1990.

The 'Basic Plan' was instantly recognizable as just a rehash of the previous reconstruction plans. The members of the reformist group gathered with Hayashi and analysed the Basic Plan and listed its weaknesses in a memorandum. It could hardly be called 'drastic'. Its overall purpose was to prevent the break-up of JNR and prolong the life of the nationally-operated, single entity JNR. The Plan's target of personnel reductions of 188,000 and its aim of selling ¥3 trillion of idle land were both almost exactly the same as points being discussed by JNR RAP. There was clearly information of JNR RAP's plans being leaked, most probably through a connection with the Director-General of the National Railway Department at the Ministry of Transport. They had fine-tuned their own plans by using the discussions at JNR RAP as a reference point. Their proposal to retain the Public Corporation to arbitrate in labour disputes and set wages, despite being a 'privatized' company clearly reflected their desire for private-sector wage levels but betrayed their lack of confidence that they could create a company that could afford to pay them. It was also obvious that this clause was incorporated in the plan to appease the labour unions. The reference to the review in fiscal 1990 showed the temporary nature of the plan. Asking the government to suspend ¥16 trillion of debt while offering no guarantee that no new debts would be incurred, was like the rest of the plan, pie in the sky. We distributed the memorandum outlining the Plan's shortcomings to the people concerned during the New Year holidays. We had to forestall the efforts the top executives of JNR would undoubtedly make in the New Year to create momentum for their plan. The important tasks were divided up amongst ourselves: Hayashi would make contact with the members of JNR RAP and the press, and we would make contact with the members of SARC and the Mitsuzuka Committee.

At the end of the first business day in 1985, the Basic Plan for Management Reform was made public. The media reaction was immediately hostile, with editorials containing comments such as 'a stop-gap measure,' 'a bogus plan,' 'neither thorough nor adequate,' and 'JNR management's self-deception'. The work we had done in analysing the plan carefully at the end of December, and Hayashi's groundwork with JNR RAP and the press had certainly had its effect.

I heard that on the final working day of 1984 when the Basic Plan was completed, a director-general, smelling slightly of liquor, openly told a group of reformist assistant directors that the Basic Plan was finally completed and that the senior management would risk their own lives to ensure that the plan was realized. All of JNR would unite behind the plan and anyone who opposed it would be fired.

However, the unexpectedly strong public criticism of the Plan soon dampened the enthusiasm of senior management. The fact that we had done our groundwork was obviously a factor, but even if things had gone according to the management's plan, they would never have received the public's support. The Plan, more or less a rehash of previous plans, was never going to revive the fortunes of the company and its management that had sunk so low. It was, however, the only weapon the management had with which to fight JNR RAP.

In order to implement the 'Basic Plan', the management first had to gain the understanding and support of the public. They would also have to produce practical and workable programmes of action. From an organization perspective, such work would normally be the responsibility of the Corporate Planning Department. However, Corporate Planning served as the contact with JNR RAP and was made up of reformists. To get around this problem, the management set up a temporary 'task force' to promote the Plan and tried to take control of its implementation by forcing all existing departments to cooperate it. Under normal circumstances, it would of course have been much easier simply to replace the members of the Corporate Planning Department with those more sympathetic to the management's position, but this would have caught the attention of the press, and besides there was no time. They therefore resorted to bypassing the existing organization with the newly formed task force, which consisted solely of those loyal to the senior executives.

Although the task force was formed as a stop-gap measure and its staff had no experience in long-term planning, they accepted the senior management's purpose at face value and made their presence felt more quickly than expected. One of their first tasks was to have key 'reformists' executives transferred out of head office. Signs of this appeared in March and April 1985, the season for regular personnel changes in Japanese companies. The first to be expelled was Matsuda as he belonged to the Corporate Planning Department, had argued for the break-up and privatization of JNR and maintained a relationship with JNR RAP. He was transferred to a newly created position, as Director of the Corporate Planning Department of the Hokkaido's Regional office. Ide had already been appointed Director-General of the Tokyo-West Railway Operating Division and I reported directly to the most powerful promoter of the 'Basic Plan' and was, therefore, seen as easily controllable.

Formally, transfers such as Ide's and Matsuda's were regarded as a promotion, but in reality of course they were a sort of banishment from headquarters. Although they were expected, it still came as a shock when the moment arrived. Matsuda himself felt that although the environment was becoming more hostile, he would avoid becoming a target because he was the key contact person with JNR RAP. He was therefore unable to conceal his shock when he was transferred to a local office. The next step was for reformists among the rank of Assistant Director to be sent out to local offices as Directors. Rumours were spread that the purpose of these personnel changes was to punish those engaged in 'factional activities'. Notwithstanding this, the former Director-General of the Personnel Department (who had become a member of JNR's board but had retained his responsibility for the Personnel Department) invited each of those affected by these moves to lunch and indicated to them that as they were capable people, they would one day be invited to return to headquarters but warned them, in the meantime, to 'act prudently'. As expected, the management were starting the process of trying to divide and break up the reform group.

It is, of course, quite normal for those who hold power and authority in an organization to hold an overwhelming advantage over those who do not. So convinced were we, however, of the catastrophe that awaited JNR without drastic measures that we ceased caring about our personal reputations. We were utterly convinced that what the people truly wanted was not a stop-gap plan but thorough and comprehensive reform. Around April, as the reformist Assistant Directors were transferred one by one to local offices, we felt a chill wind behind our backs. The transfer of Matsuda to Hokkaido created a much greater sensation than the senior management expected. The confrontation between JNR and JNR RAP was reported in dramatic tones by the mass media.

During all of this, Hayashi's role as psychological mainstay for all of us was critical. We also gave our full support to JNR RAP. We had to devote ourselves fully to our normal work duties and in order not to give people any excuse to accuse us of shirking our responsibilities, we talked with the Secretariat and compiled data after business hours or during holidays. Inside JNR talk was of nothing other than the Basic Plan. Senior executives lobbied politicians on a daily basis, and colluded with the labour unions to isolate JNR RAP. The new task force was in charge of logistics for this campaign. Despite the fact that this team was formed in haste and not staffed by people with the relevant skills and experience, the rule was that all documents and materials should be distributed to the outside through it. That period was certainly the most difficult for us.

In the autumn of 1984, the Asahi newspaper invited Matsuda to a study meeting for its own staff. Matsuda delivered a speech to an audience, which included not only the managing editor but also the department chiefs and desk people, about the current situation of JNR and how reform should be implemented. He told me afterwards that he had explained the conflict within JNR as generational. The older generation, with only a few years left to serve out, were happy with a stop-gap plan. The younger generation, however, saw things in terms of a ten or twenty year view and realized that a drastic plan was required. A reporter from the Asahi newspaper who was a member of the Tokiwa Club, a press club covering JNR issues, told me that he had found Matsuda's lecture to be very clear.

The same reporter told me that the news division was planning a number of articles along the theme of 'JNR Squarely Divided'. I told him that that would be a mistake. It was certainly true that JNR was divided, but that did not mean it would remain so until the end. Many people were against break-up and privatization because it would be a very difficult process; a lot of conflict, problems with the unions, and taking responsibility. These people would continue to oppose the break-up and privatization until JNR RAP's report came out and the Prime Minister gave it his endorsement, when their opinion would change to 'We will do our best'. They would tell the unions: 'We have not changed our opinion, but the nation has ordered us to change. We are part of a national organization and we are obliged to obey the nation's will.' The sense of conflict would soon dissolve. Thus, an article describing JNR as being 'squarely divided', would be superficial and give readers the wrong perception about JNR. The proposed article was never more than a subject of conversation and never materialized.

Despite its shortcomings, the Basic Plan could be regarded as a step forward towards JNR's break-up and privatization. By making the Plan public, the senior management attempted to undermine JNR RAP's report, which was to be released imminently, possibly trying to appeal to the public's fear of drastic change. At the same time, the Plan would provide a good stepping-stone from which to jump on the privatization bandwagon when the report by JNR RAP was released. The senior executives wanted to give the impression that the reformists were nothing more than a group of subversives and that nothing meaningful could be achieved until the mainstream came to the fore.

6 Proposal to reshuffle the top executives

The danger was that once JNR RAP issued its report and it was approved by the Cabinet, the senior management, while supporting the process of break-up and privatization on the surface, would continue secretly to resist the idea. There was obviously considerable doubt as to whether such a group would be capable of leading the company as it prepared for privatization and subsequently into the new, post-privatization world. The arguments about reform would lose their clarity and the arguments that we had been having might be seen as just a confrontation between a group of rash young turks and the cunning top executives. Even worse, propaganda might be put about that it was just about a struggle for power within JNR. Our frustration was deepening gradually. It was around the summer of 1984, when Ide was transferred from the Secretariat Section, that we started to consider the idea of documenting clearly the various issues that lay at the heart of this confrontation while they were still clear in everyone's minds and nail our colours firmly to the mast of the break-up and privatization. My idea was that we should all take responsibility for such a document by signing it and making it public. It was important to demonstrate that it was not a power struggle that we were pursuing, but radical measures to reform JNR.

The likelihood of us winning this battle was remote. If this was the case I strongly felt that we should lay all our cards on the table and demand a reshuffle of the top executives, while leaving something behind to enable people to understand what we had been aiming at. However, the members of the group were generally against this, considering it too radical, a suicidal attack, suggesting the premise that we faced certain death. Many, particularly the younger members, advised caution: to be accused of disrupting the organization was certainly a serious charge. I interpreted this as opportunistic behaviour: they were merely seeking the most advantageous position if things did not develop favourably. It demonstrated, however, that the reformists' group was not united, and the management realized this.

Matsuda was also cautious at first, but after he was transferred to Hokkaido, he changed his mind. Indeed, he urged us to have the document issued as soon as possible. With Matsuda on board, he, Ide and I decided to proceed at full speed. A young executive from the Corporate Planning Department wrote a draft, the basic gist of which was that 'JNR is now in a devastating situation, and needs drastic measures to put it right. The Basic Plan put on the table by the management is just a repetition of the stop-gap policies implemented in the past. The management will support reform on the surface but are against it deep down and the result will be implementation that is only vague and half-hearted. We therefore need to replace the top management.' Twenty-one people signed three copies of the petition. We would hand one over to Prime Minister Nakasone, and one to the chairman of JNR RAP.

Around Golden Week,[2] eighteen members of the reformist group were invited by the chairman of JNR RAP, Kamei, to dine at a guesthouse of the Sumitomo group, one of Japan's former *zaibatsu* groups, at the back of the Hotel Okura. This was arranged by Hayashi to give us the opportunity to convey our thoughts frankly. We planned to use this occasion to hand over the signed petition, but a few members had already been transferred to local

---

[2] A series of national holidays at the end of April and early May.

offices and had not been able to sign in time. It was a lively and cheerful occasion, in sharp contrast to the gloomy atmosphere at each of the JNR departments. We disclosed what each of us really thought, and Kamei earnestly listened to what we had to say with occasional comments by Hayashi. We then handed over the petition to him, indicating that we would deliver it formally when we had received all the signatures. Towards the end of the dinner, Kamei explicitly acknowledged that he fully understood our position.

While the work that such members as Kamei and Kato did was important in the proper functioning of JNR RAP, the role of Hayashi was particularly critical. He put his own career at risk in the same way that we did. There was no option for us as we worked for JNR. But as a bureaucrat with no direct relationship with JNR, he was in a position to sweep the problems under the carpet for someone else to clean up, just as many others had done. But he refused to do so and chose for himself the most difficult of paths. At the time, there would have been very few people within JNR and the Ministry of Transport, or anywhere in Japan for that matter, who thought it possible to break up and privatize JNR. There were very few who understood the seriousness of the situation and the need for drastic measures. This hopeless situation, in fact, served to strengthen the bond between Hayashi and us. He was not only a man of ability but also a man of resolute will. His self-confidence and optimistic personality was backed up by extraordinary judgement that enabled him to grasp the whole situation. What an encouragement he was to all of us!

We understood that some members of our group objected to the idea of the petition. I knew who they were. One of them had implored Ide not to present it. Just as the dinner with Kamei was breaking up, noticing Ide rolling up the signed petition and stuffing it into his pocket, I stopped him and took the petition back. In the car home, he argued that we should not present the petition to politicians and the press. He also thought that it was sufficient for the three of us to risk our careers, and not involve the younger people. 'I don't agree with you', I said to him. 'The young people who have been going along with us are thought to be the most able, not only by their peers but also by themselves.

When you put your career on the line in a situation like ours, it's those with the most talent that are the weakest as they tend to be the most risk averse. But they follow us because they believe that we will win in the long run. By standing firm ourselves, we will help them overcome their hesitation.' I then threw down a challenge to Ide: 'You say you are prepared for the fight but it doesn't sound like it to me. Why don't you just admit you're scared too?'

Shortly after I got home, there was a call from Ide. He said to me, 'Look, I don't disagree with you. But there is someone who is scared. I guess you know who I mean', referring to the young colleague who had pleaded with him. To this, I replied: 'We've got to be fully prepared for this. We have no other choice. If they really have talent, signing a petition won't destroy them: their ability should see them through any difficulties. If they are expendable, we don't need them. Just have them leave our group. But these guys are indispensable to the future of JNR. If we are defeated, we'll all have to assume responsibility for our actions. I'll quit JNR and I suppose that you will do the same. But JNR will need these young guys and they'll give them a chance: within just a few years, they will be back on a fast track for promotion. We don't need to worry about them.' Deep down, I knew there would not be any meaningful work anywhere in JNR if the break-up and privatization failed. Day by day, we were becoming increasingly pessimistic: even if the petition were to be presented, we could not be sure that it would leave the slightest impression. Since the beginning of 1985, the screws were tightened on the reformists and we all felt we were being suffocated. JNR became a virtual prison filled with a dark and stagnant air.

One episode stands out that illustrates the darkness of those times. I was lucky enough to work under a number of talented seniors that taught me a great deal at various JNR departments and offices where I worked. The newly appointed Director-General of the Finance & Accounting Department was one such person. He initially supported my research regarding the potential break-up and privatization of JNR when he was still a Director in the General Affairs Section. After assuming his new post, he was treated with hostility by the Executive Vice-President and the Executive Director in charge of personnel matters who did not share his pro-privatization views. For this reason, he was isolated from the mainstream decision-making process in the same way that we were. One day, we decided to get some relief from the stress of work over dinner and went to a sushi restaurant in Ueno, a downtown area of Tokyo. As we started to talk over a drink, he gradually relaxed. He lamented to me: 'I suspect that our Executive Vice-President has ordered my subordinate in the Budget Section to keep me out of the loop. I'm given no important information at all. I just let him do what he wants and all I can do is watch. Honestly speaking, it makes me feel very uneasy. I go home when the bell goes at five thirty, but while I am at home, I am too absent-minded to hear what my family are saying to me, and I just end up mindlessly watching television. Even though I drink, I cannot get drunk. I cannot sleep at night. In my thirty years at JNR, I have never experienced such a miserable time as the last six months.'

When I heard this, I urged him: 'You should stand up and fight. You don't have to worry about hierarchy as I do. You're their equal and you can't be fired so you should tell them your opinion is different. You want your opinion to be respected by those opposed to JNR's break-up and privatization. You are increasingly isolated, and you cannot sleep at night. It's a vicious circle. If you fight for your cause and are determined to kill them, you should be able to sleep at night. If you end up getting killed, you won't have to worry about sleep any longer. Let's fight them together.' He replied: 'You can talk like that because you are still young. I envy you.' At this, I reflected on the appalling situation in which we found ourselves.

Our thoughts were the same. The ship was sinking. While it was slipping beneath the waves, most people on board were still worried about securing a better position for themselves.

► *Chapter 6*

The floodgates open

☐1 President Nisugi's resignation (June 1985)

President Nisugi suddenly announced his intention to resign on 24 June 1985, while the Diet was in session. The news came as a bolt from the blue. Nisugi was said to have been appointed president with the purpose of promoting the break-up and privatization of JNR. However, the balance of power within JNR had forced him reluctantly to retract the statement he had made in June 1984 soon after he became President in support of privatization and he had probably been pondering his resignation ever since. I believe that with his precisely-timed resignation, together with the impact of the personnel reshuffle that followed, Nisugi played a vital role in the realization of JNR's break-up and privatization. Isolated as I was within headquarters, it was difficult for me to guess what was really happening at the centre and what was in the minds of the top executives. Looking back, however, there were some clear indications.

Towards the end of May, I visited Sejima, a member of the Administrative Reform Advisory Committee (ARAC), to give him a report on the internal situation at JNR, where the anti-JNR RAP group were beginning to make its move, as well as to explain to him why the situation called for a complete reshuffle of top management. After reviewing these issues, Sejima asked me whether JNR's national operations would be greatly disrupted if all of the members of the board left at once. 'Trains would run as if nothing had happened', I replied. 'Sadly, even if all the head-quarters' directors like myself left, train operations would not be affected at all. That sums up the hundred-year history of Japan's railway industry.' To this, Sejima responded: 'I know what you mean. I suppose that if JNR were to be broken up and privatized, the unions would stage an indefinite strike and if that were to happen, the Self Defence Forces might have to be deployed to ensure the transportation network continued to function.' After the meeting finished, as Sejima accompanied me to the lift, he said, 'What you are doing now is correct, Kasai. The nation will not desert you, so be prepared to do what you believe is right.' Although I did not exactly understand what he meant, I assumed that he just wanted to encourage me in the difficult situation and I found his words reassuring.

With the final report of JNR RAP scheduled to be submitted at the end of July, and the ordinary session of the Diet completed at the end of May, we saw a good opportunity to submit the petition requesting changes in senior management and we decided to do this just before the Diet session ended. However, the night before Nisugi announced his resignation, a political journalist at NHK,[1] whom I had known since I was Director of the Shizuoka Railway Operating Division, called me at around 2:00am. 'What's going on?' he asked. I had no idea what he meant, but he was insistent.

He explained: 'I cover Abe Shintaro and Kato Mutsuki[2] and I have been watching Kato's movements quite closely recently. There is definitely something going on as he's been seeing all sorts of people, almost on a nightly basis – Mitsuzuka, Sejima, Kato Hiroshi and Kamei of JNR RAP, Gotoda, Director-General of the Management and Coordination Agency, and Prime Minister Nakasone. Anyway, Kato Mutsuki got home drunk about an hour ago, which is rather rare for him. We expected some comment from him, but all he said was: "We have lost," and then went straight to bed without another word. It's my guess that there's going to be a change of president at JNR soon.' I told him I did not know anything and that I did not think there would be a change of president.

There had actually been a rumour that the president would be

---

[1] Nippon Hoso Kyokai, Japan's state-owned broadcasting company.
[2] Prominent LDP politicians.

replaced and that the board would be reshuffled at the end of the ordinary session of the Diet. However, we estimated the chances of this happening were very slim, perhaps less than one in a hundred. Although Kamei was sympathetic to our position, it was apparently beyond his powers to make the senior management changes. It seemed to us, therefore, the most likely scenario following the issuance of JNR RAP's final report was that JNR management would say something like 'We will do our best to conform to the government's wishes, although we are not sure how much we can accomplish'. This would be followed by more of what we had experienced in the past, stop-gap measures and appeasement of the unions.

The following day, however, Nisugi did unexpectedly express his intention to resign. Speculation about the reasons for resigning centred on his assuming responsibility for his failure to promote the break-up and privatization of JNR, but what was harder to understand was the timing of his resignation, and how the situation would develop afterwards. It certainly meant that there might be a chance for a senior personnel reshuffle and I even dared to hope that our opinions expressed in the petition to Kamei and in the memorandum to Sejima would influence the development of the situation. But I soon put them to one side, fearing that raising false hopes would reduce our fighting spirit and the momentum we had built up.

According to what I heard later from Hayashi, Kamei and Hayashi leaned heavily on Prime Minister Nakasone to replace the senior management. Apparently, Kamei said to the prime minister: 'If the current JNR management is not replaced, I am not confident that the report of JNR RAP will be executed, no matter how brilliant it might be. I am not going to write a report that is not going to be implemented. If you don't take any action, you will get my resignation instead of the report.'

I heard another story from a reporter, a member of the Tokiwa Club (the press club which covers JNR), about the Executive Director in charge of personnel. One day, in late April, the reporter, who was quite sympathetic to the cause of reform and who was therefore treated with some hostility by the JNR senior management, was called by him. He must have been confident that he could win over the reporter. After all, the newly formed task force and the Basic Plan were in place. They had been working on influential members of the LDP, the opposition, the unions and the media since January and trying to give them the impression that only the existing management had the credibility and experience to implement reform. Winning over reporters like this one would further isolate the minority of reform supporters, such as 'the trio' of Ide, Matsuda and myself. No doubt they also thought that the reporter would be useful after JNR RAP's final report came out.

The reporter was invited to a Japanese restaurant in Akasaka and spent two hours listening to the Executive Director. The Executive Director's arrogant and triumphalist air evidently made him feel uneasy. He took notes of the conversation, which he reported to us in detail afterwards. 'Those three fellows are traitors,' he said. 'They'd be the first to jump off a sinking ship and head for the lifeboat. Nobody supports them. They might expect us to be dismissed after the report comes out, but we will not oppose the report once it has been submitted. We will follow government policy, just as members of a government agency should. We won't be expelled, like a gang of war criminals. However, if I were asked whether I really support JNR's break-up and privatization, my answer would definitely be "No". I don't believe it is possible. The process will be very difficult. First, the report will be submitted and the government will announce its intention to support it. There will be the process of drafting a bill, which will be followed by deliberations in the Diet. Then, the actual procedure of breaking up and privatizing JNR will start. It will take more than one year to complete with the labour unions and opposition parties both involved. As the various parties concerned will act in accordance with their interests, the teeth will be taken out of the bill quite easily. Waging a battle is not that simple.' The reporter got the impression that the Executive Director was asking, 'Are you ready to come on board now?'

I relayed this story to Tanaka Kazuaki of the Management and Coordination Agency in the Prime Minister's Office, who had been a good friend since my SARC days. He, in turn, passed the story on to Prime Minister Nakasone, Gotoda, the Director-

General of the Administrative Affairs in the Prime Minister's Office, and a few other influential people. It revealed the real intentions of the top executives of JNR and confirmed Kamei's opinion that the report on its own without replacing the top management would make no sense. It was about the time of my visit to Sejima. But like many people in the thick of the action, I was unable to see the wood for the trees and notice the huge changes that were about to hit us.

Sugiura Takaya, the former Administrative Vice-Minister of Transport, was appointed president of JNR to replace Nisugi. All eyes were then on the members of the board to see what they would do. The president did not have authority to decide on personnel matters relating to the board. Board members were appointed by the Minister of Transport, while the president was appointed by the Prime Minister, but there was no precedent for a board member to be dismissed in the middle of his term of office and it was therefore difficult to replace them unless they consented to resign. Nisugi assembled the entire board and persuaded them to submit letters of resignation after his own resignation was announced. Faced with a request from Nisugi to let Sugiura, who had a very difficult job ahead of him, choose his own team to carry out the task, the board clearly found it impossible to refuse. With the Diet in full session, Nisugi's resignation had a dramatic impact and the behaviour of the JNR board was being closely scrutinized. Although the board members were divided on how to respond to Nisugi's request, all of them eventually submitted letters of resignation and it was up to the new president as to how to respond. Thus, although the resignation of Nisugi seemed sudden, it must have been a carefully calculated action, taken after much deliberation about how and when it should be done.

Sugiura became President of JNR in June 1985. The resignations of Nisugi and seven out of twelve board members were accepted and replacements named. With the exception of Nisugi, all seven board members had been strongly against the break-up and privatization of JNR. They had played a leading role in the creation of the 'Basic Plan for Management Reform', and in suppressing the reformist group. I heard afterwards that Prime Minister Nakasone had asked his advisers, Sejima and Gotoda,

124

who's resignation he should accept. Gotoda's opinion was that it would be sufficient to replace only the anti-reform ring leaders, the Executive Vice-President and the Executive Director in charge of the Personnel Department. Accepting the other resignations would only serve to call the attention of the public to the issue. Sejima, on the other hand, argued that there would be no difference in public reaction whether seven board members were dismissed, or only two. He urged Nakasone to go all the way, sparing no pain. Nakasone eventually sided with Sejima and it is probably the case that replacing only two board members would have greatly slowed down the process of JNR's break-up. Sejima was a former military man, while Gotoda had been a bureaucrat at the National Police Agency. The difference in their approach would be compared to that between Napoleon and Joseph Fouché.

On the Saturday evening of Sugiura's appointment, about ten members of the reform group gathered with Hayashi in Tokyo. Hayashi said: 'What we have to do first and foremost is to choose a secretary for the President.[3] I assume that the new President has no first-hand information about the internal workings of JNR, though he was an Administrative Vice-Minister of the Ministry of Transport. How he performs his job will depend entirely upon the person who sits next to him, explains to him the situation within JNR, mediates between him and other staff, and controls his schedule. After JNR was publicly criticized for the Strike for the Right to Strike and Takagi took over as President, the Personnel Department judged that labour issues were his Achilles heel and selected as secretary someone who could spoon-feed him the Department's labour policies, which Takagi followed to the letter. With this experience behind them, members of the old guard will try to exert their influence in the selection process for Sugiura's secretary. In any case, this will be the very first personnel matter. They may already have made their suggestion, since the Director of the Secretariat Section, who controls personnel assignments at the executive level, is on their side. We should make our opinions known during the course of this weekend. I will try to talk to the

---

[3] In major Japanese corporations, the President's secretary acts as an 'aide de camp', a vital role usually filled by a young executive on the fast track for promotion.

President myself, but a company insider should also speak to him directly.'

It was a gamble to try to put forward suggestions on sensitive personnel matters to a new President who had just come in from the outside. If something went wrong, it could backfire. The person to deliver the message should therefore be someone who was already close to Sugiura, but who would that be? After some discussion, we came to the conclusion that Matsuda would be the best choice. Matsuda had been assigned to work temporarily for the Railway Supervision Bureau of the Ministry of Transport when Sugiura was the Director of the Financial Affairs Section there. Matsuda could make contact with Sugiura in the most natural way and we called him in Hokkaido and told him to come back to Tokyo immediately. We then drew up a list of candidates for posts that needed to be filled as a matter of urgency, such as board members, on a single sheet of paper.

Matsuda arrived in Tokyo on the last Japan Airlines flight. He expressed total agreement with our personnel proposal and the next day, at about noon, Matsuda came over with Sugiura for about an hour to his private residence in Shimotakaido on the outskirts of Tokyo. At 1.30 pm, Matsuda joined me at a coffee shop nearby. He told me that Sugiura, firmly intent on completing the break-up and privatization of JNR, was intending to appoint the best people to do the job, ignoring the Personnel Department's policy hitherto of balancing internal political considerations in personnel appointments. He sought advice in order to help him for this purpose. He seemed quite sincere in this. The personnel appointments that were eventually made were just in line with our recommendations, and that gave the whole reform process a great deal of momentum.

As expected, the Director of the Secretariat Section had already given Sugiura two names from which to choose his secretary. Both were members of the 'Basic Plan' task force and were exactly the recommendations we had expected. As it was Saturday when he received the recommendations, Sugiura had not yet given his reply. After meeting with Matsuda, he accepted our recommendation, Otsuka Mutsutake, who is now the President of JR East. Otsuka remained Sugiura's secretary until 31 March 1987, the day of JNR's break-up and privatization. Communication between Sugiura and us was perfectly smooth, thanks to Otsuka.

Despite Sugiura's enthusiasm, there still remained a significant body of middle management within JNR who were opposed to break-up and privatization, believing it could never really be achieved. They were concerned that further personnel changes would lead to a company squarely divided into two groups. Newly appointed board members withered, concerned about further board reshuffles.

The seven former board members of the old regime remained as advisers for a while, but left JNR soon after their successors were announced. One of the seven, and my boss when I was Senior Assistant to the Director at the Finance & Accounting Department, said to me on his departure: 'You, Ide and Matsuda have done a great job as the spearhead, but you've now got to drive the organization forward as part of the mainstream. I will be watching how far you can go.' I sensed regret in his words. I answered: 'I will do my best. I am not confident, but there is no alternative. Please keep watching us.' Somehow, his words summed up the feeling within the whole of JNR. Everybody was watching us from the sidelines. Ide was appointed Director-General of the President's Office and, with this, the round of priority personnel changes came to an end. In November, Matsuda returned to Tokyo.

[2] JNR RAP submits its report (July 1985)

JNR RAP submitted its report to Prime Minister Nakasone at the end of July 1985. The report largely reflected our discussions since SARC and contained no great surprises. The outline of the report was as follows:

• The division of JNR

Honshu, the main island, would be divided into three regions with one company to be established in each: 1) JR East would combine the Tohoku and Joetsu Shinkansen lines with conventional lines in the Tokyo metropolitan area and the north and eastern part of Honshu; 2) JR Central would combine the

Tokaido Shinkansen with conventional lines in the central part of Honshu; and 3) JR West would combine the Sanyo Shinkansen with conventional lines in the Kinki and Chugoku areas. Three more companies would be established on the islands of Hokkaido, Shikoku, and Kyushu, making six passenger train companies in total. All the facilities and infrastructure of the conventional lines would belong to these new companies, while ground facilities of the four Shinkansen lines would be transferred to the Shinkansen Holding Corporation (SHC). Another independent company, JR Freight, would be established to carry out freight operations nationally. It would be allowed to own and operate freight trains and stations and would lease track from the passenger train companies.

The seven companies would be set up so as to enable them initially to post recurring profits amounting to approximately 1% of the total revenues.

• **The Profit Adjustment Scheme**

The Tohoku, Joetsu and Sanyo Shinkansen would be cross-subsidized with profits made by the Tokaido Shinkansen, using the SHC as the framework. The SHC would own the ground facilities of the four Shinkansen lines, and would shoulder debt from JNR corresponding to the market values of these facilities. The debt would be paid back over a period of thirty years using the method of equal annuity payment with interest. The SHC would collect rental charges from the three Honshu companies to pay back the debt. Profit adjustment would be made by setting lease rates for each of the Shinkansen lines based on their respective earning power. After repayment of the debt in thirty years, the SHC would be dissolved and ground facilities of the Shinkansen lines would be transferred to each of the operating companies. During that period, capital expenditure for maintenance and renewal of leased facilities would be defrayed by the passenger companies, which would operate the Shinkansen lines.

'Management stabilization funds' would be provided to each of the three island companies. Operations of existing lines would be maintained, with revenue shortfalls compensated by income from the management of these funds. The freight company would achieve and maintain profitability by negotiating more competitive lease charges with the passenger companies for the use of track.

- **Disposal of Accumulated Debt**

The total debt of JNR stood at ¥25.4 trillion ($211.7 bn) at the end of fiscal 1986. There was a further ¥11.9 trillion ($97.5 bn) of JNR-related debt, which consisted of ¥5.2 trillion ($43.3 bn) debt of the Japan Railway Construction Public Corporation (arising from the construction of the Joetsu Shinkansen, the Seikan Tunnel connecting Honshu and Hokkaido, the bridges between Honshu and Shikoku Island, and so on), ¥4.9 trillion ($41.7 bn) to compensate for under-funded pension liabilities, and ¥1.8 trillion ($15 bn) for necessary expenses related to the break-up and privatization of JNR, such as the management stabilization funds for the three island companies.

Total JNR debt was, therefore, ¥37.3 trillion ($309.2 bn), and this would be disposed of in the following way. The three Honshu companies would take over ¥5.7 trillion ($35.8 bn), which corresponded to the total amount of assets to be transferred to the three companies from JNR. The SHC would take over ¥8.5 trillion ($70.8 bn), equivalent to the value of the Shinkansen assets they were taking over. The JNR Settlement Corporation, to be established when JNR was broken up and privatized, would take over the remaining debt along with corresponding assets of idle land (¥5.8 trillion – $48.3 bn) and shares of JR (worth ¥0.6 trillion – $5 bn). Any remaining debt (¥16.7 trillion) would be borne by the state.

- **Measures for the Employment of Surplus Workers**

The optimal number of employees for JR as a whole was estimated at 183,000. Employees would be reduced to 276,000 as of April 1987 with the continuation of the recruiting freeze. Measures for the 93,000 surplus employees would be as follows:

20,000 would be encouraged to take early retirement with an additional retirement allowance; 32,000 surplus workers to be retained by the JR companies. The remaining 41,000 would have to find jobs with the help of special employment assistance,

30,000 of whom would be recruited by government or public organizations.

The 'Headquarters to Deal with Surplus JNR Workers' would be established as soon as possible, headed by the Prime Minister. The government would make efforts to ensure that not a single worker would go unemployed.

- **Establish the JNR Settlement Corporation** to implement the winding up of JNR including the settlement of such issues as the disposal of past debt and employment measures for surplus employees.

I had become aware of the outline of the JNR RAP report before its submission by participating in an informal study group set up to support Kato Hiroshi, Chairman of the JNR RAP Sub-committee. The group consisted of Tanaka Kazuaki, Sando Yoichi, Yayama Taro, all of whom had been members of the fourth panel of SARC, Matsuda and myself. When a meeting of JNR RAP was held, we would gather afterwards in the late afternoon at Kato's seminar room located at the east gate of Keio University. Kato would go through with us the most recent JNR RAP documents and the points that had come up in the meeting that had just ended. Kato would then ask for our opinions. I expect this process helped Kato summarize JNR RAP's progress in his own mind. The plan to divide JNR into six passenger companies was basically the same as the one conceived by another informal study group in which I had participated soon after becoming liaison officer for SARC in 1981. Our conclusion that freight and passenger transport should be combined within the same regional company was ignored. In coming to its conclusions, JNR RAP had to take into account not just market principles and economic rationality but the views of local people, the media and so on. The study group therefore felt that this sort of compromise was inevitable, although it was united in its opposition to the system of 'profit adjustment' through the SHC.

3 The new regime (August 1985)

Immediately on receiving the report, the Nakasone Cabinet decided in a cabinet meeting to proceed with the full-scale reform of JNR and to establish the necessary infrastructure to support it. Early in August 1985, the 'Headquarters to Deal with Surplus JNR Workers' was set up, headed by Nakasone himself and with the vice-ministers of each of the ministries as members, to tackle the biggest stumbling block to reform. A Secretariat was formed with staff transferred from the Ministry of Transport and other related ministries. The Ministry of Transport formed a special task force to carry out the numerous tasks relating to the JNR reform, including the drafting of the bill, and this resulted in large-scale personnel changes within the Ministry.

JNR also created two separate taks forces to deal with the process, the 'Reorganization & Implementation Centre' and the 'Surplus Workers Counter-measures Centre'. Both were headed by President Sugiura. The Corporate Planning Department was restructured to enable it to function as the Secretariat for the Reorganization & Implementation Centre. The Staff Relations Section of the Personnel Department was assigned to be the Secretariat to the Surplus Workers Counter-measures Centre.

However, the setting up of these bodies by both the government and JNR did not bring about a feeling of tension and change, nor a sense that the company was actually going to be broken up and privatized within eighteen months. Under board level, most of the senior JNR positions were occupied by anti-reformists. While no objections were voiced publicly, among the employees there was no sense of urgency about getting on with the reform programme.

Under normal circumstances, we would have tried to implement change through transfers of the right people to key positions at the working level, but we had no time for that. We decided on a more top-down approach to create the 'Joint Liaison Conference' of the two Centres as the sole decision-making body. At that stage, the Reorganization & Implementation Centre and the Surplus Workers Counter-measures Centre were the only two organizations that were taking the whole process of reform seriously. My plan, therefore, was that Sugiura, who headed the two centres, would meet members of the Secretariats from time to time to make decisions on all important matters related to the break-up and privatization in an efficient and flexible way. There would be no need for personnel changes, nor even the need to try to change the attitudes of the JNR headquarters staff, as most were still bystanders. Membership of the Joint Liaison Conference would be limited to the President, the Director-General of the President's Secretariat, the President's secretary, and the staff of the two Centres. Holding the meetings in the president's office effectively limited the number of participants. I proposed this to President Sugiura at the end of August and he immediately agreed. When the Joint Liaison Conference started to function, both the speed of decision making and preservation of confidentiality improved dramatically.

Within JNR, decisions usually involved many layers of meetings. A decision would normally have to be ratified by meetings of (in order): Deputy Directors, Directors of General Affairs, Director Generals, board members, senior board members and finally ratified by a formal meeting of the Board. Before this decision making process could start, preparatory meetings by departments and sections concerned with the decision had to take place, which often took several months. It was common knowledge in JNR that it would normally take at least one month to make a decision on any matter. Meetings were organized horizontally across hierarchy to include staff from all sections and departments that had the slightest connection to the subject under discussion in order to spread responsibility. By contrast, the system we proposed limited participation in the Joint Liaison Conference to the President's Secretariat, the Corporate Planning Department and the Personnel Department, using a vertical organization that directly linked top executives to section directors' assistants. This resulted in a minimal number of staff with a direct interest in the subject at hand involved jointly in decision-making.

President Sugiura attached a high value to the Joint Liaison Conference. It met as many times a week as necessary, and decisions about important issues were made with extraordinary speed. Those who resisted reform were rapidly left behind and quickly lost influence. On the other hand, the majority of JNR Headquarters management, who had hitherto adopted a wait-and-see attitude, began to sense that reform was inevitable, and reluctantly started to take action.

4 The first barrier – the launch of Employment Measures (August 1985)

The first group to dig in and confront the practical issues was the Personnel Department. They launched a series of measures to deal with the problem of surplus workers and to promote headcount rationalization. They continued working until the final moments before the bill to establish JR was enacted in the Diet, sorting out which staff should be transferred to which JR company, and who should be transferred to the JNR Settlement Corporation. I was deeply impressed by the zeal and commitment with which everyone in the Department tackled their difficult tasks.

The first, and perhaps most difficult, hurdle to overcome was the reemployment of workers. The success of the reform of JNR would depend on whether the government's public pledge not to put anyone out on the street was believed to be sincere. The Secretariat to the 'Headquarters to Deal with Surplus JNR Workers' was set up in August, staffed mainly by personnel from the Ministry of Transport, some other ministries and JNR. The 'Headquarters' would play a key role in determining whether the break-up and privatization of JNR would succeed. The ministers, however, were prone to adopt a wait-and-see attitude. Despite the Prime Minister's enthusiasm, they saw many difficulties. 'Let's not get ahead of ourselves', was very much the thinking at that stage. Despite my anxiety that the whole process would come to a stand-still, it was Nakasone's strong determination and Gotoda's hands-on decisiveness that got things moving. Judging that the head of the Secretariat was weak, the prime minister took the daring step of replacing him after only a month on the job. At the same time, Gotoda managed to persuade the National Police Agency to absorb all of the roughly 3,000 JNR police officers into the regular police force. Since Gotoda was a former Commissioner of the National Police Agency, he was able to exercise his influence over his former colleagues. This decision produced big newspaper headlines, and had the effect of making the ministries recognize the determination of the prime minister.

At the same time, the Surplus Workers Counter-measures Centre, i.e., JNR's Staff Relations Section, started to negotiate with each of the ministries. At first we were not taken seriously and we were given a number of reasons for the lack of cooperation: that the ministries were going through their own process of reform and restructuring and could therefore not afford to take on our workers; that JNR's union members were notorious activists and taking them on would undermine the efforts they had been making to build good relations with their own unions; that JNR would keep their best workers and just give them the bad ones. On the latter point, we argued, as it turned out, correctly, that the average workers would never voluntarily leave. The ones who raised their hands for transfer would be precisely those we would have wanted to retain.

After the National Police Agency, the Meteorological Agency, decided to hire JNR employees for work in lighthouses, which faced a staff shortage. Although lighthouse work was very tough, some workers volunteered. The National Tax Agency also made an early decision to hire 600 JNR workers. The JNR workers, who were sent to the National Tax College to learn the basics of taxation, passed the final examination with better marks than the average achieved by the proper staff of the National Tax Agency. It was good to see our claims about the high quality of JNR workers being vindicated.

The atmosphere within the ministries gradually changed and some ministries concluded: 'If we have to hire JNR workers, we might as well get in first and hire the best ones.' Thanks to Nakasone's and Gotoda's determination, the offer to find jobs for the surplus workers accelerated, and by the time of the JNR break-up and privatization, 46,000 workers had been re-employed, of whom 22,000 were employed in the public sector, 25,000 if the JNR Settlement Corporation is included. About 12,000 were employed in the private sector and 12,000 found jobs at JNR-related companies. This success provided the critical impetus to the whole reform programme: the process had passed the point of no return.

5 The problem of relocating JNR employees (August 1985)

Another key issue with which we had been grappling was the relocation of JNR employees to the six passenger companies and one freight company that would be formed after privatization. From both a legal and practical viewpoint, simultaneously balancing the objectives of allocating the employees among the seven companies, dealing fairly with workers who could not be re-employed, keeping the unions on an even keel, while at the same time making progress towards break-up and privatization, was extremely challenging.

The Staff Relations Section set to work immediately after the submission of the report of JNR RAP in July. The number of employees deemed appropriate for JNR had fallen from 420,000 in 1981 to 295,000 in 1985 as public criticism of JNR's inefficiency continued. The actual number of employees had been reduced from 420,000 to 320,000, mainly through natural attrition caused by the freeze on new hiring, which meant that JNR still had 25,000 surplus workers. However, further reductions were now called for as the total number of employees for all the JR companies was targeted at 215,000 (including 32,000 surplus workers), a cut of at least 100,000 in one year.

The first difficult problem that emerged in the process of drafting the law was to determine a legally correct way of relocating employees among the JR companies. We were greatly assisted in this process by a young judge who was dispatched from the Secretariat of the Supreme Court. He was able to get straight to the heart of any problem and gave unfailingly clear-cut legal answers to our questions. He would sometimes respond: 'It is legally possible, but it is up to the judgement of the management,' and at others he would say: 'Absolutely impossible'. A 'no' from him really meant 'no'. His professional advice was indispensable in helping us pick our way through the complex legal issues that confronted us.

He was very proactive and would offer extremely useful advice and ideas about the relocation of employees without being asked. It is not legally possible to order an employee to move to another company against his or her will. This has to be a voluntary action on the employee's part. He suggested that JNR should be succeeded by the JNR Settlement Corporation as a legal entity and all JNR employees would automatically become employees of the JNR Settlement Corporation. They would then leave JNR and apply for a job at the newly-established regional JR companies, which would be totally new and separate entities, and go through the normal screening process when applying for a job. The workers would be choosing which company they worked for of their own volition. When he came up with this idea, it was as if the scales fell away from my eyes.

The Ministry of Transport, however, was reluctant to accept a theoretical framework in which the JNR Settlement Corporation was the legal entity directly succeeding JNR. They argued that the underlying logic of this framework where the JR companies would not be successors to JNR was purely fictitious and would provoke the opposition parties. They also fretted that Kokuro and Doro might instruct members not to submit letters of resignation and not to apply for jobs at the JR companies. We pointed out that union members had families to support and that they would only lose members by issuing such orders. Besides, if the JNR workers did not apply for jobs, we could always recruit employees from the private sector. Discussions continued. The Ministry was completely unable to come up with any workable alternatives and they eventually agreed to our proposal of relocating JNR employees to the JR companies as new workers. The Cabinet Legislation Bureau supported this method, and the Ministry of Labour came to the conclusion that there was no alternative solution. Provisions relating to the relocation of JNR workers were contained in Article 23 of the Reform Act and although this became the most contentious issue between JNR and the labour unions, the court eventually ruled that the provisions were entirely legal.

6 An unprecedented rationalization plan: reducing the work-force by 100,000 in one year (October 1985)

As JNR workers were supposed to be relocated to their new jobs between January and March 1987, employment measures had to be implemented before that date. Calculating backwards, we realized that we needed to start asking workers to volunteer for retirement by June 1986 at the latest. Before calling for voluntary retirement, a number of steps were necessary: the passage of a bill to authorize supplementary retirement benefits; tangible progress in rationalization; and even if the number of applicants to the new JR companies was small, the establishment of a work-place for them. If you allowed one year for negotiations with the unions, the rationalization plan had to be worked out and presented to them by October 1985 at the latest.

Three major bills were required to enable the following: (1) additional payments for early retirement plans and a system of voluntary retirement; (2) the establishment of the JNR Settlement Corporation; and (3) the establishment of the six regional passenger companies and one freight company. The bills needed to be drafted by December 1985 and introduced to the Diet for deliberation and approval during the 1986 ordinary session. During that period, Kokuro could influence the JSP and JCP to try and prevent passage of the bill. We would need to create an irreversible momentum for reform to prevent major compromises having to be made during the Diet Session, which was likely to be the most unstable period for us. I spent most of the summer of 1985 considering these problems.

It was critical that I had a reliable partner in the Personnel Department to deal with these issues in the short time that was available. I asked President Sugiura to appoint Nanya Shojiro (currently the President of JR West) as Director of the Labour Section. After the senior management was replaced in June 1985, the situation in the Personnel Department had not changed. The majority of the staff took a wait-and-see attitude and there were even one or two that tried aggressively to interfere with the reform effort. When the government established its 'Headquarters to

Deal with Surplus JNR Workers', the Staff Relations Section immediately strengthened our own Surplus Workers Counter-measures Centre with extra staff. With the arrival of the new Director of the Labour Section in early September, the right team was finally established. There was a flood of extraordinary and unprecedented measures and an impressive impetus was built up within the team, which worked together for eighteen months to tackle these difficult views. As Director of the Labour Section, Nanya Shojiro contributed significantly.

By the end of October, barely a month after Nanya became the director of the Labour Section, we needed to make a proposal for the reduction of the work-force by 100,000 to the 215,000 who would be relocated to the new JR companies in line with JNR RAP's recommendation. Never before had such a large-scale rationalization taken place in such a short time. Moreover, it was essential that all aspects were rolled up to create one, comprehensive proposal. Of the three major projects with which the Personnel Department was now charged, personnel rationalization, voluntary retirement and relocation of employees, the most pressing was rationalization. Of course, I wanted to do my best, but I was not completely confident I would achieve the difficult goals we had set ourselves. To grit our teeth and get on with it was the only way.

Conventionally, rationalization measures would be proposed by the management based on the agreement for prior consultations with the labour unions. While management would insist publicly that the introduction of such measures was their prerogative, in reality unilateral implementation was believed to damage the mutual bond of trust between management and the unions, with the result that nothing was done in practice without the unions' consent. The negotiating process would start with the unions demanding that the management explain its measures, submitting what were called 'requests for explanations' to JNR. After submitting several of these requests, the unions would enter actual negotiations with the objective of having the management compromise by softening the measures. There was a margin built in to the proposed measures that could be used as leverage in negotiations, which was referred to as the 'compromise rate' or the 'back rate'. The first negotiation was held to determine whether the unions would even listen to management explanations based on the agreement for prior consultations. If they refused, actual negotiations would, of course, not even get off the ground. Much time was wasted in endless 'prior consultations' because the labour unions made numerous 'requests for explanations', or because they stopped or shelved a consultation. For example, it took more than two years for management and unions to reach a compromise over the proposal to revise the train drivers' work rules.

While we were agonizing over the rationalization proposals and how to implement them, it was again the young judge in the legal section that came to our rescue. He commented that from a common-sense perspective, JNR's way of doing things was peculiar. He pointed out that the Public Sector Labour Relations Law separates 'items for management' from 'items for negotiation' and stipulated that 'the matters for management cannot be the objects of collective bargaining'. The law further stipulated: 'Matters relating to the rights of management are themselves "items for management".' The most important task for labour-management relations within JNR was sorting out what were items for management and what were items for negotiation. Conceptually, items for management should be treated as matters for consultation, while items for negotiation should be regarded as matters for collective bargaining. Once a particular issue had been regarded as a matter for negotiation, the unions' attitude would be: 'These measures cannot be implemented without our consent.'

Distinguishing items for management from items for negotiation was so difficult that court rulings tended to define the range of items for negotiation relatively broadly. While the Trade Union Law stipulated that it was an unfair labour practice to refuse collective bargaining without proper reason, there was nothing in the law that forbade measures to be implemented without the consent of the unions. The judge advised that while we should try to persuade the unions through negotiations, if they did not accept our arguments, we should implement the proposals calmly, with management taking full responsibility. 'JNR has been doing everything upside down', he said. 'You form a line of defence around the concept of 'issues for management', but once the labour unions have broken it, they can do more or less what they want to. The real world is, however, different. Almost any item is open for discussion with the unions, but if negotiations fail, management does what needs to be done on its own responsibility. Negotiations should be conducted sincerely, but there is no obligation to negotiate until agreement is reached. If you have a lot of time, you can negotiate at length, but if you negotiate at length, you can forget about reducing the workforce by 100,000 in one year.' I couldn't have agreed more.

As we embarked on our efforts to implement the rationalization programme, we decided to adjust our negotiating strategy accordingly. We showed our proposal to Kokuro first. The Kokuro leaders sat at the negotiation table and the new Director-General of the Personnel Department who is now Governor of Shimane Prefecture, made the usual, rather formal, greeting: 'We will do our best to explain the personnel rationalization sincerely in order to get your consent and cooperation.' I then made a short greeting: 'As the Director-General has explained, we would like to negotiate with you sincerely and implement the personnel rationalization when the time comes.'

The Kokuro representatives asked us to confirm our position: 'There seems to be a difference in nuance between the Director-General's words and those of the Director. The Director-General said that you will do your best to explain the personnel rationalization in order to get our consent and cooperation. Our understanding of his statement is that you will not implement any personnel rationalization without our consent as has been usual practice so far. On the other hand, the Director said that you would explain and negotiate the rationalization sincerely and implement it when the time comes. Our understanding of that statement is that you intend to implement rationalization, even without our consent. Which of our understandings is correct?' I replied: 'Both the Director-General and I are saying the same thing. The words we use may be different, but our intention is the same. Am I right, Director-General?' The Director-General answered, 'Yes, that's right.' The leaders of Kokuro seemed to be offended and said to me rather curtly: 'So when did you become such a big-shot?'

Then we started to explain. Frankly, a package that aimed to reduce a work-force by 100,000 was quite unprecedented for a rationalization programme. This plan contained every conceivable measure. After hearing our explanation, Kokuro confirmed: 'We have now heard the outline. Next, we would like an explanation of each of the measures contained in the plan. We assume that each measure will be put on the table for negotiation individually.' I replied: 'I don't think so. We have finished our explanation for today. If there is anything you do not understand properly, please ask us for further explanation.' They responded: 'There can never have been anything this unreasonable in the entire history of JNR. It is completely unacceptable. We will assume that we have not heard any explanation today, so we will leave your proposal on the table.'

The conversation then went as follows: 'You did in fact hear our explanation so you cannot pretend that you did not hear it.' 'No, we will not accept to take the proposal documents with us.' 'If you don't accept it, we will send it to you by registered mail. You have already heard our explanation, so it is up to you as to whether or not you read the mail when it is delivered.' Finally, they asked: 'If we remain silent and ask no more questions, what will you do?' In the previous JNR mode of negotiation, if the labour unions did not submit a 'request for explanation', prior consultation, which was a precondition for the start of negotiations, would not take place. The management would then bow to the unions, earnestly requesting their cooperation. But this time, we replied: 'If there are no questions and you do not exercise your right to collective bargaining, we will naturally assume that you have agreed to the proposal, and we will implement the measures as planned.' This made them extremely angry: 'We have never experienced an approach like this. Since there appears to be no scope for discussion, we will leave.' And they left. These were the negotiations with Kokuro.

The other unions listened to our explanation and left the room saying nothing. Negotiations progressed smoothly, and the rationalization measures were implemented on schedule, probably something unprecedented in the history of JNR. Indeed, we exceeded JNR RAP's goal of 215,000 workers: the final number was 195,300.

7 Questionnaires to ask workers their company of choice (December 1985)

As the drafting of the bills progressed during the autumn of 1985, one government agency after another decided to proceed with the hiring of surplus JNR workers. The government also announced the number of JNR workers it wished to hire and then started the actual process of recruitment.

Needless to say, even if the workers had secured employment, many did not begin their new jobs immediately. Some were actually hired during fiscal 1985, others in the following year. Some were transferred temporarily to the JNR Settlement Corporation until they received formal notification of employment. Others, who were awaiting notification, went to the agencies at which they expected to work in future and received on-the-job training. In this case, wages were paid by the JNR Settlement Corporation.

If a vacancy at a government agency was filled by a former JNR employee, it had the effect of reducing the number of graduates the agency could hire. To get around this, the Ministry of Finance, who had the authority to appropriate money for wages, and the Management and Coordination Agency, who had the authority over each agency's headcount, created an extra incentive to promote the hiring of former JNR workers, whereby for every JNR worker an agency hired, it would be allowed to increase its authorized head-count by 0.5 person. Agencies would not lose anything. If they hired two good JNR workers, they could expect to have the two assigned jobs performed well, and by hiring two JNR workers, the agency could increase its fixed head-count by one and hire a new graduate. With this, the government changed its attitude and started aggressively hiring JNR workers. The smooth progress in the hiring of JNR workers by the government and government agencies gave momentum on a broad front to the process of JNR's break-up and privatization and the determination they showed no doubt gave an air of irreversibility to the entire reform programme.

On 28 December 1985, the second Nakasone Cabinet was inaugurated and Mitsuzuka, who had become an expert on JNR affairs, was appointed Minister of Transport. The bill was already in the final stages of drafting, and with the impetus created by Mitsuzuka's appointment, it was completed rapidly, with the bill scheduled to be introduced to the Diet one month hence. With the New Year approaching, I came up with the idea of giving JNR employees an opportunity to consider their future carefully while relaxing at home during the year-end and New Year holiday. After discussing this, we decided to send a questionnaire to all employees, asking which company they would like to work for if the break-up and privatization of JNR were realized. The purpose of the questionnaire was to get direct feedback from the employees rather than allow unions to filter their views. It was inevitable that Kokuro would resist with all its strength and, with the cooperation of the opposition parties, try to block the passage of the bills in the Diet. This direct approach of trying to get employees to reveal their intentions was, in my view, the only way to reduce the resistance of Kokuro, with whom it would have been impossible to obtain agreement through negotiations, however hard we tried. We distributed the questionnaires to each worker on Christmas Day and they were asked to fill them in and return them after the New Year's holiday.

We received strong criticism from Kokuro; sending questionnaires without the bill having even been introduced showed a 'reckless disregard of the Diet'. Kokuro ordered its members not to answer the questionnaire under any circumstances. The other unions took a different attitude for the time being and let their members write what they thought. The fact that many of the employees had already applied for jobs in government agencies, and some had been informed of their acceptance, showed that most of the workers did not expect JNR to survive for very long. Under such circumstances, an attempt to stop the break-up and privatization process through a boycott of the questionnaire was quite ineffective. This was demonstrated by the fact that many Kokuro members answered the questionnaire.

Before the replacement of the JNR senior management the previous summer, measures like the questionnaire would have been considered oppressive and provocative, and therefore unacceptable. It was the creation of the Joint Liaison Conference, which took place in the President's room, that enabled such decisions to be taken quickly, and then implemented.

[8] The joint declaration of labour unions and management (January 1986)

The Directors and Senior Assistants to Directors of each section of the Personnel Department were in the habit of gathering daily. This meeting took place from 8.30am to 9am and participants would exchange information concerning the previous day's events, confirm policies with each other, and then return to their offices. With so many difficult issues to handle within a short time, probably unimaginable to our predecessors, we had to be as one, sharing information promptly and making decisions based on that information, and the briefings were invaluable for that purpose. At one meeting towards the very end of the year, as our next move following the questionnaire, we decided to propose to the labour unions that we issue a joint declaration at the beginning of the New Year. We had to think of ways of creating constant communication with employees to monitor their intentions, and we considered this a good method. I instructed the staff to come up with a draft during the New Year's holiday.

A first draft of the declaration was composed early in the New Year, based on the ideas presented by the staff. This policy was approved at the Joint Liaison Conference held on 10 January. The declaration contained such phrases as 'Let's work together towards rationalization,' 'Refrain from disrupting train operations until business performance has been improved,' and 'Let's improve passenger services in order to regain trust and esteem.'

On 13 January, we proposed the joint declaration to each of the labour unions. I had proposed to the president that, as a joint declaration of this kind was unusual, we should invite the union leaders to the President's office and have the President address them directly. It was the first time the leaders of the labour unions had ever been allowed to enter the President's room, which was equipped with a working desk, a set of comfortable chairs, and an oval conference table.

Since the unions were invited in order of size, Kokuro came first. I assumed that the Kokuro representatives had read and understood the contents of the joint declaration draft and knew what the meeting was about. The Kokuro chairman and the other

144

leaders stood before the conference table and looked at the document laid out before them. 'What is this?' they asked in a rough manner. President Sugiura responded: 'The paper on the table states: 'Until an improvement in JNR's performance has been achieved, we have to gain the public's trust and strengthen our management base. In order to achieve these goals, we must carry out the rationalization measures and refrain from industrial action. We must also improve passenger services.' Our proposal is that the labour unions and management should agree on these goals and make public that agreement in the form of a joint declaration.' At this, the Kokuro representatives said: 'We cannot accept such a ridiculous suggestion' and left the room without even picking up the document. Then it was Tetsuro's turn. Its leaders said: 'It's about time! We have been urging you to do this sort of thing for a long time. We agree to it.' Doro's response was: 'As we are now in an emergency situation, we agree that unions and management should cooperate.'

The responses of the labour unions were thus divided. This was quite predictable. The unions that had agreed to the proposal and the president of JNR held a joint press conference; together they announced the joint declaration. Kokuro chose isolation again. As the largest union, they may have been expecting the opposition parties to kill the bills in the Diet and at that stage appeared still to be placing their bets on that outcome.

Soon thereafter, the decision was taken to introduce the relevant bills related to break-up and privatization in the Diet in March. The major items were a bill to enable retirement plan payments to be increased and separate bills relating to the establishment of the JR Companies and the JNR Settlement Corporation. An official of the Ministry of Transport remarked in a very self-satisfied manner: 'It took us only six months to do what would normally take a hundred years!'

In February 1986 I was appointed Deputy Director-General of the Personnel Department. Since the most recent personnel reshuffle, in July 1985, I had in fact managed the Personnel Department in cooperation with Nanya, the Director of the Labour Section, but with the creation of this new post, my position of responsibility was clarified. With the joint declaration announced, the issue of worker discipline seemed to have turned a corner and we could also see light at the end of the tunnel in the rationalization process. However, with the Diet deliberations coming up, we had to prepare for the most difficult and critical phase of reform.

Despite the fact that we had made steady progress during the preceding six months, it still seemed to me that I was still not confident that we had made enough progress. The mountain we had to climb could be seen in the distance. It was an unclimbed peak and there were no maps, but we only had a limited amount of time to reach the summit. The scenery changed as we made our way and new landscapes and scenery appeared. But if we looked down at our feet, all we could see was the roughness of the road and the obstacles that kept appearing. We could perhaps keep going for three months at best. It seemed the odds for reaching the top were about a hundred to one. All we could do, though, was to keep walking in the direction of the mountain. Labour-management relations and employee reassignments had to be managed by JNR itself. I would even go as far as saying that the whole reform programme was all about personnel and employment issues. This was the *raison d'être* of the Personnel Department, we simply had to keep going.

9 Inter-regional transfers (March 1986)

Given the number of obstacles and the scale of opposition, we understood that losing momentum for even a brief moment would put us on the defensive. It was essential, and very much part of my strategy, that we keep finding new problems to solve, new initiatives to launch. With the rationalization process on track, the questionnaire and the joint declaration behind us, it was time for a fresh initiative.

The joint declaration had had a big impact because it had been quite unexpected. We understood, however, that the impact would gradually fade and that those who opposed us would take advantage of even a brief unguarded moment to go back on the offensive. We needed to move on, and keep several steps ahead, so that even if they counter-attacked, it would be against old ground, old issues, and there would be only a limited impact. Our next move was to initiate the 'inter-regional transfer'.

The number of employees that could be hired by each of the new JR companies was determined by JNR RAP. With the rationalization process in place and with the impact of the hiring freeze, it was much easier to determine where the greatest number of surplus workers would be. It was in Hokkaido and Kyushu where the problem was the most serious. In both regions, there were many excellent employees who intended to continue working for a railway company. If they were willing to work on Honshu, they could certainly find more attractive positions in Tokyo, Osaka or Nagoya, where the respective JR companies were authorized to hire larger numbers of workers, and we decided to implement a scheme to facilitate this, which came to be called 'inter-regional transfers'.

In later years, this method was applied within Honshu, whereby we promoted transfers from areas such as Tohoku (the northern part of Honshu), and Niigata, where transportation density was low and therefore less demand for staff, to Tokyo. Kokuro was outraged, as they had been after we had sent out the questionnaire. They accused us, again, of treating the passage of the bills in the Diet as a *fait accompli*. Although we did not make any explicit promises to employees who volunteered for transfer, there was certainly a tacit understanding that their willingness to leave their native home in Hokkaido and move to Tokyo would be rewarded when the time came for the new JR companies to start hiring workers.

There were altogether three rounds of inter-regional transfers, and in all, more than 3,000 employees were transferred. A programme aired by the Japanese Broadcasting Corporation (NHK) highlighted the case of one worker who moved from one part of Japan to another to start work at a new work-place. He had sold his old house and the story of moving a gravesite from Hokkaido nearer to his new home caught the attention of many viewers.

The implementation of the inter-regional transfers was another important milestone for the management of JNR in particular because it preceeded the formal decision about the break-up and privatization of JNR. It also served to increase the share of personal responsibility for the successful break-up and privatization as there were now so many more lives and careers at stake following the transfers. The Joint Liaison Conference approved the plan for immediate implementation. At the same time, there was no way back for the employees who applied for transfer. The same thing could even be said for the unions to which they belonged.

10 Doro withdraws from Sohyo and drops its support for the Japan Socialist Party (May 1986)

Early in 1986, prior to the Diet deliberations, Ide, Matsuda, Nanya and I received through Mitsuzuka a request to meet the Minister of Labour, Yamaguchi Toshio, and the other top labour officials such as the Director-General of the Labour Policy Bureau. Yamaguchi told us: 'Your way of dealing with the labour unions is problematic. Kokuro is one of the pillars of the labour movement. Unless you make the relationship with Kokuro central to your strategy, everything will eventually fail. Change your attitude.' Responding to pressure from Sohyo (the General Council of Trade Unions of Japan), he was trying to lean on us. Doubtless, even greater pressure would be imposed by politicians and the mass media when Diet deliberations got under way. I explained to Yamaguchi: 'It is not our intention to isolate Kokuro, but since Kokuro don't seem to be able to make any decision, we are not able to coordinate with the other labour unions. We cannot hold up progress towards JNR's break-up and privatization simply because of Kokuro. You should address your comments to Kokuro rather than to us.'

On the following day, the Director-General of the Labour Policy Bureau called Sugiura, saying: 'Your staff, particularly Deputy Director-General Kasai, seem to have a very rigid attitude. If you allow them to manage industrial relations like that, you might find yourself out of a job.' The President asked me: 'What did you say to them?' I gave the President a verbatim account, ending with my suggestion that the Minister address his remarks to Kokuro, given their complete opposition to the break-up and privatization process. On hearing my explanation, the President laughed and made a rather dismissive remark.

Given Doro's recent behaviour, the relationship between themselves and Sohyo continued to deteriorate. Kokuro was an important part of Sohyo and this made Sohyo take a very harsh attitude towards Doro. With the arrival of spring, the unions which had signed the joint declaration formed the Conference of Labour Unions for JNR Reform (Kaikaku-kyo). However, Tetsuro's distrust of Doro had not waned since the productivity movement, and they wished to impose various conditions on Doro before cooperating. Tetsuro belonged to Domei (the Japanese Confederation of Labour), and supported the Democratic Socialist Party, and they suggested that if Doro intended sincerely to work with them, that they should withdraw from Sohyo and drop their support for the JSP. Doro met all these conditions, first withdrawing from Sohyo and then cutting its links with the JSP.

Sohyo, the JSP, the public security authorities, and the leaders of other labour unions asserted that Doro's transformation was just a ruse and that the radicals had only done it to keep the organization together. We replied to them: 'You may be right, but so long as their actions are in line with their words and they continue to support the reform process, we will work with them. If it proves otherwise, our attitude will certainly become very antagonistic!'

Deliberation of the bills in the ordinary session of the Diet started. The government realized that the schedule would not permit passage of both the Law for the Break-up and Privatization of JNR and the Law for Voluntary Retirement in the ordinary session. For fear that either of the bills might simply be dropped, the government's strategy was to focus on the Law for Voluntary Retirement. If the break-up and privatization was going to proceed as scheduled, we needed to start the process of calling for voluntary retirement by the summer of 1986. As the passage of the Law for Voluntary Retirement would be a watershed in the entire process, the JSP and Kokuro made desperate efforts to block it. Despite this, it was enacted on 21 May 1986, with the government thus becoming fully committed to JNR's break-up and privatization.

On the day the Law for Voluntary Retirement passed, I returned from the Diet and addressed my staff: 'The Law for Voluntary Retirement and the Law for the Break-up and Privatization of JNR are inseparable. There can be no turning back. If the government cannot enact the Law for the Break-up and Privatization of JNR in the autumn session it will not survive. We must make thorough preparations for that. However, we must also prevent any slip-ups in the rationalization process and implement the Voluntary Retirement Law without a hitch.

We set about immediately calling for volunteers for early retirement. Applications came thick and fast. Although we expected 20,000, applications eventually totalled 40,000. With this many voluntary retirees, the number who required special employment support was reduced significantly. Of the 40,000, 16,000 quit JNR and found jobs by themselves. I believe the reason why the voluntary retirement programme and the transfer of JNR employees to the public sector proceeded smoothly lay in the conflict within Kokuro, which continued to oppose the break-up and privatization, and the individual union members who found it increasingly difficult to follow the leadership. In the spring of 1986, we were to witness yet more conflict and turmoil within Kokuro's organization.

11 The split of Kokuro and the passage of the law for JNR reform (July to November 1986)

Simultaneous elections for the Upper and Lower Houses of the Diet were held on 6 July, resulting in an unprecedented triumph for the LDP in both houses. It gained 304 seats in the Lower House, while the JSP suffered a sharp decline to 86 seats. Since the reform of JNR was one of the biggest policy agendas in the election, the landslide victory of the LDP was regarded as a full endorsement by the public for the government's plan. It was quite natural, therefore, for people to assume that the privatization process would now be a formality. There was no time, however, for the Personnel

Department even to breathe a sigh of relief. We had to make meticulous preparations for the Diet deliberations scheduled to start in the autumn, anticipating every conceivable question and compiling the relevant data. Meanwhile, progress was being made on the voluntary retirement programme and the relocation of workers.

It was clear that with the passage of the Law for Voluntary Retirement and the LDP's landslide victory, Kokuro felt more and more uneasy. Kokuro consisted of many different groups with many differing opinions. Although the overwhelming majority of Kokuro's members were ordinary workers, the leadership was clearly divided along ideological lines, which caused a great deal of bitterness and antagonism. The mainstream group belonged to the relatively moderate Mindo-saha (Minshuka domei-saha), which supported the JSP. The anti-mainstream group was divided into two factions: Kakudo (Kakushindoshikai), which was under the influence of the JCP; and Shakaishugi Kyokai-ha (Socialist Conference Faction), a Marxist group. Mindo-saha seemed willing to abandon its opposition to the break-up and privatization of JNR, at least at some point in the future, but when the matter was discussed by the union as a whole, opinion was always divided. Mindo-saha supporters accounted for almost half of the total union membership, with Kakudo and Kyokai-ha accounting for about a quarter each. Reflecting their political leanings, the Mindo-saha faction was a moderate, even loose, organization, while Kakudo and Kyokai-ha were doctrinaire and belligerent. Since the factions could agree on almost nothing, consensus never went much further than the basics of the union platform. While the leadership probably wanted to break the deadlock and change direction, they were simply unable to, and in the meantime the individual union members were left to decide their own fate.

Under such circumstances, there was an increase in members withdrawing from Kokuro between July and August 1986. They tended not to join either Tetsuro or Doro immediately, as that would be a 'leap too far', but instead started to form new unions as a means to avoid isolation within JNR. After the July election, for example, white-collar members of Kokuro formed a number of small groups in each of the Railway Operating Divisions. Similar groups spread throughout JNR.

Tetsuro and Doro seem to have suspected that the Personnel Department was manipulating the union members behind the scenes. In fact, a Democratic Socialist Party Diet member who was a former employee of JNR, asked me bluntly: 'Kasai, why don't you encourage workers withdrawing from Kokuro to join Tetsuro, instead of allowing small groups to spring up like mushrooms after rain? Matsuda is saying the same thing.' I replied: 'Whether we permit them or not, they are doing this of their own free will.' The member replied: 'They're doing this because you let them. Otherwise, the former Kokuro members would have joined Tetsuro.' I countered: 'That is incorrect. It's enough of an emotional wrench for them to leave Kokuro, having been members for such a long time. It's quite natural for them to resist joining Tetsuro, which has been so antagonistic towards Kokuro. Forming their own small groups is quite natural.' But he insisted: 'I think that everybody would join Tetsuro if the Personnel Department told them to.' I emphasized again, before leaving his office: 'I have never said that the Personnel Department is encouraging members to leave Kokuro.'

The membership of Kokuro started a precipitous decline from about 180,000 in April 1986 to around 120,000 when the Diet session began in September. Moreover, the decline showed signs of accelerating. The leaders of Kokuro were finally forced to confront the peril that threatened their organization's very existence.

During the summer, to deal with the problem of underemployed workers at the work-place, which worsened as rationalization progressed, special units, known as 'Human Resource Utilization Centres' were set up at worksites around the country. Surplus workers were beginning to undermine discipline and safety in the work-place with serious implications for morale and possible consequences for the reform process. The main objective of these centres was, therefore, to train and shift human resources to areas where they were required.

Coinciding as it did with the beginning of Kokuro's collapse, Kokuro believed that the establishment of the Human Resource Utilization Centre network was the trigger that started the decline. The real reason was, of course, quite different. The gap between the union leadership's policies and the day-to-day realities faced by its members had grown too great. While in ordinary times it might have been all right for members to 'pay their union dues and say nothing', at this critical juncture, if they had simply followed the union directive to take industrial action to prevent or slow down the reform process, they would have lost their jobs and the basis of their livelihood. Forced finally to make a choice, they decided to withdraw from Kokuro.

Public attention began to focus on Kokuro's next move. In September 1986, as deliberations of the bills got underway in the Diet, the mainstream Mindo-saha faction of Kokuro formed a 'Central Struggle Committee'. However, bitter criticism from the anti-mainstream prevented any consensus, and having exhausted every possible avenue for agreement, it was decided to hold an extraordinary conference in Shuzenji – a famous hot-spring resort in Shizuoka Prefecture. With this very much on the minds of the public, the outcome of the conference was eagerly awaited.

Meanwhile, with the Nakasone Cabinet and the LDP firmly behind the reform programme, deliberations were proceeding smoothly in the Diet. Given the controversial and wide-ranging nature of the bills, one would normally have expected stiff confrontation between the ruling and opposition parties and even complete standstill from time to time. In reality, however, the Law for Voluntary Retirement had already been enacted in the spring and given LDP's large majority in the Diet, opposition was quite muted.

The Shuzenji conference was held in October in clear anticipation that the bills would be passed in the Diet and turned out, as we feared, to be a repeat of the 'Central Struggle Committee' held in September. The union was completely divided, with the mainstream faction arguing that break-up and privatization should be accepted as a reality, and the anti-mainstream faction arguing for the continuance of total opposition. Eventually, the mainstream faction broke away from Kokuro and formed a new union called the Japan Railway Industrial Workers' Union (Tessanro). With 30,000 members joining the new union, the membership of Kokuro declined to only 40,000.

While the Diet deliberations progressed, we continued steadily with preparatory work. Recruitment procedures, for example, needed to be established. This involved preliminary work, such as compiling the necessary employee data, and for this purpose, a workplace performance and vocational aptitude evaluation was carried out, and the results stored in the various administrative offices around the country. An 'Establishment Committee' had been set up for each of the JR companies that had laid down the criteria for recruitment and the conditions of employment. We would then make an evaluation of each employee based on the information we had already gathered, listing them in the order of our evaluation. The list was then presented to the Establishment Committee which would use it to decide who would be employed and where. We were also making steady progress in rationalization, and it now seemed certain that we would be able to exceed by quite a margin the numerical targets that had been set by JNR RAP.

The day after the conclusion of the Shuzenji conference, three JSP Diet members who were closely involved in matters relating to JNR invited three senior members of the Personnel Department, including myself, to dinner. It was held at a restaurant specializing in turtle dishes in Akasaka, a well-known entertainment area in Tokyo. Since the deliberations on the bills were nearing an end, we anticipated a request of some sort.

We arrived slightly before the Diet members and took our seats. When they arrived, they said: 'You are our guests, so please sit at the head of the table.' I replied: 'We cannot possibly sit at the head of the table and ignore you, our great *senpai*. We've already taken our places so why don't we forget about guest and host seating for today?' After agreeing to this, the Diet members bowed deeply and said: 'We would like to ask you a special favour today. You started the productivity movement but this failed because we blocked it. On that occasion we did not seek a 100% victory over you as this would have led to a collapse of the company's management. We therefore stopped at 90%. That 10% represented the mercy of the samurai towards the management. This time, victory will be yours and if the current situation continues, Kokuro will collapse. They tried at Shuzenji to get its members to agree to the break-up and privatization. It failed and the result has been that 30,000 have left Kokuro and formed a new union. We believe this group will support the break-up and privatization, so we would like to request that you do not oppress them or discriminate against them.' This remark betrayed the JSP's recognition that there was nothing they could now do to prevent passage of the bills. We concluded by saying: 'We have no intention of being antagonistic towards Kokuro. We simply want to rescue JNR from its current situation. You needn't worry.'

In the Diet, the opposition parties focused their attacks on the Human Resource Utilization Centres. Their main argument was that being assigned to go to these centres was as good as being told you were not going to be employed by the new JR companies and that this was causing great unease among the Kokuro members. They also claimed that workers were forced to engage in inhuman work at the centres and demanded that they be disbanded. With Kokuro membership shrinking by the day, such demands gradually increased. At the request of Kokuro, the JSP and JCP threatened to make informal on-the-spot investigations to ascertain what was happening at the centres. With the memory of their success in blocking the productivity improvement still fresh in their minds, they clearly thought this was another opportunity to rescue Kokuro from the brink of extinction. JNR steadfastly refused to accept these demands to investigate the Centres.

Some staff members irresponsibly advised the President that we accept the opposition parties' request for an informal investigation in order to show our sincerity. It was quite clear, however, that the purpose of the investigation was not to know the reality at the centres but to seek a means to denounce them and thereby undermine the reform process. The mass media would doubtless feature the investigation just out of curiosity. The frontline managers' confidence in senior management, yielding to political pressure just as they had in the bad old days, would have been profoundly shaken. The proper way would have been to exercise the Diet's right to make a formal investigation if necessary. Calling their bluff and standing by our decision was absolutely correct.

When deliberations began drawing to a close in November, the government, especially Minister of Transport Hashimoto Ryutaro (who succeeded Mitsuzuka in July 1986), seemed to encourage us to respond to the opposition's request to disband the Human

Resources Utilization Centres as a means to get opposition support for the bills. By that stage, however, there had been great progress in the relocation of employees and the problem of surplus workers was on the wane, and the decision to close the centres did not present us with any difficulties. The Centres had been the most contentious issue during the deliberations, but they had served their purpose.

[13] The transition to JR (from November 1986 to March 1987)

On 28 November 1986, the eight bills relating to the reform of JNR were enacted. We only had four months left, until 1 April 1987, before the law came into effect, and JNR was formally broken up and privatized, and the JR companies established. One of the major issues remaining was the relocation of employees to each of the seven new JR companies. Much preparatory work on relocation had already been done, and in December the Establishment Committees asked us to present the list of the employees that it needed for recruitment.

The situation was greatly influenced by the fact that we had received such a large number of applications for voluntary retirement, far beyond the 20,000 that the plan called for. The result was that all JNR employees in Honshu who wanted jobs would be able to join one of the JR companies. Kokuro began an aggressive propaganda campaign along the lines of: 'Given that the aim of the break-up and privatization was for the management to do away with people they didn't like, the fact that everyone has been able to join the JR companies is a disastrous result for them.' Faced with this, some JNR staff went so far as to suggest we call a halt to accepting any more applications.

We were not deflected, however. Applications could be accepted until 31 March 1987 and if we stopped half-way, we would be infringing the right of employees who were still in the midst of considering their futures. We would not let rumour and irresponsible criticism deflect us from our purpose. Notwithstanding Kokuro's comments, the purpose of the reform process was not to single out employees or groups of employees but to re-establish the right of the management to manage, and to re-instil discipline in the work-place. Fair and equal treatment of workers in the voluntary retirement process was therefore essential. In the end, 40,000 workers retired voluntarily, and on Honshu there were hardly any workers who had not found employment, and the fact that 16,000 of these had found employment under their own steam greatly helped to ease the problem of finding jobs for the surplus employees.

The situation was more difficult in Kyushu and Hokkaido. While the 'inter-regional transfers' had helped somewhat, these efforts were not sufficient to cope with the large number of surplus workers in these regions. Eventually, 8,000 workers, mainly in Kyushu and Hokkaido, were left without jobs at any of the JR companies and had to be transferred to the JNR Settlement Corporation. On the whole, however, the voluntary retirement programme and the employment measures we introduced were more successful than many had expected.

Although JNR had frequently been criticized for its inefficiency and lack of discipline, I had been particularly impressed with the energy with which the organization tackled the reform process. The compilation of the list of employees was a good example. The Personnel Department cooperated with numerous colleagues of various divisions around the country and in an extremely short space of time managed to draw up a list consisting of the names of every single person that eventually joined the JR companies. They were all ranked in order: there were no overlaps and not one name was missing. This was the power of JNR's one-hundred-year history.

Early in September 1986, there occurred what appeared to be a coordinated attack on workers who had withdrawn from Kokuro and were sympathetic to Doro, resulting in a number of serious injuries and even deaths. Soon after the start of the New Year 1987, a top-three Doro official was attacked and was badly injured. Police reports indicated that these attacks were the result of violent internal strife among radical sects inside Kokuro and Doro. There were also a number of arson attacks, with communications equipment and residential buildings as frequent targets. A number of police officers, politicians and union leaders went as far as to blame the Personnel Department for putting Kokuro in a tight spot and commenting that labour problems were much preferable to public disorder.

While the outcome of the Diet deliberations remained uncertain, there remained a powerful forward momentum for reform within JNR. When the outcome became clearer, however, the natural instincts for self-protection came to the surface among bureaucrats. This instinct would have been behind the urging of some staff members that we accept the Socialists' and Communists' request for informal inspections at the Human Resource Utilization Centres. The same thing could be said about the mass media. After critical editorials about deteriorating discipline and the collapse of management of JNR passed their peak, the tone changed rapidly to one of sympathy for Kokuro. The media aggressively reported incidents of workers committing suicide caused by the stress of reform. If we relaxed even a little, there was no telling what could happen. It was not until the very last minute that I felt I could say to myself: 'we've done it!'.

On 31 March 1987, just one day before the establishment of the seven JR companies, the attention of the majority of the employees at JNR Headquarters had already shifted to the new companies. Some felt sentimental about the conclusion of JNR's long history. For them, the work on JNR's break-up and privatization was long finished, and their minds seemed to have moved on to their new jobs. At the Personnel Department, however, there was neither sentimentalism nor enthusiasm. Until the final day, work continued as usual, and I felt nothing but gratitude, admiration and pride for hundreds of staff in the various sections of the Department. They had been the vanguard, then the driving force and were now acting on the rear guard, all during the most difficult of times. When I thought of the tense period to come in the next days, I felt nothing other than numb with cold.

Distrust and friction still clouded labour relations. For a hundred years, JNR had been a fairly straightforward organization, but with the break-up, that was about to change drastically. If these new companies failed to function in an orderly way, there could be tragic consequences: there was always the possibility of train accidents and paralysis in the chain of command. There were many people who had been hoping that the break-up and privatization would fail and they were not pleased with its success. Obstruction and even sabotage could not be ruled out. In a new and unfamiliar organization, communication might not go smoothly, despite everyone's best efforts. In that sense, for a while after 1 April 1987, we were left very exposed, like a crab out of its shell. The break-up and privatization of JNR had been successfully accomplished, but there were still grave concerns about what the future held in store.

► *Chapter 7*

Summing-up: the establishment of JR – 15 years on

Fifteen years have already passed since the break-up and privatization of JNR and the establishment of the seven JR companies in 1987. It is twenty-one years since the Second Administrative Reform Committee (SARC) initiated discussions of radical reform in 1981. As the Japanese saying goes, 'Ten years is an age' and for most people JNR is an artefact: its break-up and privatization is just part of ancient history.

During this period, the performance of the newly-established JR companies except JR Freight has generally exceeded expectations. Although initial expectations were that their recurring profits would reach only 1% of total revenue, this level was exceeded from the beginning as the JR companies benefited from the 'bubble economy' of the late 1980s. This was particularly true of the three Honshu JR companies, which posted recurring profits of around 10% of total revenue. Even during the depressed economic environment after the burst of the 'bubble' in the early 1990s, these three companies have managed to maintain a level of more than 5% of total revenue. Furthermore, they have been able to avoid fare hikes despite the expectation in the government's original plan that fares would have to be raised by 3% annually. Fares have increased only once, by approximately 7%, and that was carried out only by JR Hokkaido, JR Shikoku and JR Kyushu. These favourable results have enabled the three Honshu JR companies to list on the Tokyo Stock Exchange and business performance since the listings has been steady. With the JR Company Law having been revised and enacted in June 2001, the regulations governing the operations of the three Honshu JR companies were formally relaxed to the same level of other private railway companies[1] as of 1 December 2001. It is envisaged that shares of these companies still held by the government will be gradually sold off.

However, there are a large number of people who believe that with the revision of the Law and the full privatization of the three Honshu JR companies that will take place when the government's remaining shares are sold, we can all sit back as market forces will ensure that things will automatically go well for these companies. Some people even argue that the shares of the JR companies in Hokkaido, Shikoku and Kyushu, as well as JR Freight should follow the three Honshu JR companies and list on the stock market sooner or later. As the primary purpose of this book is to examine the collapse and privatization of JNR, I will perhaps set out a more detailed description of events after privatization in a future book. I would therefore like to conclude with a very broad-based view of the problems experienced in the post-privatization era. I greatly fear that the management of the JR companies have been intoxicated with their own success and that a new myth, that economic and social structural reform can be achieved through the privatization of public corporations, seems to be taking hold of the nation.

[1] The essence of the break-up and privatization of JNR – forming a national consensus

(1) Are the JR companies completely private companies?
The break-up and privatization of JNR, which was initiated by its collapse, had two objectives: firstly, to resolve the conflict in having both to serve the public and to make a profit, and secondly, to

---

[1] Other than the former JNR companies there are many other private railway companies in Japan, for example Tobu, Seibu, Odakyu, Keio, Meitetsu, Kintetsu and Hankyu. Most of these are based around the large urban areas such as Tokyo, Yokohama, Nagoya, Osaka, Kyoto and Kobe. As well as operating suburban railway lines, many of these companies operate in other sectors, particularly retail and property.

introduce to the fullest extent possible the discipline of the market mechanism in the company's management. With the completion of the Tohoku and Joetsu Shinkansens, the focus was shifting from the development of the railway network to its efficient management. The market mechanism, and its application through the process of break-up and privatization was how this was supposed to be achieved. This was very much the line of SARC's arguments, but once JNR RAP started to draw up a concrete and workable plan, politics started to intervene and it became clear that the reality of the reform process would be determined by mostly politically motivated decisions.

The blueprint for the break-up and privatization of JNR was drawn up by JNR RAP, and based on this, the government drafted a detailed bill. After debate and enactment by the Diet, the law would be implemented. While this process was typical of the Japanese national consensus building process, the paradox of the privatization (i.e., the application of the concept of the profit-seeking enterprise and market forces) would need to be resolved through political means. The ensuing compromise between 'profit-seeking' and the 'public interest' would mean the JR companies would be set up on the same unsatisfactory premise as JNR had been under the MacArthur administration. Clearly, a comparison of JNR and the JR companies shows that the JR companies are much more market-oriented. However, this is more to do with the vastly different operating environment that existed in 1987 compared to 1949. Firstly, there is much more competition from other modes of transport and secondly, with the completion of the Tohoku and Joetsu Shinkansens, the railway system was completed and the railway industry itself entered into a mature phase.

The reform of JNR was part of Japan's national policy to clear away the debt that the public corporations had accumulated. In order to achieve this goal, all related parties, such as tax-payers, railway passengers and JNR workers, needed to share the burden. This burden sharing was possible only because there was an understanding that public services, such as railway transportation, could not be left entirely to market forces.

The law passed in 1998 stipulated that the public should

shoulder ¥28 trillion ($233.3 bn) of JNR-related debt, which would be paid off with tax-payers' money over a period of sixty years. In return, the people expected significant improvements in service by the newly-established railway companies. However, during the deliberation leading up to break-up and privatization, the government undertook in the Diet that all railway routes inherited from JNR would be maintained. Even after the revision of the JR Law, the fact remains that the railways are a provider of public services.

(2) Compromise to make a consensus. Efforts to make concrete programmes
Taking into account the three gravest concerns of the LDP and the opposition parties regarding privatization and break-up, namely closure of unprofitable lines, fare increases and job losses, JNR RAP went to great lengths to draft a plan that would be acceptable to politicians and the public alike. It was clear that the tax-payers would no longer tolerate the funding of JNR's huge operating deficit (more than ¥700 billion per annum). Increasing JNR's debt would inevitably mean using taxpayer's money to write it off in the future. In this situation the application of market principles would lead to drastic measures such as line closures, fare hikes, wage cuts and redundancies. However, such measures would obviously not have received the necessary support from other key parties. There would certainly not have been any consensus even within JNR RAP itself. Ultimately, the government treated the issue of employment with the utmost care, giving a guarantee that 'no one would be thrown out into the streets', thereby underwriting not only financial debt, but also 'human debt', the overmanning that had been caused over the years by inefficient management or by political considerations.

In order to assist the three island JR[2] companies, which suffered from low transportation density and, hence, many unprofitable lines, a 'Management Stabilization Fund' was established for each company, totalling ¥1.3 trillion ($10.8 bn). With the interest

---

[2] 'Three island JR companies' is used throughout as a collective term for JR Hokkaido, JR Shikoku and JR Kyushu.

income from the management of the funds, these companies would be able to compensate for the shortfall in passenger income and would be able to maintain existing railway networks in their respective regions. Despite the fact that the three island JR companies were losing money on their railway operations, they were obliged to maintain as a long-term objective the listing of their shares on the stock exchange. This would suggest that the listing of the JR company shares, which was an integral part of the process of the break-up and privatization of JNR, was no more than a theoretical or nominal objective. The conventional wisdom even for the three Honshu JR companies was that it would be impossible to achieve a listing within ten years of their incorporation. The common understanding was that the privatization process would be reviewed after a suitable interval. The thing to focus on for the time being was to avoid racking up more losses. One obvious problem would be that if the three island JR companies were listed with the Management Stabilization Fund as the mainstay of profitability, investors could conceivably acquire the companies and make a quick profit by separating the cash assets from the railway business and abandoning the unprofitable railway business. This kind of possibility could of course not be entertained.

(3) A defective system: the Shinkansen Holding Corporation (SHC)
A perfect illustration of where political considerations made their impact felt was the profit adjustment among the three JR companies in Honshu. JNR RAP had come to the conclusion that some kind of cross-subsidization be required to provide financial support to JR East and JR West by taking advantage of the profits earned by the Tokaido Shinkansen, which was to be operated by JR Central. This would make all of the three Honshu JR companies profitable and ensure the continued operations of all of the lines which they would inherit from JNR. Although this kind of internal cross-subsidization occurred naturally in JNR, which was a unified national organization, one of the primary purposes of the break-up of JNR was to reduce them so that they would only be permitted within each of the regional JR companies, not across them. However, with the unprofitable lines in Honshu that had to be maintained, there would have to be a new source for the

'external subsidy' after the break-up of JNR and it was for this purpose that the SHC was established.

The system of cross-subsidy, or 'profit adjustments', through the SHC would work in the following way: the ground facilities, including the track, of the four Shinkansen lines (Tokaido, Sanyo, Tohoku and Joetsu) would be owned by the SHC, a separate organization from the JR companies. The lines would then be leased to JR Central, JR West, and JR East for operation. Profit adjustments would be reflected in the lease charges paid by the three Honshu JR companies. This was, in a sense, the functional division of rolling stock, ground infrastructure and superstructure that was mentioned in Chapter 1, being introduced specifically for the operation of the four Shinkansen lines.

The book values of the Tokaido Shinkansen, Tohoku/Joetsu Shinkansen and Sanyo Shinkansen were ¥0.47 trillion ($3.9 bn), ¥4.49 trillion ($37.4 bn) and ¥0.69 trillion ($5.8 bn), respectively, totalling ¥5.65 trillion ($46.3 bn). Following a market-based revaluation in April 1987, these amounts increased to ¥2.44 trillion ($20.3 bn), ¥4.67 trillion ($38.9 bn), ¥1.43 trillion ($11.9 bn), respectively, a total of ¥8.54 trillion ($71.2 bn). The SHC took over the assets of the four Shinkansen lines and JNR debts amounting to ¥8.54 trillion, which was set as the amount of the revalued assets. The SHC would lease the assets to the three Honshu JR companies for the amount of charges equivalent to the present value of principal and interest equally paid off over 30 years. The SHC would then repay the debts by using the income from leasing the lines.

The Ministry of Transport determined that lease charges for the three Honshu JR companies should be charged according to a formula considering the volume of traffic carried by each of the Shinkansen lines. Based on this method, lease charges for each of Shinkansen Lines were calculated as follows: charges for the Tokaido Shinkansen would be ¥5.02 trillion ($41.8 bn) (58.7% of total lease charges compared with 28.6% of total asset value), for the Tohoku/Joetsu Shinkansen ¥2.39 trillion ($19.9 bn) (28.0% of total lease charges, compared with 54.7% of total asset value), and for the Sanyo Shinkansen ¥1.13 trillion ($9.4 bn) (13.3% of total lease charges, compared with 16.7% of total asset value).

Lease charges exceeding the actual asset value was regarded as the amount available for profit adjustment or external cross-subsidies. Initially, lease charges were to be reviewed every two years taking into account actual transport volume.

The system, proposed by Sumita Shoji, a member of JNR RAP, and a former vice-minister of the Ministry of Transport, was strongly opposed by Hayashi. JNR RAP Chairman, Kamei Masao, who was the Deputy Chairman of Nikkeiren (the Japan Federation of Employers' Association), and Sub-Committee Chairman Kato Hiroshi were also sceptical. On the day the system had been discussed at JNR RAP, the informal study group that had been set up to support Professor Kato Hiroshi consisting of Tanaka Kazuaki, Sando Yoichi, Yayama Taro, Matsuda Masatake and myself gathered as usual at Kato's private seminar room. The opposition to the system was unanimous. They argued that it would be irrational to revalue only the assets of the Shinkansen Lines for profit adjustment purposes. Some of the existing conventional[3] lines such as the Yamanote Line operating in the centre of Tokyo posted large profits, and were inherited by the JR company at book value. There was no consistency or logic to it. The biannual review of the lease charges for the Shinkansen Lines was also fatally flawed. Not only did this create balance sheet uncertainties, it also meant that independent management of the JR companies would not be possible as our common fates were inseparably and artificially linked to the reviews. From what I heard, Hayashi counter proposed that the profit adjustment should be calculated according to the estimated earning power of each of the JR companies. The amount of debt inherited would be based on this figure and the assets of the Shinkansen lines would belong to the JR companies which would operate them. While we all supported this idea, ultimately, despite widespread opposition, the SHC plan was pushed through. Attempting to refute Hayashi's arguments the Cabinet Legislation Bureau, whose

---

[3] It is worth noting that Japanese conventional railway lines are narrower than Shinkansen lines. Shinkansen lines are 'standard gauge' (1435mm), whereas the Japanese conventional lines, at least those used by the JR companies, are the 'Japanese standard gauge' or 'narrow gauge' (1067mm).

senior officer in charge of the MOT was a close subordinate of Sumita Shoji, commented: 'We cannot legislate based on the vague future earning power of each of JR companies.'

Eventually, after four-and-a-half years, the SHC was disbanded and Hayashi was totally vindicated. With hindsight, with a willingness to listen and share knowledge on all sides, this problem could have been solved. Hayashi asserted that the establishment of the SHC was the biggest mistake in the entire JNR reform process and every time the issue arose, he would, with a deep sigh, say 'it was unforgivable'. It had also been the biggest bone of contention within JNR. With the handicap of the SHC system, a listing for the three Honshu JR companies would have been inconceivable. While none of us actually believed deep down that a listing was possible anyway (just seeing the new JR companies breaking even and not incurring any new debt would have been quite sufficient), the establishment of the SHC was concrete evidence that none of those who were responsible for the break-up and privatization of JNR believed it was going to happen. The SHC was a provisional arrangement, with the details and specifics to be reviewed at a later date.

(4) Disbanding the SHC – Remaining problems

In reality, the three Honshu JR companies performed much better than expected and by 1991, fully met the listing criteria. This development, beyond everyone's wildest expectations at the time of the establishment of the JR companies, meant changes would have to be made before a listing could take place. On 1 October 1991, the SHC was disbanded and its assets and liabilities allocated to each of the JR companies. The revalued assets of the four Shinkansen Lines as of October 1991 amounted to ¥9.17 trillion ($76.4 bn) including the salvage value of ¥1 trillion, with the Tokaido, Tohoku/Joetsu, and Sanyo Shinkansen accounting for ¥2.96 trillion ($24.7 bn) (32.2% of the total), ¥4.42 trillion ($36.8 bn) (48.2%) and ¥1.79 trillion ($14.9 bn) (19.6%) respectively. With liabilities being also allocated on the basis of their share of the leasing charge burden, the allocated amounts for the Tokaido, Tohoku/Joetsu and Sanyo Shinkansen were ¥5.09 trillion ($42.4 bn) (55.5% of the total liabilities), ¥3.11 trillion ($25.9 bn)

(33.9%) and ¥0.97 trillion ($8.1 bn) (10.6%) respectively. In other words, the Tokaido Shinkansen was requested to accept additional liabilities of ¥2.13 trillion($17.8 bn) (¥1.31 trillion – $10.9 bn – from the Tohoku/Joetsu Shinkansen and ¥0.82 trillion ($6.8 bn) from the Sanyo Shinkansen) over and above the value of the assets it was inheriting to provide an 'external subsidy' to the other two Honshu JR companies (JR East and JR West). JR Central had been urging the government to allocate liabilities based on the real earning power of the three Honshu JR companies with reference to their business performance since incorporation and taking into account not only the Shinkansen lines but also conventional lines. As only four years had passed since the establishment of the JR companies and the shares were still entirely owned by the government, this kind of an adjustment could easily have been made, had there been a will to do so. However, we were unable to overcome the rigidities of the annual budget system and the tendency of bureaucrats to stick to something unless it is afflicted with a truly fatal flaw.

I will admit that the new system represented a great improvement over the SHC. Around 85% of JR Central's total revenue comes from the operation of the Tokaido Shinkansen, and it was obviously essential for the company's business to maintain and improve this asset. Needless to say, we were not allowed to depreciate the ground facilities at all under the SHC lease system. Therefore the depreciation costs accounted for a mere 7% of total revenue, which was extraordinarily low compared with other railway companies. Normally, lease charges for facilities and machinery include maintenance and replacement costs. While these were reflected in the calculation of the SHC lease charges, as the entire lease income received by the SHC was appropriated for the repayment of JNR debt, it did not cover maintenance or replacement costs at all. Thus, the JR companies had to pay these costs out of net income and external borrowing. Thus, total debt would continue to mount unless they chose to neglect maintenance and suppress investment. With SHC disbanded and its assets allocated to the three JR companies, cash-flow immediately increased, and this put us in a better position to fund maintenance and replacement costs, as well as pay back debt. During the eleven years from fiscal 1991 to 2001, JR Central reduced debt by ¥1.2 trillion ($10 bn), but it still remains at ¥4.3 trillion ($35.8 bn). Despite the extremely low interest rates that currently prevail in Japan, interest payments account for around 20% of total revenue in 2002. Compared with power companies and private railway companies, whose debt is about twice and a little less than three times of their annual revenues respectively, JR Central's debt (approximately four times annual revenues) and interest burden is excessively high. It is quite difficult to predict how long the current favourable interest rate environment will continue. Repaying as much of the debt as possible as quickly as possible is the most urgent issue for the company.

The structure whereby the source of funds for debt repayment gradually tapered off was artificially and politically created. Of JR Central's ¥5 trillion ($41.7 bn) of Shinkansen-related debt, ¥2.3 trillion ($19.2 bn) was included to reflect the value of land holdings (as of 1 October 1991). The original book value of the land held by the Tokaido Shinkansen was ¥40 billion ($333 mn), which should be regarded as a 'sunk cost'. However, the land is actually on the balance sheet at a value more than 50 times this amount. As the land cannot be depreciated, earnings are artificially inflated. The value of the land is equal to the amount of the profit adjustment in nominal terms. Currently, capital expenditure has been kept below levels of depreciation, which generates free cash flow, which is used for debt repayment. However, if capital expenditure continues to be kept at a low level for a long period, depreciation costs will start to reduce and eventually dry up as a source of funds for debt repayment. It was for this reason that we asked that measures to facilitate debt repayment be put in place in advance of complete privatization. Nowhere in the world will you find a private sector company which is burdened by government with such excessive debt and interest payments. There was an obvious and serious problem for JR Central, which took assets on to their balance sheet at greater than their repurchase price through the profit adjustment. However, there was also a potential problem even for those who did the reverse (i.e., JR East, JR West), as depreciation levels would be insufficient to generate sufficient cash flow for maintenance and replacement investment. In virtually treating the three Honshu JR companies as a single entity, the profit adjustment system through the SHC was no more than 'window dressing'. With the revision to JR Company Law in 2001, consideration started on ways to enable JR Central to accelerate repayment of debt with internally generated funds. This was realized in changes to the tax law in fiscal 2002 which allowed JR Central to create a ¥500 billion ($4.2 bn) reserve for large-scale repair work on the Tokaido Shinkansen. With the timing for these works on the Tokaido Shinkansen still far off in the future, these reserves can be appropriated for the early repayment of the excessive debts imposed by the government.

(5) Self-contradictory transportation policy

The profit adjustment framework not only reflected the self-contradiction embedded in the break-up and privatization of JNR, but also caused a distortion to the entire Japanese transportation framework. More specifically speaking, as a result of the profit adjustment, passengers of the Tokaido Shinkansen are forced to pay fares at least 20% higher than they should be in order to support the railway system in the rest of Honshu. Let me elaborate further. The daily frequency of Shinkansen departures between Tokyo and Osaka has reached 192, which is triple that of airlines. This means that, at the current service frequency, the Shinkansen service can offer seven times more passenger seats than all planes flying daily on the same route. It is therefore the case that intrinsic costs per passenger are much lower for the Shinkansen than for the airlines. Even including additional costs imposed by the profit adjustment policy, if one factors in access costs to Shinkansen stations compared with airports, costs for passengers using the Shinkansen come out much lower than those for the airlines. With the advent of the Nozomi Shinkansen, travel time between the central business districts of Tokyo and Osaka is almost the same as going by plane. The overall level of convenience is much higher, given the greater frequency of the Shinkansen and the direct connections between the two central business districts. If additional costs caused by the profit adjustment system were abolished and fares were reduced by 20% from the current level it would not be possible for planes to compete between Tokyo and Osaka. However, during the last ten years, the Civil Aviation Bureau has permitted the airlines to increase flights between Tokyo and Osaka from 30 to 76 per day. With increased air capacity between Tokyo and Osaka price competition intensified forcing airlines to lower fares with the result that the share of air transport on this route increased from 10% to 20%.

Subsidizing unprofitable local lines by keeping fares of the Tokaido Shinkansen artificially high on the one hand and increasing airline capacity between Tokyo and Osaka is clearly an inconsistent policy. Not only is it unfair to the Shinkansen, which offers a low cost and convenient service, it represents inefficiency and wastage of scarce resources.

In energy usage, for example, the Shinkansen is superior in every way. The emission of CO_2 per unit of transport volume of the 700 Series[4] Nozomi is one-tenth that of a Boeing 747, and its energy consumption is one-sixth. The total capacity of Haneda, Tokyo's domestic airport, is about 720 departure and arrival slots per day, of which about 110 are for flights to and from Osaka, Okayama and Hiroshima. If the 700 Series Nozomi replaced these flights, CO_2 emissions would be reduced by 200,000 tons per year. This is the equivalent of one month's CO_2 emissions from all domestic flights in Japan. Scarce slots at Haneda would be much better utilized for long-haul and international flights where planes, of course, have a clear competitive advantage. The twisted logic of the profit adjustment system has been greatly to the detriment of the Japanese people.

We are now in a world of deregulation and the application of market principles in all walks of life. I would argue that unfettered competition is not always appropriate and that in such sectors as transportation the public interest is best served with some limitations on the market mechanism. However, what is important is that the regulators ensure firstly, that competition is fair and

---

[4] There are many different types of Shinkansen trains, reflecting improvements in rail technology over the past three decades. The original design is known as the 0 series, an example of which can now be seen at the National Railway Museum in York (England). Subsequent models used on the Tokaido and Sanyo Shinkansen lines have been 100, 300, 500 and 700 series. On the other lines, the 200, 400, E1, E2, E3 and E4 series have been utilized.

secondly, that they take into account external diseconomies, such as the destruction of the environment, in important policy matters. As far as I understand, this is what is being considered in many European countries, and it is essential that this kind of comprehensive thinking is applied if the JR companies are going to function properly after their complete privatization.

2 Seeking sound management and sound industrial relations

People often said, 'The reform of JNR means the reform of the labour unions'. In other words, the true purpose of the reform of JNR was to attempt to bring into the mainstream of industrial relations two unions, Kokuro and Doro, which had always existed on the extremes. They were overtly politically motivated with the manifest aim of helping to establish a socialist regime, and would stop at nothing, paying scant regard to the travelling public, to achieve their aims. Soon after the privatization of JNR, people often talked about the 'Miracle of the privatization', referring to the fact that the attitude of the JNR workers seemed to change overnight. Against this we would argue that there were no overnight miracles. The simple objective was to try to balance the books. By stripping out debts accumulated in the past, we could greatly reduce the interest payment burden. Through thorough rationalization we were able to slash personnel costs. Expenditure could thus be reduced to a level to match revenues. Needless to say, reduced political and bureaucratic interference in the management was an important prerequisite for success. People, however, do not change overnight. What you see is what the workers have always been. In the process of privatization, they were just able to express themselves more freely.

By coincidence, soon after the privatization of JNR, the Berlin Wall collapsed in 1989 and in the ensuing wave of freedom that swept through Eastern Europe the communist regimes of the Eastern bloc fell one after another. On a smaller scale, a similar transformation occurred as JNR turned into the JR companies. The fate of the Soviet and Eastern bloc illustrated that even the strictest political and economic social controls extending over half a century could not suppress the souls of a nation forever. There are interesting parallels between the collapse of the labour movements led by Kokuro and Doro, guided as they were by the idea of class struggle, and the collapse of the totalitarian political regimes of the Soviet bloc.

Industrial relations, being about human relations, is a living organism. In the case of JNR, labour-management relations had developed over decades and could not be changed overnight with the establishment of the JR companies. Rather, it was as if, in the process of the curtain falling on an old play, a new drama started. In the process of privatization, Kokuro split in two, and Mindo-Saha, which constituted the main stream, established Tessanro. With the radical Doro making concessions to the moderate Tetsuro, the unions formed the Japan Confederation of Railway Worker's Unions (JR Soren) which was expected to be the first step in uniting all unions under one umbrella. There were many, particularly among industrial relations experts and the security authorities, who regarded Doro's policy shift as a tactical and temporary disguise to increase its membership and to maintain its influence. But it seemed to me that, despite some difference still remaining between the Doro and Tetsuro organizations, Doro had through their actions demonstrated that it had passed the point of no return: supporting the revised train drivers' work rules and the major rationalization measures, participating in the labour-management joint declaration, supporting inter-regional personnel movements, the secession from the General Council of Trade Unions of Japan (Sohyo), and the withdrawal of support for the JSP. At the time of JR Soren's inauguration, we expected the unions would take care to maintain a semblance of unity despite the differing legacies they had inherited from their former organizations, and as time passed, new employees would eventually account for the majority of union members and true unification would be realized.

But the situation did not develop as expected. The mutual distrust between former Tetsuro and Doro members came to surface again soon after the establishment of the JR companies and finally led to a split in the union. Now, sixteen years on, two labour union groups exist within the JR group reflecting the contrasting characteristics and philosophies of Tetsuro and Doro. The largest union group, the Japan Railway Trade Unions Confederation (JR Rengo), with 61,000 members as of November 2002, accounts for the majority of the union members of JR Central, JR West, JR Kyushu and JR Shikoku and is a minority within JR East, JR Hokkaido, and JR Freight. JR Rengo is now one of the major industrial unions under the umbrella of the Japanese Trade Union Confederation (Rengo). Their guiding principles are those of the democratic labour movement within the private sector, upholding the freedom of speech and criticism, and decision-making by a majority of elected representatives.

On the other hand, the union group which constitutes the majority of the members of JR East, JR Hokkaido, and JR Freight is the Japan Confederation of Railway Worker's Unions (JR Soren). The leadership of this organization consists of former Doro members who maintain hard line principles. How industrial relations will be influenced by the divided union structure is a critical issue for the future of the JR companies. The notion in the JNR era that the essence of managing JNR lay in managing labour relations fully reflected the characteristics of railway business. The same still holds true of the JR companies.

The way industrial relations develop will be determined not only by union activity but also by the attitude of management. In this regard, I would like to quote the words of Kamei Masao, chairman of JNR RAP:

> The substance of management can be summarized in three intrinsic rights: to determine personnel issues, to make capital expenditure decisions, and to set prices. Managers should protect these rights at the risk of their careers from interventions of any outside pressure, labout unions or politicians. Managers who allow labour unions to interfere with these issues should not be called managers

His words carry weight because he himself was directly engaged in industrial relations issues as Vice-Chairman of Nikkeiren, the employers' federation. This is sound advice and by sticking to it, management should be able to maintain sound labour-management relations.

3 Imperfect and unstable ownership of facilities and property

The break-up and privatization process was completed a little over one-and-a-half years from the announcement of the report by JNR RAP in July 1985. With so little time, emphasis was on speed rather than caution in the process to determine which one of JR companies would own which assets held by JNR. As far as personnel were concerned there could be no ambiguity. Every single worker was properly assigned to a new position in each of the JR companies and started to work on 1 April 1987. There were no dual or overlapping positions. As far as facilities and the property were concerned, however, the allocation process proved to be extremely difficult as in many cases, such as stations and the buildings around them, that were used jointly by several JR companies, drawing a clear line of ownership between them would have been a long and awkward process.

Ambiguous division of the facilities and the property would definitely cause trouble in future years. In principle, ownership of all assets should have been clearly determined in light of their use and the function after their division, with their use having clear legal definition. Practically speaking, however, it was impossible to do this so thoroughly in the time available. Those who were concerned, therefore, had to resort to expedience and stopgap measures. The ownership of assets commonly used by several functions within JNR was allocated to a certain successor company thought to be in the best position to manage the asset in question. It was then up to the new owner and the users to redefine the usage of the assets through new business agreements. A similar approach was taken in regard to sales and marketing arrangements between the firms. There was indeed an underlying sentimentality in the whole process with the JR companies being treated as the offspring of JNR who would amicably and flexibly use the assets after the break-up, as if they were brothers and sisters. The vague legal environment gave rise to many problems which would usually never occur among completely independent companies. My feeling is, however, that if we were able to assign all the JNR workers to their respective new employers, a complicated and difficult process made even more troublesome by having to respect the subjective wishes of the employees involved as to where they would like to work, then there is no reason why an equally thorough job could not have been done on the separation of assets. It would appear to be the result of wishful thinking bordering on negligence, and started with the assumption right from the outset that the listing of the three Honshu JR companies was not a real possibility. Some of this was put right as part of the revision of the JR Company Law in 2001, when some of the critical issues governing rights over assets was more clearly defined. Much vagueness remains, however, and until such time as these matters are completely resolved, the provision of basic services to passengers will be affected.

④ Political decision required to solve the problem of Japan Freight Railway Company

It is impossible to grasp the logic of JR Freight's establishment as a national operator. The decision was certainly not consistent with the overall logic of the break-up process. To break the freight company up into six regional companies along with the passenger companies would have been entirely rational as, in most cases, the transportation of bulky goods is conducted within one region. The operation of long-distance freight trains carrying containers and so forth could have been conducted across several JR companies: a fairly straightforward logistical matter. The JNR employees engaged in the freight division also wanted to have a unified, regional passenger and freight company: for them, the mix of passenger and freight work would provide more variety in their careers. This is how JNR had carried out its personnel rotation hitherto.

Notwithstanding these arguments, the separation of the freight division as one independent and nationally-operated company had been pre-ordained, and a team dispatched from the Ministry of Transport took the initiative in drafting the plans. The management of JNR's freight division had been against the regional break-up of the freight business and even before JNR RAP's report was released, supported their position by arguing that the operation of long-distance freight container trains required a national network. This argument was reflected in the report of JNR RAP, and thus no doubt contributed to the eventual decision to have the freight services operate as a single entity with a national network. It is perhaps also significant that the plan was conceived during the 'bubble economy' when land prices were skyrocketing. In this environment, there were some people who thought it plausible that the freight company could turn itself into a real estate developer and use its vast land holdings for commercial purposes. However, it gradually became clear that it was a combination of the interests of the private freight forwarding companies (e.g. Nippon Express) and the concerns of the management of JNR's freight division that were the driving force behind this plan. It was feared that if the freight division was divided regionally as with the passenger division, the freight division of each newly created JR company would be treated very much as the poor relation on account of its low profitability, and would continually be restructured, gradually diminishing in size and importance.

The private freight forwarding companies and the JNR freight division apparently overreacted to what they saw as the 'euthanasia of the freight companies', and put strong pressure on the Ministry of Transport to agree to a single, national freight entity. A professor of transport economics, who was closely involved in this process, recounted that Hirose Shinichi, the Chairman of Nippon Express (the largest private freight forwarder in Japan), who had been a former Administrative Vice-minister of Transport, with the cooperation of a former subordinate at the ministry, who was a Director in charge of relations with JNR, were the main forces behind the establishment of JR Freight. The main actors in this drama were Hirose, Tanahashi and his ally within JNR the then Executive Vice-President Hashimoto Masashi. The fact that they became the successive presidents of troubled JR Freight, i.e. Hashimoto followed by Tanahashi, fits in with this explanation. In recent years, JR Freight has been suffering from a gradual decline of freight volume and chronic losses. Moreover, accidents have recently been on the increase because of poor maintenance and insufficient training of workers. The passenger companies should be greatly concerned by this development as passenger trains and freight trains run on the same conventional track. I would, therefore, like to take this opportunity to lay out some structural and theoretical issues related to the establishment of JR Freight:

(1) As the passenger companies own the track and the freight company has the right to rent it, how access charges are set is obviously a critical matter. These are based on 'avoidable costs', a technical term meaning, in this case, 'the expenses that could be avoided if the freight business were to be abolished'. This concept is applied when trying to determine how to allocate production costs between a main product and by-products when one company produces multiple products using the same production facility, and only has validity when the production facilities have excess capacity. With fluctuations in sales of a company's main product, they will adjust production levels of the by-products in order to maximize profitability. Close coordination of the production levels of the various products is therefore critical in the process of profit maximization. Pricing on the basis of marginal, or 'avoidable' costs is often done by companies that are trying to recover as much fixed cost as possible by raising even slightly the utilization rate of facilities with excessive production capacity. JR Freight is an example of an independent company established by the government to produce only by-products, with pricing and production levels being rigidly determined and virtually imposed on the JR passenger companies by the government: surely something unique in the business world. The Tokaido Line,[5] the busiest and most profitable freight line, for instance, operates at full capacity with an extremely congested passenger time-table. Securing time for essential maintenance is therefore very difficult. In such an instance, there is no excess capacity of which advan-

---

[5] This is the conventional line between Tokyo and Osaka (actually, Kobe, located near Osaka) and should not be confused with the Tokaido Shinkansen.

tage can be taken to recover even the smallest portion of fixed costs.

(2) In reality, there is a big difference between the actual access charges paid to the passenger companies and avoidable costs. Taking one example, the amount of repairs a track requires is obviously determined by how much they are damaged by train operations. Except for a few night trains, passenger trains are all electrified and use lightweight EMU technology, causing little physical degradation to facilities such as track. On the other hand, the damage caused by freight trains, which are much heavier and consist of a large number of connected rolling stock pulled by a locomotive, is quite substantial. In the case of the Tokaido Line, with 200 freight trains running in both directions daily, most of the damage is therefore caused by freight trains. It follows that the majority of repair costs for track on lines like the Tokaido can be avoided if freight trains do not run and such costs can therefore be described as avoidable costs for the passenger train company. Repair costs for tracks, overhead lines and other facilities caused by damage from freight trains on the Tokaido Line is estimated to amount to ¥30 billion ($250 mn) every year. By contrast, the access charges are only around ¥3.5 billion ($29.2 mn) per year. This is only one of many irrational cases, and there is no other way to describe this phenomenon than a compulsory transfer of wealth from the passenger companies to the freight company enforced by the government. It is difficult to conclude that a company which has an irrational burden like this imposed by the government is completely privatized. What kind of explanation can be made to shareholders? It is a particularly damning indictment of the reform process that a small group of people in JNR, the bureaucracy and the distribution industry, pushing their own particular agendas, and disregarding national consensus, could produce such an outcome.

As JR Freight has already started operations as an independent company, it makes no sense to argue the case from square one. However, this problem was created by government interference in the privatization process and their misjudgement as to what was required for the freight business to become a viable entity. It is therefore the government's responsibility to seek a solution, one that takes into account the reality of the situation and the original purpose of JNR's privatization.

(3) Industry experts are often heard to say that increased dependence on railway freight would conserve energy and therefore reduce the overall burden on the environment. I cannot help having the impression that these arguments just popped into their heads without serious thinking. In order to support such arguments, it is necessary to carry out the following quantitative analysis: how much CO_2 emissions would be produced by other modes of freight transportation (e.g., trucks and ships) transporting cargo from the freight stations to their point of delivery; how much capacity does railway freight have in the current situation to meet increasing demand, if any; how much additional capital expenditure would be required to improve rail freight infrastructure and capacity; what are the inherent fixed costs and how should freight rates be structured to cover these costs; how much economic benefit can the people enjoy through increased railway freight; how can we calculate the total unit distribution costs by train, truck and ship.

Given Japan's industrial structure, and its likely future course, what are the prospects of rail freight set against truck and sea freight? The establishment of a single, national freight company has reduced the flexibility of rail freight. The majority of the idle land, which was created as a result of the closedown of freight yards and depots, has been transferred to the JNR Settlement Corporation or sold to make up for some of the losses incurred by JR Freight. JR Freight, therefore, is no longer the mass transportation organization it used to be. JR Freight can have a bright future only if the role it is expected to play is properly defined and its raison d'être clarified. It is the responsibility of the government to do this, in particular to examine its role in the context of the entire freight market in Japan and its likely future development. According to legal statute, JR Freight is expected to aim for a stock market listing in the future. However, considering the situation of access charges and the state of the rail freight market, the prospect of a listing is completely unrealistic, so much so as to make a mockery of the law in which this objective is laid out.

⑤ Peach and plum blossoms: the future of Japan's railway industry

As explained above, the privatization of JNR and the establishment of the new JR framework was achieved through a process in which many compromises were made and was by no means 'perfect'. However, it is significant that the reform succeeded in correcting the fundamental defects that had plagued JNR. The Chinese saying, 'With the root established, the tree will grow' is quite appropriate in summing up the reform of JNR. Although the JR system was born needing life-support at the beginning, at least the three Honshu JR companies have made great progress for fifteen years and have established a sufficiently stable platform to enable the government to sell off their entire holdings of these companies. With the break-up and privatization of JNR we had 'the root established', and we were able to build a solid foundation and from this 'the tree will grow'. The objectives have been achieved, more successfully than most expected.

JNR was weighed down by a myriad of restrictions that were imposed to ensure that the company fulfilled its 'public mission' and it was this factor that ultimately caused the collapse of its management structure. However, it was the critical importance of this very same public mission which justified the enormous financial burden imposed upon taxpayers and passengers to finance JNR's reform and regeneration. The idea of the public mission was very much woven into the fabric of the newly-born JR companies.

In May 2001, I had the opportunity to deliver a welcome speech to the newly-hired graduates who were starting their careers at JR Central. Thirty-eight years had passed since President Sogo had addressed us. Fate had determined that it was my turn to speak.

JR Central has made steady progress and there are currently no indications that things will change. We are responsible for the operation of Japan's most vital transportation artery that is at the heart of the nation's social and economic activity. We have verified that nothing can compete with our Shinkansen for reliability and safety. The 500 km between Tokyo and Osaka that make up the Tokaido Shinkansen and is served by JR Central is the optimal distance for rail transportation. The scale of the transportation density is perhaps unique in the world and the combination of these factors has enabled the Tokaido Shinkansen to overwhelm other modes of transport in terms of speed, efficiency, flexibility and cost. So long as these conditions continue to hold, our *raison d'être* will also remain unassailable. Since the establishment of JR Central, we have sought relentlessly to extend the advantage our services enjoy with constant improvements. With the completion of the part of Shinagawa Station serving the Tokaido Shinkansen scheduled for Autumn 2003, access to the Tokaido Shinkansen for passengers in the western part of Tokyo will be greatly enhanced. At the same time, all Shinkansen services will operate at 270 km (168 m) per hour. Currently the Nozomi Shinkansen runs twice-hourly in both directions, but this will be increased to seven per hour. As a result, the relative advantage of the Tokaido Shinkansen over airlines in terms of services and cost will become even greater. It will have taken fifteen years to complete the new Shinagawa Station and to realize the plan to operate all Shinkansen services at 270 km (168 m) per hour, both of which were launched soon after the company was established in 1987. This is a clear illustration of what is required in the management of the railway business: a broad, long-term perspective combined with a great deal of persistence. With this recognition, we will continue our efforts to develop new technologies, make the appropriate investments to improve and maintain our facilities, and to provide safe, accurate, reliable and comfortable service for passengers.

The final essential prerequisite is the human factor, the loyalty, skills and morale of our employees. This human factor, combined with the judgement of the management and improvement of facilities, can work together to establish a permanent advantage over competitors and further enhance our raison d'être. Whether the privatization of JNR was perfect or only a product of compromises ultimately is not the point. There is a famous phrase in the Chinese classic The Book of History by which we should be guided: 'Although Peach and Plum Blossoms Do Not Speak, a Path Will Naturally Appear Underneath Them.' (In other words, if you produce something of beauty, a small road is formed naturally by people who are attracted to it.)

In some ways this expression is quite similar to 'Fight to the death with a rail as your pillow,' a phrase I heard as a young man which I now recall with a sense of nostalgia.

▶ *Appendix I*

Panel discussion on rail privatization held in Frankfurt, 6 September 2002

PARTICIPANTS

YK   – Yoshiyuki **Kasai**, President, Central Japan Railway Company
DS   – Diethelm **Sack**, CFO, Deutsche Bahn AG
SR   – Sir Steve **Robson**, non-executive director of Cazenove and former Director of Finance, Regulation and Industry of the UK Treasury
DF   – David **Freud**, UBS Warburg

DF: In his book, Mr Kasai has given an excellent account of the rationale for and the history of railway privatization in Japan. Mr Kasai has offered us valuable insights into the way the privatization approach in Japan was worked out between the JNR management and the political decision-makers and into the issues that were encountered in a number of areas such as finance and industrial relations. The purpose of today's discussion is to compare a number of key issues of railway privatizations across different countries: the UK, where the ownership of Railtrack is currently being restructured, Germany, where Deutsche Bahn is preparing for its privatization and Japan where the remaining shares held by the government are now being sold.

Let's start with the objectives of railway privatization. What benefits of rail privatization were foreseen in Japan and the UK and what would they be in Germany? So I think we start off with Mr Kasai.

YK: I would like to highlight three aspects: the enormous debt burden of ¥25 trillion ($208.3 bn) accumulated during the Japanese National Railways (JNR) era, the issue of political interference and the need to increase productivity. With hindsight, the privatization and break-up of JNR was the only comprehensive solution to reducing the railway debt by transferring part of it to the government and also to make sure that debt levels remain healthy in the future. Without the initial reduction in debt, there would have been no future for the railways in Japan. Naturally, privatization forced us to maintain a healthy balance sheet, and, therefore, the initial privatization approach had to ensure that the burden of cross-subsidizing railway networks in less populated areas was kept to a reasonable level. This was a central theme in the privatization of JNR, which eventually created the need to break up JNR in commercially viable entities operating in Honshu, where traffic density is sufficiently high, and entities in less populated areas like Hokkaido, Kyushu and Shikoku, where it is virtually impossible to operate a sizeable railway network at a profit unless you can adjust wages and other cost items. Another benefit was the reduction of political interference in management: prior to privatization management had to attend Diet sessions on, say, 200 days a year to answer what were very often meaningless questions. Politicians intervened regularly in key management issues, for example, investment plans, setting of fares and wages and other operational aspects. Finally, we could halve our head-count, from 400,000 to 200,000.

DF: What were the objectives of privatization in the UK and how far were they achieved?

SR: Well, I think the motivation for privatization in the UK was to improve efficiency and also to improve service to the users of the railways. Those improvements were seen to come from replacing the flawed structure of state ownership, and the flaws in state ownership. I think, there were seen to be four, some of which have been mentioned already. Firstly, there was a lack of clarity about the objectives of all enterprises in the state sector in the UK, and hence, there was no definition of success and so no real accountability for performance. The second problem, was the interference in the activities of the enterprises by civil servants and politicians, which is obviously part of the lack of clarity of objectives. The third aspect, I think, was that the public sector generally in the UK is motivated by aversion to risk and this means that it is motivated to avoid doing new and different things and if you want to improve anything, you've got to do new and different things, so effectively it was motivated not to improve. And finally the finances of state enterprises in the UK are often constrained by the state's own fiscal position.

Now, privatization caused a shift from that environment to an environment where the objectives were clear. There was a more balanced incentive set because there was reward for success as well as punishment for failure. And, finally, the finances were determined by the performance of the privatized entity without reference to the state's own fiscal position. So you changed a debilitating environment for the enterprise into one which was potentially empowering and this change, in general, led to an improvement in efficiency and customer service. And, indeed, for the rail industry prior to November 2000 privatization was having some of the same effects, although the improvement in performance wasn't as marked as we might have hoped.

DF: Let's go to Germany where the railway activities have been incorporated in separate subsidiaries under the umbrella of Deutsche Bahn AG's ownership, but where the share capital of Deutsche Bahn is still fully state-owned. How much of what has been said previously do you recognize in terms of Deutsche Bahn's current situation?

DS: I believe there are a lot of parallels between Deutsche Bahn and the situation prior to privatization in Japan. Political interference has been high in the past. A steady decrease in market share, combined with extremely low efficiency, resulted in an operating loss of about €8 billion p.a. and a combined debt position of €34 billion at the end of 1993. The finances we obtained from the government were not used for maintenance and modernization but to pay interest. This caused a vicious cycle with service quality deteriorating and accumulated debt increasing to astronomical levels. Everybody was clear this process had to be stopped. So what we did was to reduce the debt and to form a company which could potentially become a player in the transportation market. Finally, we also aimed at reducing rail services in areas where they were not needed. But the main objectives were reducing the debt burden and increasing or stabilizing market shares. And to this end it was decided that Deutsche Bahn had to be run like a private-sector company.

DF: What did you gain from incorporation, considering that your shares are still fully owned by the government?

DS: First of all, there is the change in mentality, which in our case led to an increase in productivity: by approximately 160% in eight years. Due to improvements in efficiency we are now generating positive operating cash-flows, which help us funding new investments, e.g., in new rolling stock, in infrastructure and in remodelling our train stations. We are also well positioned to tap the capital markets to finance major investment projects. All this leads to a much better service for our customers. Secondly, there is less interference from the politicians. We believe that transportation functions just as any other market and the public interest can be protected through industry regulation.

DF: Why couldn't the German approach have worked for British Rail?

SR: What we have in Germany is a state-owned rail monopoly which operates partly at arms' length from the government, but which is still in the public sector.

One thing that was driving us in the UK was the experience of earlier privatizations where we had seen that moving entities from the public sector to the private sector did improve performance, did improve efficiency, and did improve customer service. This improvement was much greater if that change was associated with the introduction of competition into the activity concerned. So we sought to create a structure for the railways which was not simply moving from the public sector to the private sector, but was also introducing, as far as possible, competition which in some cases was competition in the market-place and sometimes was competition for franchises to run trains for a period. And I suppose the best way to illustrate that is by pointing out that when we started the privatization, British Rail was a monopoly employing about 120,000 people, whereas at the end of the privatization the only monopoly element left was Railtrack employing some 10,000 people. That was a very fundamental part of the process because it was seen as the way to get the most improvement in efficiency and customer service.

DS: I believe that introducing competition through privatization is somewhat tricky in the case of railways, at least in Germany. In order to create competition, operators and investors need to be convinced that operating a railway can be a profitable business. There is a major difference to other privatized state monopolies, for example in the telecom or electricity sector, because these businesses have always been highly profitable due to their high user tariffs. No private-sector entity would have been interested in running a railway business in Germany prior to 1993, given the disastrous state the railway was in. The progress Deutsche Bahn has made since incorporation has demonstrated that it is indeed possible to run a railway network and generate profits, which in turn has created competition in areas such as local passenger services and increased competition in freight services. The idea of breaking up the railways for the sake of introducing competition seems to me somewhat far-fetched, especially if one considers all the complications that come with it.

DF: Let's move on to discuss the various types of privatization. Mr Kasai, in Japan you went the regional approach – keeping an integrated company but dividing it into essentially three majors – and one of the things that you describe in the book is how you managed to push the speed of the Shinkansen from 220 to 270km/h. Your view is that you were only able to do that very complicated exercise because you had been broken up into regions, rather than being the old JNR monolith, private or public. Could you explain why that was the case.

YK: In the JNR era, we used to invest about ¥40 billion p.a. in the Tokaido Shinkansen. After privatization, we could increase investments to ¥90 billion, because we could invest the cash-flow generated by the Tokaido Shinkansen which had been hitherto used to subsidize unprofitable networks, for example in Hokkaido in the northern part of Japan. Part of these funds are invested into a new Shinkansen terminal in Shinagawa in Central Tokyo, which will open in Autum 2003 and will further enhance our market position *vis-à-vis* other transportation modes, e.g. domestic air travel. In addition, we have been investing ¥50 billion per annum (a total of ¥800 billion by the end of 2003) to increase the operating speed of the Shinkansen from 220 km/h to 270 km/h. These investments are absolutely critical to retain the competitiveness of the Tokaido Shinkansen.

DF: Let's go to Germany now because you have set your eye very much on remaining an integrated national railway. So you would disagree with Mr Kasai on the benefits of regionalization?

DS: In Germany the situation is slightly different: first, because the local governments have funds available to order local passenger services, and second, because we now have considerable freedom to abolish unprofitable services. Until 1993 the local passenger services were financed by the federal state, and there were considerable fears that a lot of these services would be abolished following the incorporation of Deutsche Bahn. To solve this conflict of interest, the finances of local lines were transferred to the regional governments, who in turn received the right to restructure their operations. The regional governments so far prefer to have an integrated operation of local and long-distance passenger services, which is one reason why Deutsche Bahn operates a nationwide rail network.

But we have taken a number of decisions in terms of closing unprofitable lines, both in freight and in long-distance passenger services, which has resulted in a lot of pressure from the press and the general public over the last two years. But in the long term, there is no benefit from running some of these unprofitable lines. We have already realized the first and second step of our programme to close uneconomical lines, and we expect to complete this programme by the end of this year.

YK: In Japan, the original idea behind the regional break-up was to have each passenger company set their own fares – according to their cost and revenue profile – and service standards and let the passengers decide whether they would like to use the service or not. In reality, the three regional railway companies continue to receive indirect state subsidies in order to support low fares and existing service standards. So, if we had had the opportunity to terminate unprofitable services, we may not have considered a regional break-up of JNR. But the political reality was and is that there would be no massive closure of lines.

DF: Let us move on to the issue of asset separation. I already know the views from Japan and Germany, but I think before we get them, it's up to Steve to say why the British went the disaggregated route rather than, say, the regional route when the privatization decision was taken.

SR: Well, part of the reason goes back to my earlier description of what we were seeking to do which was to introduce competition and the regional model would have meant regional monopolies as opposed to a national monopoly with the same intrinsic problems. There was a second layer of problems which was related to the very complex structure of the rail network in the UK. There was no regional breakdown in which you could have given regional companies some track on which only their trains ran. You were inevitably going to have regional breakdowns where a particular company's trains, first of all, ran on other people's tracks part of the time and other people's trains ran on its track part of the time, and there were two problems seen with that. One is potentially an anti-competitive one, namely if someone's else train is trying to get across your track you are potentially going to give precedence to your own trains and to disruption of service to the detriment of the other providers. And the other is a safety one. I have to say that this was a British Rail view and British Rail was strongly opposed to the break-up, so this was not a view they would have advanced lightly, which was there would be very real safety issues as a train was handed over to the controllers in one region as it passed to controllers in another region as the train crossed from one region's track to another region's track. So the decision turned on this combination of a dislike of the monopoly element, a dislike of the potentially anti-competitive element and a concern about the safety. And it all flowed from the complexity of the network in the UK.

DF: The regional solution wasn't there.

SR: Well it was there, but it was there at a real price.

DF: Let's ask President Kasai. Do you think it was a mistake to go on the disaggregated approach in the UK?

YK: From our experience in Japan, I am led to conclude that it would be very difficult to make integrated decisions in a functionally separated railway system like the one we have in the UK. For example, to increase the speed of our Tokaido Shinkansen we needed to develop and invest in new rolling stock, reinforce the ground facilities and, at the same time, re-model the operations and the timetable. Infrastructure, rolling stock and operations all have to be adjusted in an integrated manner to be able to eventually deliver a high-quality service, in particular a punctual service. I am not sure this would be possible if infrastructure and operations belonged to different companies.

DF: If what you say about integration is a kind of necessity, you just can't get separate bodies to bring about improvement.

SR: If one looks around other parts of the economy you can see examples of industries where there are interdependencies between assets which are owned by different operators, and where cooperation is possible. For example, airlines need airports, but airports are not owned by airlines. In the UK, someone who produces gas needs to be able to get gas to the home, but that doesn't mean the gas producer owns the infrastructure of the Lattice Group or the regional distribution, so the idea that you can have industries which are interdependent and can operate perfectly satisfactorily with different parts of the industry in different ownerships seems to me to be demonstrated in other areas of the economy and I don't think the railway industry is that different.

DF: Mr Sack what do you think? What's special about the railway industry that makes it different?

DS: I think there is a much stronger link between operations and infrastructure in the railway industry compared to other industries. The quality of a railway service is basically a function of punctuality which in turn is dependent on the efficiency of the infrastructure. If you are not able to manage the infrastructure yourself, not only the capital expenditure but also the day-to-day running of the tracks, you are in no position to improve or to even guarantee a certain service level to your customers. If a train is late, customers don't ask whether it was the infrastructure company's or the railway station's fault. The train operator is answerable to the customer. So the main backbone of the 'production system' in the case of railways is the infrastructure.

SR: But the same is true, for example, in the electricity industry. It is even more complicated because you can't actually slow the electrons down in the wires. You can slow the trains down if necessary or speed them up. It doesn't mean that to get the necessary level of service and costs to the customer that the whole electricity system needs to be in one ownership. In fact, it would appear in quite a lot of countries it's rather better off when it's not in one ownership. I would have thought that actually managing an electricity group is even more complicated than managing a railway group.

DS: I think I should mention two issues here that have particular importance in the railway industry. First, there is a lot of manual work required on the track, especially in the case of very busy lines. This is more complicated to manage in the case of railways, because the infrastructure is used by different types of rolling stock, e.g., express trains, local trains, freight trains etc. Second, the interdependencies are much more pronounced than in other industries. As Mr Kasai mentioned before, investing into a new line requires an integrated decision-making process for both the rolling stock and the infrastructure. The same is true for a myriad of other areas, for example, technical advice and maintenance. If the infrastructure is not well maintained, it causes damage to the rolling stock; and vice versa, if rolling stock is not maintained appropriately it will damage the tracks leading to an increase in infrastructure costs. To integrate rolling stock and infrastructure is not just a strategic matter, it is part of our day-to-day business.

DF: Mr Kasai, what do you think of this?

YK: In rail transport, ground facilities (e.g. track bed, track, signal system and stations) and train operations are inextricably interwoven. In the case of highways for example, management of ground facilities and ownership and operation of vehicles is like an open system, i.e., vehicle owners can use the roads based on pre-agreed rules. There is obviously hardly any need for coordinating vehicle operation and road management, which is very different from railways. The Japanese bureaucrats are now discussing the possibility of a functional break-up of the Japanese electricity industry. I don't think such a system is really going to function well in the long term.

Furthermore, free access to infrastructure is in my opinion not the most optimal way to increase efficiency.

DF: Let Steve have the last word on this. You've have had fierce opposition.

SR: Well, in terms of the separation of the electricity industry, we've got it in the UK. We've had it for twelve years and the system works incredibly well. And service standards have gone up and prices have come down and down and down. And, as I say, I think it is actually more challenging to run an electricity system because you can't change the speed at which electrons move like you can change the speed of trains, than it is to run a railway system. If you can disintegrate an electricity system, then you can disintegrate a railway system.

DF: That was the theory. In practice what happened was the big failure in Railtrack. One major reason seemed to be that it lost control of the quality of its maintenance. And that created all kinds of crises, and that is where the British experiment blew up. So I think the question is was that an inevitability of the system or was it just an incompetence of the particular example of Railtrack?

SR: It is clear that incompetence is part of the story, but there are other probably more important aspects of it too, although I don't think any of them were inevitable.

DF: What do you think, Mr Kasai?

YK: I think a major issue in case of Railtrack was that the facilities it had inherited were relatively old. In contrast, the old JNR invested around ¥1 trillion p.a. until 1980, meaning that at the time of the privatization the facilities were modernised and well-maintained. Following privatization Railtrack had the enormous task of upgrading many of the old facilities, and I continue to believe that a functionally separated railway is not an ideal framework for achieving such a large-scale upgrade. In addition, there were many rail operators using the same tracks. That must have added to the complexity in managing the infrastructure. In the case of the Tokaido Shinkansen it would be unthinkable that other Shinkansen operators, e.g. JR East would use our tracks to operate their trains. First of all, because some of the specifications are different, but even if it was possible it would almost certainly result in confusion and inefficiencies. We would prefer not to have other operators using our track for the reasons explained by Mr Sack earlier.

DF: Mr Sack, is that what you think? Was it the system?

DS: British Rail was in a similar situation as most other European railway operators, for example in France, Germany or Belgium. If the infrastructure is very old it is important to focus investment at critical points. For example, we had to spend about €40 billion on improving infrastructure and stations over the last eight years because after the war investment had been severely neglected. The UK government spent substantial sums on subsidising train operators, but because of vertical separation there was no guarantee that an adequate share of these funds would be invested in the infrastructure. So in order to use public money effectively, it is critical to have a vertically integrated railway. Secondly, the management of Deutsche Bahn AG is still convinced that vertical separation is not workable in the long term. This view has been formed over many years of improving the railway system in Germany. If you look at the US, Canada, Japan, you will not be able to find a precedent for a privatised railway which is vertically separated.

DF: I think we have exhausted that subject, so we should probably move on. One of the interesting things in Mr Kasai's book, I think, is the discussion of what happened to the debt. In Japan, the newly created JRs were handed huge amounts of debt and it was not forgiven, although in some ways you say that might have been rather helpful to concentrate the mind. But let's ask the question. In the UK, the railway was shrunk to a minute capital base, about £2-2.5 billion I think from memory, with very little debt. Similarly, in Germany there was a huge debt-forgiveness programme and the size of the financial burden was very substantially reduced. So Japan is very different in the financial restructuring approach that had been taken.

YK: In relative terms, there may not have been such a big difference between Japan and the rest, because our high revenues could support very high debt levels. This comes back to the issue of traffic density, and we are fortunate enough to have very high passenger volumes on many major lines. In the case of the UK or Germany, railways are less profitable due to lower passenger volumes, meaning that a certain amount of debt forgiveness is essential to make privatization work. However, at the time of privatization no one can predict exactly what the revenues of the privatized company are going to be, say, in five to ten years, so taking on a lot of debt basically means taking on risk as well. Hence, we would have of course welcomed a certain amount of debt forgiveness.

DS: We were completely released from all legacy debt at the end of 1993, but in return we were obliged to finance all the investments necessary to modernize the rolling stock, main stations, and last but not least we had to shoulder the burden of integrating the East-German Deutsche Reichsbahn. Without the debt forgiveness, we would have had to spend our cash-flow on servicing the legacy debt with no room for further investment. The debt-forgiveness programme enabled us to invest a total of about €60 billion in the railway system.

DF: Steve, what do you think now of the decision to have a very small capital base?

SR: The capital base wasn't artificially small in the sense that it was what was left after you stripped down all the other bits of the railways, e.g. the rolling stock, the operations, the maintenance and so forth. So you were left with an entity that had a certain enterprise value. We saw the historic level of debt as totally irrelevant. We looked at the cash-flow over the next five or so years, taking account of the likely internal cash generation, the investment programme that Railtrack thought it needed to undertake and the likely levels of dividends and everything else that goes into cash-flow and deciding whether or not within that cash-flow there was scope for it to service some level of debt because if there was (a) we thought it would increase overall the receipts for the government and (b) if it looked as though the cash-flow was too lax the investing community might actually reduce the rating of the company rather than increase it because they had seen how previous privatization companies, which had turned out to have an insufficiently geared balance sheet, had gone and spent their money rather recklessly and actually had produced nothing for the shareholders as a result. So we tried to get a level of gearing which could be handled within the cash-flow and which would give investors some confidence that the management would stick to its business and give us the best proceeds.

DF: The problem in the UK, or one of them, was that the companies' balance sheet or just its capital base was so small relative to the kind of expenditure that we are now talking about. I think Railtrack started off with a £2.5 billion capital base where a project like the West Coast mainline is costing in excess of £10 billion, so quite simply, it had a capital base out of scale with the immensity of its spending requirement.

SR: We had the capital base that was in scale with its spending requirement as seen at the time. One of the things that wasn't foreseen at the time was the growth in the volume of passenger and freight activity that happened with privatization. Prior to privatization, the railways had been in relative decline in terms of passengers and freight, however, about four years following privatization, both grew by about 30%. The need for investment in enhancements and, as you were saying, higher maintenance suddenly became much greater than had been foreseen. I don't think that in the right environment that could not have been handled. The trouble was that the privatization approach we adopted for the railways in the UK did not provide the right incentives. At the time this was becoming apparent, the UK regulator started to behave in a less predictable and less stable fashion and the new government introduced a new agency into the game called the Strategic Rail Authority. Suddenly, you had a number of agencies operating without clarity about what their roles and responsibility were; consequently, you had a degree of political involvement which was rising quite rapidly. I think in that the management at Railtrack became quite distracted from the job of running the railways into a job of trying to deal with these agencies. They lost control of their costs whether it was the costs of maintenance, the costs of their response to the Hatfield crash or the costs of the West Coast mainline and from that point the rest is history, as they say.

DF: Let's move on to the question of new projects and ask whether they can be done in the private sector because it's very noticeable that the Japanese railway system was basically a modern system. What's your view Mr Kasai? Is it possible to undertake a major rail project in the private sector?

YK: If we are talking about constructing a completely new line, the answer is clearly no. For example, a new line, like the Chuo Shinkansen between Tokyo and Osaka, would cost about ¥8 trillion. Now consider the benefits: part of it goes to the user who pays a fare, but the greater part – the external benefit – goes to the local economy or even national economy and can only be collected through taxes. To justify a project of this scale both external benefits and user benefit have to be compared to the total cost, which implies that the state must also have a key role in financing such a project. At the time of our privatization, the construction of Japan's rail infra-structure network was thought to be complete. The major task left for the JR companies was to operate the existing rail network effi-ciently and improve the rolling stock, the facilities and access for passengers. The Chuo Shinkansen would be direct competition for the Tokaido Shinkansen implying double capacity between Tokyo and Osaka at first, until passenger numbers would increase gradually in one, two or three decades up to full capacity utilization. In other words, a lot of capital needs to be invested up-front to achieve the desired economic impact in the long term. Therefore, large-scale infrastructure projects of strategic importance to the nation, for example railway lines, roads and airports should be financed by the state, and while part of the funds can be collected through fares, the rest has to be financed through taxes.

DF: Mr Sack, what do you think? If Deutsche Bahn were listed, could you build a new line?

DS: In theory, the railway could finance large-scale investments by simply increasing fares, but in practice, most railway users would avoid paying high fares by using cars. In Germany, the total road capacity is about ten times higher than the capacity of the railway and there are no tolls. Hence, trucks and passenger cars can use the infrastructure without paying for it. In such a situation, it is impossible to construct a new line, such as our new high-speed rail link between Cologne and

Frankfurt with private sector funds, because the line could not compete with cars. Consequently, providing the necessary infrastructure is the government's responsibility. We spend about €1.25 billion p.a. on maintenance and small re-investments and this has to be paid out of the operating cash flow. But a new line would be impossible to finance within the current transportation framework.

SR: By and large, most of the big rail projects that I see and looked at in the past aren't paid for out of the fare box. You have to pay in the external benefits. Almost all those external benefits arise because road transport doesn't pay its costs. If road transport paid its external costs in terms of environmental damage and congestion, then there would be no external benefits worth paying for in rail projects and you could build a lot of rail projects in that environment out of the fare box. But because road transport doesn't carry its external costs, if you're going to build rail projects, the only way you can do it is through government money.

DF: I think that's the basic consensus there. One more interesting thing that has happened in Europe in the last weeks is that Deutsche Bahn has bought Stinnes whose main asset is Schenker. Schenker operates a hub-and-spoke network of road trucking services which traditionally has competed with the rail. So I think it would be interesting for Mr Sack to describe the rationale to that in railway terms and then we can ask for comments from the others.

DS: As I mentioned earlier, we operate a very high volume of freight, mainly steel, coal and capital goods, derived from 400 or 500 customers. To create a commercially attractive freight business, we needed a much wider customer base in a broader range of industries, customers operating on a pan-European basis and an extended range of services. We also needed advanced logistics know-how. Schenker offers all of that. For example, Schenker is very strong in the automotive industry, in the electronics business, in inventory management and other logistics services, and they have sufficient global reach. With Schenker we now have a European-wide sales force, which can generate additional load for our railway freight business.

YK: In Japan, the amount of freight moved by the railways is very small compared to Germany and most European countries. At the time of the privatization, we proposed to break-up JNR's freight division together with the passenger business which would have resulted in a number of integrated passenger and freight businesses, but as I have described in the book, the logistics lobby succeeded in preserving the pre-privatization structure of the freight business. JNR's freight business had suffered enormously from the ongoing labour disputes prior to privatization, and even after privatization the freight company's competitiveness has been diminishing constantly. When I was younger, the freight division was still a remarkable business, and we often discussed the rationale for acquiring one of the large Honshu freight forwarders, for example Nippon Express. If we had been in a position to combine the freight business with a logistics business at that time, I am sure we would have been able to improve performance significantly. Because we were a public sector company at that time, we could not buy it, and now I would think it is too late to make such a drastic step.

DF: So you actually were looking to buy the equivalent logistics capability if you could have.

YK: Correct, if we had had the opportunity thirty years ago, i.e. in the early '70s, because at that time the rail freight service was still very important in Japan. At present, bulk cargo is being moved along the seashore and high value goods are moved on trucks because they require timely delivery. For example, in the automotive industry, inventory is a critical cost item because parts and raw materials are of very high value. That is why even thirty years ago the automotive industry hardly used JNR's freight service. In the case of rail transport, we could have promised delivery on a certain day, but a truck company could promise delivery within a thirty-minute time-frame. Hence, while railway transportation was cheaper than trucks, inventory costs would have risen enormously. Given the rise in value of parts and other commodities over the last 30 years and the change in the structure of the Japanese industry, I am sure that the railway freight business in Japan will continue to lose its importance and, therefore, it does not make sense to acquire additional logistics capabilities.

DF: Steve, what do you make of this?

SR: All I would say is that if I were someone running a German freight-forwarding company, and I saw the federal railway system buy one of my competitors, I would feel rather worried about whether competition in the freight forwarding industry was going to be as fair as it might be.

DF: It is interesting that we now have the two big logistics networks in Central Europe – they are more than freight forwarders – essentially owned by the German government. The Schenker network is owned by Deutsche Bahn and the Danzas network is owned by Deutsche Post. So it is a rather peculiar competitive situation there. I don't know what the government thinks of that.

DS: Well, in both cases the government had no concerns. Deutsche Post is already listed and it is commonly known that the government intends to sell its remaining shares subject to market conditions. Similarly, in the case of Deutsche Bahn, the basic direction is that the company will be privatized and listed in the near future. The restructuring process prior to privatization simply requires acquisitions of private sector companies, and the acquisition of Stinnes was a unique opportunity to strengthen our freight business. If we had waited for another four or five years, this opportunity would have been lost with potentially serious consequences for the freight business. I don't think this transaction creates unfair competition. Danzas and Stinnes are very large and attractive companies, so it was clear that they would come at a certain price, and there are only a few players globally who can pay that kind of price. We all know that the logistics business has been consolidating over the last two to three years and we foresee this trend to continue over the next two to three years.

DF: You have all agreed earlier that the state has got to support the railway business one way or another. Could we just discuss what is the most efficient way for the state to support the railway industry. Do you want to start Mr Kasai?

YK: The construction or fundamental improvement of infrastructure has to be financed by the state. But as far as the efficiency of the operations is concerned, I don't see any reason why the state should interfere with that. For example, our company is planning to construct what we call the new Chuo Shinkansen Line, which will run from Tokyo through the mountainous areas West of Tokyo all the way to Osaka in one hour using our latest super-conducting

Maglev technology. Of course, if this line is not going to be constructed, it won't compete with our existing Tokaido Shinkansen Line which will be forever profitable. But if it is constructed, it would be potentially very important for Japan as a whole because it will support the development of new technologies and thereby strengthen the Japanese industry and create the potential to develop the area between Tokyo and Osaka. The government has granted us the right to operate both the Chuo and the Tokaido Shinkansen. But to be clear, this would be a very complex and difficult situation for us. We are currently in the process of developing a financial framework which will satisfy both the national interest as well as the interests of our shareholders; however it is very clear that the government pays at least for the infrastructure.

DF: Mr Sack, what do you make of that? What's the most efficient way?

DS: Deutsche Bahn is in the process of privatization and we have a mandate from the state to compete with other players in the transportation market. Consequently, the government should not continue to financially support the railway. In general, there are a number of serious issues related to traffic and transportation throughout Europe which need to be addressed urgently. There is a steady increase in passenger and freight services both on roads and railways and also in air freight. What the government can do is to come up with a basic policy about an optimal transportation framework for the future. The best support for us would then be to internalize some of the external costs caused by roads as we discussed earlier. But this needs to be a pan-European process. Mobility is very important for a modern society, and hence, it is time the governments paid more attention to transportation issues. If the basic framwork remains unchanged you can imagine that in the near future we will not be able to travel anymore – not on roads at least.

DF: But let's say a high speed line is required to construct a new line, say, between Frankfurt and Berlin. How would that best be constructed, if you think that you will be listed in three years' time, five years' time, whenever. How most efficiently can the government support that?

DS: Certainly, if we had to build a new high-speed line, this investment would have to be financed by the state. In Germany, we have just opened a high-speed line from Cologne to Frankfurt and in 2006 we will complete construction on a high-speed line between Frankfurt and Munich. So there will be only one left: from Munich to Berlin. Once these lines have become operational, we don't foresee the need to construct additional railway lines. But as I said, creating an evironment where the railways can compete with the cars on equal terms is more important. Without such an environment we should perhaps not even invest into new infrastructure, because that infrastructure will not be competitive: it's like the race between the hare and the tortoise.

DF: Steve, what about the UK?

SR: I agree that the most efficient way the government can support the railways would be to make road transport pay its environmental and congestion costs. And if it did, that that would be the end of the whole issue and there would be nothing more to be addressed. If it doesn't do that, there are two circumstances in which the railway may need public support. One is if it is required to operate uncommercial operations and needs day-to-day operating subsidies to run certain lines, in which case I think the efficient way would be to hold a competition to see who could run those lines most cheaply in terms of subsidy. The other circumstance would be if there was a desire for a big rail infrastructure project, which wasn't financially viable, but which was economically viable because of these uncharged externalities and the efficient way for the government to do that would be to make its finance intra-marginal. In other words, the government would quantify the external benefits and pay this as a subsidy to the operator who bears the risk for any construction cost overruns. So the risks fall on the railway and shareholders.

DF: What would you say, Mr Kasai, are the key lessons of the Japanese privatization, what would you want to tell other countries, particularly Germany, as they are contemplating privatizing?

YK: Privatization decisions in Japan are made by the Diet, and therefore based on a political consensus. This itself constitutes a contradiction in this whole system of privatizing companies, because privatization can only be successful if it takes into consideration the market environment and investor expectations, which often conflict with political considerations. Therefore, I think there needs to be some flexibility to be able to make adjustments if something goes wrong later. One way to retain this flexibility is for the government to keep a certain stake in the privatized company, so that it can intervene if needed. Obviously, this only replaces the old dilemma with a new dilemma. The railway privatization in Japan has so far been very successful, but ten years down the line things could change dramatically. For example, prior to privatization the government decided not to construct any new Shinkansen lines, but just three years later this decision was reversed. Consequently, the operator had to bear part of the financial burden.

DF: What do you make of that Mr Sack? The advice there is that once you are privatized they'll make you do things that you don't want to.

DS: Well, it's the normal course. But the roles should be clear. The railway is part of the market and has to be competitive. The worst thing would be that the privatization process gets under way and then suddenly the politicians decide to stop this process. We have 200,000 employees and we tell them every day that Deutsche Bahn has to be competitive, that we need to improve our service and our productivity. Once the company is listed, we have to pay attention to our investors, in other words the business needs to be profitable and we cannot pile up debt in the same way as we did when the business was still part of the federal budget. This requires an enormous change in mentality. Now, if after five, six or eight years the government decided to change the rules, I think this would send shock waves through the organization. The government started the privatization process, consequently we would like the government to decide as early as possible that Deutsche Bahn will be listed. This will accelerate the process of improving service quality and productivity.

DF: It seems Steve what you said earlier was that one of the major problems for Railtrack was exactly this point, that the rules got changed half-way through.

SR: I agree with what's been said. It seems to me that the message or the lesson is that the private sector can deliver a better railway than the public sector can, but it needs a clear and stable regulatory and political framework to be able to do so. That doesn't mean that the framework will never change, it needs to be changed driven by a clarity of objectives of the various players involved in it and it needs to change through processes which carry the confidence of all parties. And I think in the UK we've failed that test.

DF: And what was it that allowed JR Central to improve it's productivity and if you had to isolate three key factors, what was it about privatization that allowed you to do those things that you couldn't have done prior to privatization?

YK: First, industrial relations were improved because there was much less political interference post privatization. Second, we could afford to spend more on improving the services of the Tokaido Shinkansen and commuter lines. Last but not least, quick decision-making became possible because we did not need to consult anymore with the politicians and bureaucrats about key decisions. We judge and decide ourselves, and once we have decided we put this decision into practice very quickly.

DF: What do you think Mr Sack? Do you think you're going to get those benefits once you are listed or have you already got them?

DS: Some of the things Mr Kasai described have already become reality for us. In the past, management used to make only notional investment decisions; the real decision was made by the Ministry of Finance. But now we are part of the market. We have started a complete restructuring, because we have to achieve a change in the mindset of our employees and the best way to do this is through a complete reorganization. This is not just a name change from 'Deutsche Bundesbahn' to 'Deutsche Bahn AG'. The business units are now responsible for achieving returns on the investments we make. They are responsible not only for making the investment but also for the results. This has brought about a huge change in mentality. Our employees want to improve our performance now, and this is critical for our success. Improving performance will become ever more important once a decision about a listing of

Deutsche Bahn has been made, given the additional pressure from shareholders.

SR: I think there is an important point here. It applies to almost all public sector bodies, not just railways. The point is that almost all public-sector bodies are insulated from any external pressures. There is no real pressure from the customers, and there is no real pressure from any sort of banker. There is obviously no pressure from shareholders. So if you are going to improve that organization, all the drive for change has to come from within and it very rarely does. When you have the prospect of privatization, and when you've actually done it, suddenly the people in the organization who want to improve it can make reference to external pressures in selling the case for change internally. Either the prospect of those pressures – coming along shortly when they are privatized or they've actually come along and they have been privatized means that they can point to competitors trying to take the market or to shareholders demanding performance or to bankers wanting to ensure money is paid back. I think this is a tremendous weapon in the hand of the people who want to change and improve the organization. And it's a weapon which simply isn't there when you are a public-sector organization, which means that the people who do want to make change in public sector organizations have a tremendous battle in selling the case for change internally. The power of the external forces in the hands of change agents is, I think, highly significant.

DF: Well I think that was an interesting final comment. Thank you very much.

▶ *Appendix II*

List of Figures

1. JNR Organization Chart (Sept. 1979)

2. Shizuoka Railway Operating Division

3. JNR Financial Reorganization Plans

4. JNR Reform Committees

5. Japan's Conventional and Shinkansen Lines, Nov. 1982

6. Japan's Conventional and Shinkansen Lines, April 1987

7. Japan's Conventional and Shinkansen Lines, Jan. 2003

8. Breakdown of JNR Debt Dispersal and Means of Repayment

9. Valuation of the Shinkansen Assets of the Three Honshu JR Companies

10. Chronology of Events, 1949–2002

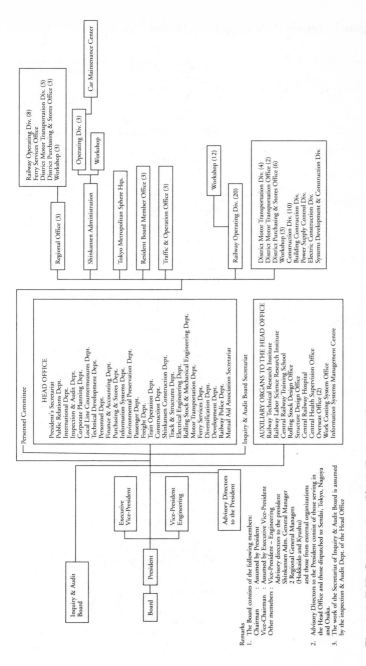

Figure 1 JNR Organization Chart (Sept. 1979)

Figure 2 Shizuoka Railway Operating Division

Administration Department	Planning Section
	General Affairs Section
	Legal Affairs Section
	Personnel Section
	Human Resource Development Section
	Labor Section
	Health and Welfare Section
	Safety Management Section

Finance and Accounting Department	Budget Section
	Accounting Section
	Audit Section
	Procurement Section

Marketing Department	Administration Section
	Passenger Section
	Freight Section
	Railway Police Section
	Freight Marketing Center

Train Operation Department	Administration Section
	Train Operation Section
	Transport Safety Section
	Locomotive Section
	Passenger Car and Freight Car Section

Tracks and Structures Department	Administration Section
	Land Contract Section
	Tracks Maintenance Section
	Structures, Buildings and Machinery Section
	Construction Section
	Level Crossings Safety Section

Electric Engineering Department	Administration Section
	Electric Power and Catenary Section
	Power Transformation Section
	Signals Section
	Telecommunications Section

| Business Development Department | Administration Section |
| | Business Development Section |

Field organizations	Station
	Signal Station
	Conductor Depot
	Locomotive Depot
	Electric Multiple Unit Depot
	Passenger Car and Freight Car Depot
	Train Driver Depot
	Tracks Maintenance Depot
	Machinery Maintenance Depot
	Electric Power and Catenary Maintenance Depot
	Power Transformation Maintenance Depot
	Signals and Telecommunications Maintenance Depot
	Electric Facilities Maintenance Depot
	Information Facilities Maintenance Depot
	Railway Police Station
	Structures and Buildings Construction Depot
	Structures Inspection Center

	First* Reorganization Plan	Second** Reorganization Plan	Third Reorganization Plan	Fourth Reorganization Plan	Fifth Reorganization Plan	Sixth Reorganization Plan (Management Improvement Programme)
Plan period	1969 – 78	1972 – 81	1973 – 82	1976 – 77	1977 – 79	1981 – 85
Target	Repay in 10th year and generate profits	Balance earnings and expenses in 10th year	Balance earnings and expenses in 10th year	Balance earnings and expenses in 2 years	Balance earnings and expenses by FY 1979	Balance main line system earnings and expenses by FY 1985
Major contents	- Rationalize to needed number of employees - Interest supply - Focus on capital expenditure - the Sanyo Shinkansen construction (Shin-Osaka to Okayama) - Construction start for the Tohoku Shinkansen - Convert from local lines to road transportation	- Rationalize to needed number of employees - Fare hike - Interest supply - Government assistance - the Sanyo Shinkansen construction (Okayama to Hakata) - the Tohoku Shinkansen Construction - Convert from local lines to road transportation	- Rationalize to needed number of employees - Fare hike - Interest supply - Government assistance - the Sanyo Shinkansen construction (Okayama to Hakata) - the Tohoku Shinkansen Construction - Convert from local lines to road transportation	-Rationalize to needed number of employees - Fare hike - Interest supply - Government assistance for local lines - Past debt on shelve	- Rationalize to needed number of employees - Interest supply - 50 % hike in fare (two times in 2 years) - Past debt on shelve - Government assistance for local lines	Balance main line - Rationalize to needed number of employees (decrease by 70,000) - Flexible fare revision - Revise nationwide uniform fare - Government assistance for local lines - Additional shelving of past debt - Measures taken against structural losses - Control capital expenditure scale

* Each Reorganization Plan is named in order conveniently.

** Deliberation incomplete at the Diet meeting, Plan abolished.

Figure 3 JNR Financial Reorganization Plans

	Second Administrative Reform Committee (SARC)	JNR Reorganization Sub Committee of the LDP (Mitsuzuka Committee)	JNR Reorganization Advisory Panel (JNR RAP)
Established	March 1981	February 1982	June 1983
Location	Advisory committee for Prime Minister (Located in the Prime Minister's Office)	Sub committee located in the LDP	Advisory committee for Prime Minister (Located in the Prime Minister's Office)
Purpose	Deliberation of measures for financial reorganization of the government	Investigation of present situation and exploration of potential measures for JNR reorganization	Deeper deliberation of specific measures for radical reform of JNR management, based on discussion in SARC
Main members	Doko Toshio (Chairman) Sejima Ryuzo Kato Hiroshi (Chairman, the fourth panel) Yayama Taro Sando Yoichi Tanaka Kazuaki (Chief Examiner, the fourth panel)	Mitsuzuka Hiroshi (Chairman) and other members of the Diet at the Transport Division of the Policy Deliberation Committee of the LDP Kasai Yoshiyuki (unofficial Secretariat) Ide Masataka (unofficial Secretariat) Matsuda Masatake (unofficial Secretariat)	Kamei Masao (Chairman) Kato Hiroshi Sumita Shoji Hayashi Junji (Deputy Secretary General) Kasai Yoshiyuki (Reformist within JNR) Ide Masataka (Reformist within JNR) Matsuda Masatake (Reformist within JNR)
Report publication	July 1982	July 1982	July 1985
Content of report	(JNR related only) - Regional break-up of JNR within 5 years. - Start with gradual opening of stock and eventual privatization of government-affiliated corporations - Locate JNR Reorganization Advisory Panel in the Prime Minister's Office to organize implementation structure	- Aim toward reorganization by FY 1985, based on the Management Improvement Programme. - Break up and privatize JNR by 1987 if reorganization is impossible. (Exit theory) - Divide JNR into 4 segments – Hokkaido, Honshu, Shikoku and Kyushu.	- Break up and privatize JNR as of 1 April, 1987 - Break up JNR into 6 passenger railway companies and 1 freight railway company. - Establish the Shinkansen Holding Corporation to adjust profits for 3 passenger railway companies in Honshu - All JR companies to start successively selling stocks as soon as conditions are ready for transfer into net private companies. - Establish the JNR Settlement Corporation to deal with excess personnel and sell assets such as land and stock.

Figure 4 JNR Reform Committees

Figure 5 Japan's Conventional and Shinkansen Lines, Nov. 1982

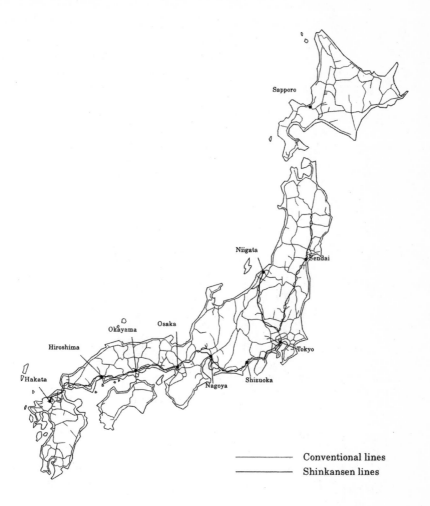

Conventional lines
Shinkansen lines

Figure 6 Japan's Conventional and Shinkansen Lines, April 1987

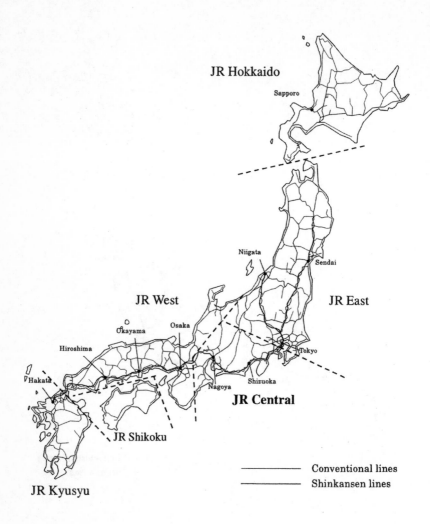

Figure 7 Japan's Conventional and Shinkansen Lines, Jan. 2003

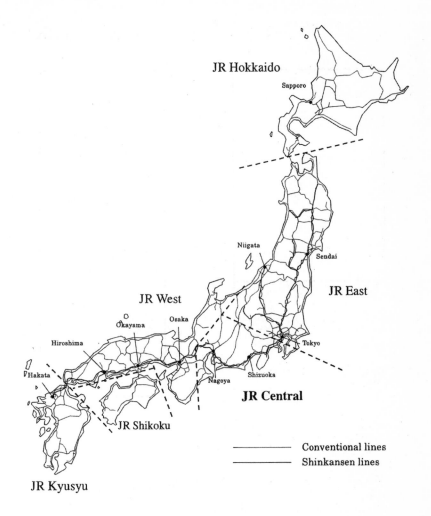

Figure 8 Breakdown of JNR Dept Dispersal and Means of Repayment

(trillion yen)

Aggregate debts (1987. 4)
37. 1

Debt Disposal and Means of Repayment
37. 1

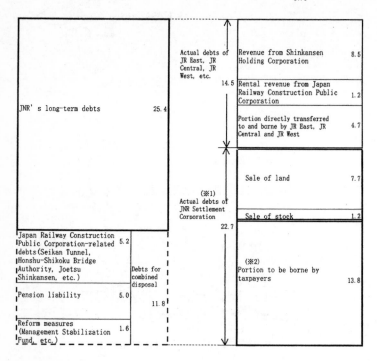

※ Sums are in rounded numbers and may not exactly correspond to
the total calculated from the exact figures.

(※1) The debt of 25.5 trillion yen of JNR Settlement Corporation includes
2.8 trillion yen to be paid by JR companies to Shikansen Holding Corporation.

(※2) Following decisions taken at Cabinet meetings on January 28th 1986
and January 26th 1988, it was expected that the 13.8 trillion yen to be borne
by taxpayers would be reduced as much as possible by an increase in gains
from stock and sales of land.

214

Figure 9 Valuation of the Shinkansen Assets of the Three Honshu JR
Companies

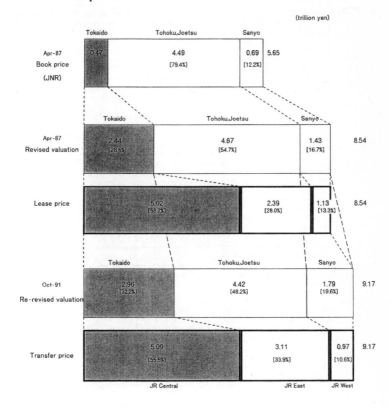

Figure 10 Chronology of Events, 1949–2002

Year	Month	JNR and JR	Government and Ruling Parties
1949	June	Inauguration of JNR ordered by GHQ (Starting business as a financially independent public corporation), Shimoyama Sadanori assumed the post of President	
1955	May	Sogo Shinji assumed the post of President	
1962	May	Mikawashima Accident (Death toll: 160, Injuries: 296)	
1963	May	Ishida Reisuke assumed the post of President	
1963	Nov.	Tsurumi Accident (Death toll: 161, Injuries: 65)	
1964	Oct.	Opening of the Tokaido Shinkansen (Tokyo to Shin-Osaka)	
1965	August	In FY1964 statement, JNR registered its first loss in a single fiscal year	
1969	May	First Reorganization Plan launched	
1969	May	Isozaki Satoshi assumed the post of President	
1972	March	Opening of the Sanyo Shinkansen to Okayama (Shin-Osaka to Okayama)	
1973	April	Third Reorganization Plan launched	
1975	March	Opening of the Sanyo Shinkansen to Hakata (Okayama to Hakata)	
1975	Nov.	Kokuro (National Railway Workers' Union) and Doro (National Railway Locomotive Union) went on strike for the right to strike (8 days)	
1976	March	Takagi Fumio assumed the post of President	
1976	May	Subsidy for Local Lines capitalized for the first time in FY1976 budget (17.2 billion yen). Interest payment on liabilities of 2.5 trillion yen shelved	
1976	Nov.	Approx. 50% fare hike carried out	
1977	April	Fifth Reorganization Plan (Former Management Improvement Programme) approved by Minister of Transport	
1977	Dec.	Bill enacted for partial flexibility in JNR fare hike	
1980	April	Interest payment on liabilities of 2.8 trillion yen in FY1980 budget shelved	
1981	March		Second Administration Reform Comittee (SARC) established
1981	May	Sixth Reorganization Plan (Management Improvement Programme) approved by Minister of Transport	
1982	Feb.		JNR Reorganization Sub Committee of the LDP established (known as the Mitsuzuka Committee)
1982	June	Opening of the Tohoku Shinkansen (Omiya to Morioka)	

Year	Month	JNR and JR	Government and Ruling Parties
1982	July		Mitsuzuka Committee announced "Measures for JNR reorganization"
1982	July		SARC submitted third report focusing on the break-up and privatization of JNR
1982	Nov.	Opening of the Joetsu Shinkansen (Omiya to Niigata)	
1982	Nov.		Nakasone Yasuhiro Cabinet elected
1983	April	Japanese National Railways halted new hires of high school graduates	
1983	June		JNR Reorganization Advisory Panel (JNR RAP) officially established
1983	August		JNR RAP advanced emergency measures for JNR reorganization
1983	Dec.	Nisugi Iwao assumed the post of President	
1984	July		Mitsuzuka published "The Only Way Forward for JNR"
1985	June	Sugiura Takaya assumed the post of President	
1985	July		JNR RAP submitted a "View on JNR Reform" to Prime Minister Nakasone
1986	Jan.	JNR, Doro (National Railway Locomotive Union) and Tetsuro (Railway Labour Union) announced Joint Declaration between Labour and Management	
1986	July		At the double election, the LDP won an overwhelming victory, gaining 300 seats in the Lower House
1986	Oct.	Kokuro (National Railway Workers' Union) held the 50th extraordinary national convention in Shuzenji. Emergency countermeasure bill approving of the break-up and privatization of JNR was rejected	
1986	Nov.	Eight bills related to JNR reform enacted. It was officially decided that JNR would be reorganized into JR companies on 1 April, 1987	
1987	April	JR companies were established	
1991	Oct.	JR companies in Honshu took over ground facilities of the Shinkansen. The Shinkansen Holding Corporation was dissolved.	
1991	Nov.	Central Japan Railway Workers Union dropped out of Japan Confederation of Railway Workers' Unions (JR Soren)	
1992	May.	Japan Railway Trade Unions Confederation (JR Rengo) formed	
1993	Oct.	East Japan Railway Company listed on market	
1996	Oct.	West Japan Railway Company listed on market	

217

Year	Month	JNR and JR	Government and Ruling Parties
1997	April	Central Japan Railway Company and Railway Technical Research institute started running tests on the Yamanashi Maglev Text Line	
1997	Oct.	Central Japan Railway Company listed on market	
1998	Oct.		Law enacted governing disposal of debt by the JNR Settlement Corporation
1999	April	Manned world record 552 km/h established on the Yamanashi Maglev Test Line	
2001	Dec.	Amendment to the Law concerning Passenger Railway Companies and Japan Freight Railway Company eases regulation of 3 JR companies in Honshu, making them the same as private railway companies	
2002	June	Allowance for Large-Scale Renovation of the Shinkansen Infrastructure established, according to the Partial Amendment to the Nationwide Shinkansen Railway Development Law	
2002	June	Government sold all East Japan Railway Company stock	

Japanese Yen Exchange Rates vs US Dollar and Pound Sterling (1960–90)

Year	Currency	
	1 GBP=JPY	1USD=JPY
1960	1,010	360
1961	1,010	360
1962	1,013	360
1963	1,011	360
1964	1,011	360
1965	1,010	360
1966	1,012	360
1967	999	360
1968	864	360
1969	856	360
1970	858	360
1971	848	308
1972	757	308
1973	664	308
1974	682	308
1975	659	308
1976	536	308
1977	468	308
1978	403	195
1979	466	240
1980	526	204

1981	445	220
1982	435	235
1983	360	232
1984	317	252
1985	307	201
1986	247	160
1987	236	122
1988	228	126
1989	226	143
1990	257	135

Source: Bank of Japan, Reuters
Notes:
US Dollar: 1960-77 BoJ Basic Rates, 1978–90
Interbank Rates
Pound Sterling: Cross rates

Index